Travelling for the Over Sixties

Timothy Blewitt

Printed by CreateSpace

Copyright © Timothy Blewitt 2013

All rights reserved

ISBN 978-1492346333

First printed in Great Britain by
CreateSpace 2013
2nd print 2014

No part of this publication may be reproduced, stored in a retrieval system, or transmitted in any form or by any means, electronic, mechanical, photocopying or otherwise, without the prior permission of the publishers.

All the information in this book was correct at the time of going to press. Nobody has been mentioned by name and cannot be identified by other readers.

All photographs were taken from the author's private collection. They have been converted from colour images to black and white thus reducing their quality.

Cover design by Tim Blewitt

Contents

1. Introduction..................6
2. Planning..................15
3. What to take..................22
4. Backpacking around the World..................31
5. Trekking..................49
6. Overlanding..................63
7. Train journeys..................94
8. Organised trips..................111
9. Cruises..................119
10. How tough can it get?..................144
11. Flights..................171
12. Accommodation. Where are you going to stay?..176
13. Health..................186
14. Safety..................194
15. Preparation. Get fit..................208
16. Communication..................230
17. Solo travelling..................237
18. Insurance..................244
19. Looking after things back home..................259
20. Money..................263
21. Tipping, begging and taxis..................270
22. Food..................279
23. Car hire..................286
24. Places to get to soon..................293
25. Traveller's tales..................304
26. We want the world and we want it - Now!..................314
27. Memories..................319
28. Who are the worst tourists?..................327
29. A final word..................329
30. Directory..................330
31. Index..................333

1 Introduction

"The traveller sees what he sees. The tourist sees what he has come to see."
G.K. Chesterton 1874-1936

You have retired and each day is your own to enjoy as you wish. Now you can do all those things that you have for ever been putting off. For many people it offers the perfect opportunity to travel. You may have retired unwillingly, regretfully, thankfully or as in my case with much rejoicing, but here you are, ideally with that perfect combination of time and money. Even if you do not have much money there is still nothing to stop you setting out on your travels. Penniless students have always done it as a 'gap' year and we were the generation that created that rite of passage.

The world is a large place and you want to see it all. You may think that you have plenty of time but at your age time is not on your side so the sooner you get started the better. You cannot foresee what the future holds but you have say x amount of years before illness, incapacity or something worse may prevent anymore travelling. So if you delay a year then you have x-1 years left. To a certain extent I had to wait until my wife retired so I started at x-2. Of course while you are waiting for your partner to retire you can always be travelling on your own. My wife did not want the challenge of Kilimanjaro nor do the Everest Base Camp trek, so I took the opportunity to go off on my own. If you both have individual travel ambitions to fill, then take separate trips. There are a lot of single travellers out there. Little else should matter except the day that you are travelling. Life is not a practice for something else, there are no second chances so get out there and do it.

Back in the days when Miss World was thought of more as a celebration of female beauty than being politically incorrect or degrading to women one of the questions was,
'What would you like to do if you won this competition?'
The answer from the pretty girl was often,
'Travel and see the world.'
There are of course many people who do not want to travel or at least do not want to go everywhere. My cousin hates even leaving Cornwall. Other people have no wish to visit hot countries or cold countries. The true traveller will want to go everywhere and there is no reason to place any restrictions upon yourself. You may have preferences but try not to impose limitations upon yourself. You do

not really know how you will feel about a place until you get there. Every destination has something to offer, cities, the countryside, mountains, islands, deserts, lakes, rivers and so on. Why limit your options? Go to the middle of Siberia just to see for yourself that there is nothing there. There must be something, after all it covers 10% of the earth's land mass. Maybe people with the travel bug still need to fulfil something in their lives. I am sometimes quite envious of those who are so happy and content with their way of life that they do not want to go anywhere. Are you happy with your life? I am, but even more so when travelling.

We were born at a fortunate time and it can be difficult to explain to younger generations just how exciting life was in the 'Swinging Sixties'. Such a period of optimism, economic prosperity and changes in life style also took place forty years earlier in the 'Roaring Twenties' and forty years prior to that the 1880's were by all accounts pretty good. Any recurring cycle unfortunately did not repeat itself with the noughties, being dull in comparison. If you were a teenager in the sixties you may not fully remember it all. If you do remember it all then you were not really there. It all seemed to pass so quickly, whatever you were doing it all swept by in a purple haze. One problem concerns the nature of time itself, as you get older time seems to speed up. One minute the grand children are sucking dummies then suddenly they are at school and asking your opinion about organic food and endangered animal species. The weeks fly by and somehow you cannot recall actually doing much at all. It could get even worse, you may even become boring. How could that happen to a child of the sixties, one of the beautiful people? You must avoid becoming boring at all costs, keep up with things particularly technology, music and entertainment. Anyway, to get back to the point, as you get older time seems to speed up. For a four year old child one year accounts for 25% of their lifetime and seems to be a relatively long time as compared to a 25 year old for whom one year is just 4% of their lifetime. For a 60 year old that drops to 1.6% and one year does not seem very long any more. If you have a set routine and nothing changes then the years will seem to fly by even quicker. Maybe, just maybe you can slow time down by doing something different and travel is the perfect solution.

If you are over sixty then you grew up in post war Britain. Your parents lived through the Second World War or fought in it for their country. In the late forties and the fifties families started taking holidays again. Just about everyone took their vacation at an English seaside resort. We went to Margate, Broadstairs, Bognor Regis and sometimes to stay on a farm in the country. My wife was from the north of England where she and just about everyone else up there went to Blackpool every single year. Only the super rich took holidays abroad. The English resorts were geared up for holiday makers and we had great fun. In the 50's and 60's we went on holiday to do nothing, many people still do, but travellers are looking for something more. Also the weather seemed better in the 'good old days'. Now it has become generally accepted that a holiday is taken abroad. Prices have come down and there are plenty of bargains to be had particularly out of school holiday times. Above all being retired you can grab that last minute bargain and leave at the drop of a hat. So, 'don't let me hear you say life's taking you nowhere in those golden years'.

We are the Baby Boomers, the chosen ones, the generation that have had everything and perhaps continue to do so. We even have our own edition of Trivial Pursuits. As children we had the perfect diet. We did not over eat as food was still rationed. Our mothers were generally at home and prepared fresh food from scratch every day. There was no unhealthy junk food and people did not have freezers. We had a balanced diet of meat and two vegetables and fish on Friday, so many of us are healthy by accident or default. Our mothers often gave us a spoonful of cod liver oil daily. They were not sure why, but now we know the benefits of Omega 3. As the bulge generation, society invested heavily in our future. Whether by accident or design the grammar schools gave us access to the best education system devised so far. (The tragic destruction of which by liberal progressives leaves only 164 today for the benefit of our own grandchildren and it is of no surprise that they are massively oversubscribed.) Then we became the biggest work force relative to population size, and the economy boomed. It was easy to get a job in the sixties and the spirit of optimism was all pervasive. We invented or at least reinvented free love, rock and roll, the gap year and managed to change society. When Spike Milligan said that Queen Victoria died in 1960 he meant that this is when old fashioned Victorian values finally began to fade away to be replaced by the sexual revolution. We were all part of that, however small it was it all added up to an avalanche of protest and change. We invented teenagers, before that it was a rapid transition between boy and man. Now though, as the baby boomers change into silver surfers, we are becoming a financial burden with fewer people working to support us. This still leaves many of us in an enviable position with a better pension than the next generation may expect, able to retire younger and with fewer health problems. Travelling just might help you to live longer. According to a report in 'USA Today', geriatrician and author Dr. David Lipschitz believes that travel helps senior citizens live longer lives. So squeeze as much as you can out of your remaining years. Each day is the beginning of the rest of your life.

By no means have I been everywhere and vast areas of the world for me remain unexplored. The intention though is to go to as many places as possible. Neither does this book cover the world as there are just too many places to see. My wife and I do consider ourselves well travelled but we are constantly meeting people who have seemingly been just about everywhere. We have one golden rule, never to go the same place twice regardless of how wonderful it happened to be. The rule has only been broken once, to Goa, one of the best places on earth to live out that hippy dream.

Goa has that feel good factor and you will have a good time

This book is intended to encourage older people to set out again with confidence because at some stage you lose the confidence of youth. I have tried to present the realities of travelling, how it really is and what to expect. Travelling is not really a holiday as such but more like exploring, seeing different places and experiencing other cultures. My wife and I are well over sixty now and still have that spirit of adventure. I am not advocating a return to the hedonism of the sixties, although it does have an attractive ring to it. However, after forty years or so of work it is time to attempt to turn back the clock a little, try to change and regain some of that lost youth. My life was interrupted by a career in teaching. For many people it is only when you retire that you can get on with what you really want to do. Irving Goffman theorised that people start to take on the persona that their job expects of them. So an accountant will look like what you may expect him to look like, different from a car salesman, builder or teacher. It is never too late to change and become a more interesting and adventurous person. Every journey starts with a single step.

SAGA magazine will now have been dropping through your letter box for at least 10 years. You did not request it and maybe you do not really want it, but they know where you live. It offers safe holidays to a certain sort of person. Not your sort, you are going to be more independent and adventurous. Do you want to be travelling around with a group of old people even if you are one of them? Travelling is not really about following someone holding up a flag so that you do not get lost. The firms that canvas the older age groups are not necessarily going to be cheaper, despite what they say. There may well come a day when it is you who are infirm and slow to get on and off coaches, but that time has not yet arrived. There will be no impromptu stops to circumnavigate lakes, play football with the locals or walk up hills. You will be safe and mollycoddled and will not have to think for yourself. This is not really travelling. Travelling is for the independent person who sometimes is not quite sure where they are going and what will happen. If you are going to travel with a company, shop around the same as you would for any other product such as motor insurance. With all the unsolicited mail that arrives targeting the older person you could just send the envelope back empty or with a message like 'thank you for the pen, it was very kind of you to think of me', or maybe ask for further information without an address. All good practice for when you really are senile and that purple haze does get in your brain.

I must at this point make it clear that nobody should be judged by their age alone. Once on a cruise I signed up for the table tennis tournament. In the first round my opponent was considerably older than me with a hump back. I smashed the first two points past him and he remarked upon my good shots. I felt a bit sorry for him but then he started to return all my shots and however hard I tried they still kept coming back. Subsequently I lost and he tottered off to the next round. On a recent African trek our guide was an elderly gentleman wearing an old suit, what looked like slippers on his feet and carrying a shopping bag. My heart sank as I was hoping for an exhilarating walk. He set off uphill through the jungle at a cracking pace and continued non stop. He had been thinking that we might not be able to keep up as we were the oldest but ended up commenting upon our stamina. Some younger members of our party could barely keep up, and then half way up we met some local women carrying gallon cans of palm oil wine on their heads. This is coma inducing stuff but he filled up a litre container and drunk the lot! We had a small sip but it is, say, more of an acquired taste. Duly fortified he then seemed to speed up. Similarly I no longer judge anyone by their appearance. Years ago I was with my family in France trudging up a steep rocky slope to a waterfall. We were all getting out of breath and stopped to rest. As we caught our breath a woman in a tight skirt, high heels and carrying a poodle under her arm came stepping up past us!

Travellers often go as a couple but there are also a lot of people out there on their own. In recent years I have noticed far more single women on the road than single men. Solo travel is ideal in that you can go exactly where you want to and do not have to consider anyone else. Also the age of travellers is increasing. There are noticeably more older people on the road, in hostels and generally travelling around the world. As a couple a really long trip in hard conditions can, at times, test the strength of your relationship. There will be some tough times when you wish that maybe you were safe in the comfort of your own home. If you decide to undertake a long overland trip through a continent with other friends then you may have found out what you dislike about them by the time you get home. Travelling alone may have advantages but travelling with other people has the satisfaction of the shared experience.

In the past you may have been content to go on some sort of package holiday every year and enjoyed it but why not try something slightly different. We went to Libya just before Colonel Gadaffi fell from power. One of our friends simply said,

'Why?'

Our friends are getting used to us going to adventurous and remote places now but still respond with incredulous statements,

'You are going where?'
'You are doing what?'
Our own daughter once said, 'I cannot think of anything worse.' What is more I do not even blame them. When I look back on some of our trips I cannot believe we actually enjoyed them, but we still keep going back for more.

My wife always says that I take her to places that she would not normally consider and that she often gets out of her comfort zone. She does do a bit of whining but ultimately enjoys the experience. Afterwards she can certainly entertain and impress her friends with traveller's tales of adventure. You have to do something adventurous to acquire some bragging rights. If you are in charge of holiday planning and want to do something more exciting, you can swing it by telling your partner a few half truths about how hard the trip actually is going to be. I try always to include a relaxing bit at the end but ultimately we would both get bored just lying on a beach.

Do not put your plans off or you will regret it. Make sure you have no such regrets later in life, if you do not do it now the chances are that you never will. So many older people say to me that they wish they had done more travelling when they were younger and that now they feel they have left it too late. A survey by the British Heart Foundation revealed that some of the main regrets for British people were, not seeing more of the world and not taking a gap year. Top of the 'to do' lists was, to travel more. The middle classes have always had the idea of deferred gratification, but whoever you are, now is the time to cash in. Some people have been saving all their life for the future and now is the future, so do not be afraid to spend some of your savings. Seize the moment, do it now while you still can and before the care home takes your money from you or before something even worse happens.

People have differing attitudes towards money. All our friends have varying amounts of it but many of them are reluctant to spend it. They have worked hard all their lives, saving for a rainy day or for their retirements, but still they cannot bring themselves to dig into their savings. I have one friend who has a million pounds in cash in an account giving a poor rate of interest, but he is still very cautious. Just how much money do you need? Lord Carnegie said that,

'The man who dies rich, dies disgraced.'

He was a philanthropist, at that time the richest man in the world and gave away a substantial part of his fortune to good causes. If you have £1,000,000 and you are 60 then that could be £50,000 a year for the next 20 years. That does not even take into account the accumulated interest, company pension and state pension that may be coming in. Sometimes it seems that it is more difficult to spend money than to save it. Most of us have far less than my friend in our bank accounts, but it is still there to spend. When my father retired he had saved up £40,000 and still had it when he passed away. Towards the end he said,

'We have all this money, why can't we spend some of it?'

However, because of ill health it was too late. Increasingly younger people are taking gap years and sometimes I wonder how they can afford it. The answer often is that most of them have scrimped and saved to create the opportunity. Inspired by their offspring exploring the world, more and more older people are travelling independently.

Perhaps you are just continuing your travels after work so inconsiderately interrupted them. Maybe you did not have the opportunity for a gap year or worse still you have seen all your children travel the world and grown envious. From now on, every year can be a gap year. In 2011 it was estimated that a quarter of over 55's were planning to take a year out travelling. You do not have to travel with a company, it is very easy to do it all yourself. Now is the time to travel because you are going to get even older. The older you get the harder adventurous travel will become and the more comfort you may feel you will need. If you haven't done it yet, do it now. If you don't make it happen, no one else will, so get out there and you will have a lot of fun.

Africa is always good for bird watching

Get to see some of the world's great iconic architecture

Try to visit some remote places

2 Planning

"Here today, up and off to somewhere else tomorrow! Travel, change, interest, excitement! The whole world before you, and a horizon that's always changing!"
Kenneth Grahame 1859-1932

First of all you have to decide what type of experience you want? Back packing independently is the classic and one of the best ways to travel as it allows the ultimate freedom to go anywhere you please. Even more adventurous would be to rock up at the airport and just book a vacant seat on a plane going anywhere and work your way around the world with only a rudimentary plan. There are always some empty places going somewhere and sometimes they get sold off at the last minute, cheaper. For a round the world trip there are plenty of routes on offer from lots of companies. A quick surf on the internet will give you hundreds of ideas. Generally these ready made offers represent great value and save a lot of time. There is nothing to stop you booking your own flights but with multiple connections to coordinate it is hardly worth it. Overlanding companies offer adventurous trips, sometimes to places that are difficult to travel to, or travel through on your own. Do not rule out package holidays. They may not fit in with the ethos of travelling but the flights can be so cheap that it is worth booking up just for that alone. We once got a great deal to Goa for two weeks and after a couple of nights in the hotel we hired a scooter and just took off down south and then up north having a great time just winging it. At some time you have to experience one of the great train journeys of the world such as the Trans Siberian Railway, the longest in the world. It can be extended by adding something extra to the start and end. Cruises also have their travelling possibilities if they go to places that cannot be accessed by any other means.

If you are anything like me then you want to go absolutely everywhere. My world map shows vast areas where I have never been and probably will never get to. There are also hundreds of little islands dotted all over the oceans and huge continents to explore. Sometimes my wife does not share my opinion, for her anywhere that is warm will be more likely to be top of her list. As you are unlikely to cover anything more than a fraction of the world it is best to make a list of priorities. Try to think ahead and plan accordingly. Anything that involves a cruise can be put off until you are less mobile. While you are still relatively young and fit go for the more challenging and adventurous trips. Something like an overland camping trip is best done sooner rather than later and then there are all the trekking challenges to test yourself out on. The essential thing is to get out there and do it. We try to fit in the holiday experience of a lifetime every year and on top of that several shorter trips.

Planning the journey is one of the best parts of travelling and one of the nicest things about returning home after a long trip can be the excuse to plan another. A world map is essential in order to visualise your route. You may have a destination in mind but it is always worthwhile looking at possible stop overs, particularly if your flight is not direct. A globe is also a nice way to explore and realise your ideas.

If you intend travelling a lot it is worthwhile investing in a whole range of travel guide books. This may seem a bit old fashioned but I still need the enduring quality of the written word. Everybody has their favourite but I stick to Lonely Planet books mainly because they are the ones I know and love and they all take on a nice collective identity on the shelf. They contain information to suit every budget, however, I do find that other guide books are better for certain countries and activities. The only problem with physical books is that they can be heavy and bulky if you want to take them on holiday with you, especially if you are visiting lots of countries. A download on to a Kindle or something similar may be more practical.

Although having said all that 'Triposo' could render written guide books redundant. This app is free to download to your phone or iPad and once information is downloaded it can be read offline. Just start the Triposo Travel Guide and pick the country you will be visiting. Download maps, city guides, information on all the major sights, restaurants and night life. Use the currency converter, weather information and useful phrases. This app is essential for the serious traveller.

Silvertraveladvisor gives personal advice for mature travellers, by whom they mean over 50's, and is a valuable source of all sorts of information.

www.silvertraveladvisor.com

The weather has to be one of the first considerations. You may have found a really cheap deal to go to Sri Lanka but this may well be cheap because it is the monsoon season. There is an excellent book, 'Weather To Travel. The Traveller's Guide To World Weather'. I find this essential at the planning stage. Good websites to check out are:

weather2travel.com

worldweather.wmo.int
weather.com
The internet is now the major place to research your ideas but once you have got your ideas and a route put together it is worthwhile going to a specialist agent such as Trailfinders who will tell you the practicalities of it and perhaps suggest further ideas. The huge advantage of booking through such an agent is that you have instant insurance cover for the trip itself.

What did we do before computers took over our lives? How did we manage? There is just so much information out there ready to be saved in your 'favourites'. Organise all that essential information that you find on the internet into subsidiary folders all under a main folder labelled holidays or travelling. Save all your favourite travel websites and cut and paste anything of interest into word documents. You need to be really well organised if you want to retrieve them easily so create a structured system that you understand. I list all the places I want to go to and this extends to countries, weekend breaks in cities, specific areas, as well as places to visit in England. There is also a priority list and one detailing ideas for specific routes as I become aware of them. I only sign up for a few web site mailings, my two favourites for bargain deals being:

dealchecker.co.uk
travelzoo.com

Over many years I have collected all the travel articles of interest from the newspaper travel sections and catalogued them into a series of folders. All articles relating to a certain country get put in a separate folder. This archive has increasingly become an excellent source of ideas. As we visit places I tend to discard this information just to keep it all manageable. Most Sunday papers have interesting travel sections and there are also some excellent travel magazines, Lonely Planet and Wanderlust being among the best. Travel brochures are another great source for copying ideas and showing routes that someone else has worked out for you. Look at the itinerary and consider if you could put it together better and more cheaply. Do not get too carried away and make sure your itinerary is sensible as someone of your age might need a little more comfort.

If you are already well travelled and beginning to slow down a bit you can always do the same stuff, but tone it down. By now you will have accumulated lots of great travel experiences and may no longer need to be searching out new thrills and excitement.

Find out as soon as possible if you need a VISA for your destination. The FCO site will tell you exactly what is required. Some applications can be extraordinarily difficult, expensive and time consuming. Russian tourist Visas involve lengthy obscure questions most of which are totally irrelevant. Why do they need your last two work addresses even if you are retired? Some countries charge tourists differing amounts depending upon how much their own citizens are required to pay to enter your own country, in some sort of tit for tat arrangement. It is convenient if application forms can be downloaded online and sent off by post, but make sure it is by registered post as your passport is enclosed. Even more convenient is to get visas at the country's border. Much less convenient is to have to visit the embassy in person, once to take it and normally a few days later to collect it. Most embassies will be located in a major city such as London. For our trip through West Africa that meant 5 separate applications. To apply for a Nigerian visa you first had to have one for Benin and Cameroon. The Cote d'Ivoire took three weeks as they constantly wanted proof of everything and further information about where we were staying. When we tried to speed things up they told us that they thought we were being set up for kidnapping. For a lengthy journey involving multiple countries it can be difficult just to acquire all the necessary visas in time, bearing in mind that you can only apply for some 3 months in advance and they then only last for a further 3 months. Thus if your trip is for 3 months you can only apply for the final visa at the last minute, so make sure that you allow plenty of time. Visa costs can mount up, including travel to embassies, and for a trip through West Africa, visas alone cost a whopping £1189 for two travellers. That was doing it ourselves, if you go through an agent, as companies often recommend, then it would have been considerably more. Most applications are fairly straight forward and if you have to apply in person then it is a great excuse for a weekend in London or wherever the embassy happens to be.

    www.doyouneedvisa.com
    www.worldtravelguide.net is also useful for VISA information and lots more.

    Once a holiday is planned or booked up it is a good idea to put all the information into a word document and save it on your computer or at least write the details out in longhand. This is essential for easy access and to ensure nothing gets forgotten. I print all the essential details off to be stored in a folder with all the information and reservations that still get sent through the post. Sometimes there are three or four folders of planned holidays on the go. All the important information gets entered into the diary, such as last day to settle the balance, departure and return times. It is essential that you adopt some sort of organised system.

I then find it useful to create a little pocket sized book of information. This will contain details of the entire itinerary, flights and accommodation plus many other things such as:

- currency exchange rates
- passport details
- insurance information
- brief essential details for every place we intend to visit
- pasted in small maps and pictures culled from travel brochures
- phone numbers of friends and emergency contacts
- coded information for internet pass words (bank etc.)
- important dates (birthdays, rugby internationals?)
- weather in the countries to be visited
- reminders such as departure taxes
- information regarding local transport from airports
- details and phone numbers for places of interest, museums etc.
- a list of hotels, hostels with prices, addresses and phone numbers
- possible restaurants
- local food and drinks
- local customs
- essential words in the local language

This little book becomes an essential part of the holiday, an easy and quick way to access information. I reinforce it down the middle with staples and cover it with a clear sticky plastic. It is much easier to do all this research in the comfort of your own home before you set off. I still prefer to store information like this rather than on a digital device, but I do also take a netbook on holiday and store even more information on it such as web pages to read later off line. A basic mobile phone is also becoming essential as prices come down and it is easy to change sim cards from country to country.

If the first place of arrival or any of the other places you are visiting is a really popular destination and in season then it is best to book up accommodation before leaving home. Never ever pay everything up front but only a small deposit. If you feel safer then you can book up everything in advance, but you lose flexibility and the accommodation may not suit you. If the hotel has your credit card details then you may get charged if you decide to go elsewhere. It is much better to find somewhere to stay upon arrival and generally it is easy. In many places people will come running towards you as soon as you get off the bus or boat desperate to get your custom. I have never yet been stuck even at 11pm. We just rock up and hope for the best.

Once you have everything confirmed then decide how you are getting from home to the airport. For short holidays driving and parking at the airport are the most convenient option and the cheapest for trips up to two weeks or so. Quite often you will not have to pay the full price if you are an AA member or of some other organisation that offers a discount. Tescos sometimes have really good offers with their clubcard. For where we live APH parking and Purple Parking near Gatwick and Heathrow offer occasional deals and if you join their mailing list will send a 10% discount from time to time. For long trips it has to be either local transport or a taxi. If trains are booked up in advance then there are some incredible deals to be had. Cheap tickets come on line 12 weeks before the intended date of travel, but you have to get in quick. Various rail groups have offers from time to time to keep a watch out for, such as special deals travelling to London or wherever you are flying from. You could always use your bus pass if you have plenty of time then it would cost you next to nothing. For a single person a taxi will seem expensive but with two or more it is could be better value than the train and sometimes it is the only option if your plane is first thing in the morning.

It may seem silly to suggest reading up on the place you are visiting before going but a surprising amount of people don't. Others prefer to do only some general research and leave the details to be discovered as a pleasant surprise on arrival. For most travellers it should be an essential part of planning and will add enormously to your enjoyment. Get an idea of what other travellers think of your ideas by checking hotels and attractions out on internet sites such as tripadvisor. Do not, however, rely too heavily on the opinion of

others, the vast majority of satisfied travellers never post any comments, whereas dissatisfied ones may feel a need for retribution.
tripadvisor.co.uk

If you book with a company check that they are ABTA or ATOL bonded so that you will be protected if they go bankrupt.

Try to visit some travel shows, the one staged at Earls Court in London annually is an excellent source of ideas and an opportunity to talk to people who can give you so much essential information, advice and tips. We rarely get there because at that time of year we are already travelling and escaping the English winter.

Some roads can get a bit muddy

3 What to take

"Anyone who needs more than one suitcase is a tourist, not a traveller."
Ira Levin 1929-2007

In years gone by when our children were young and holidays consisted of a two week package of some sort, to a Mediterranean resort, we stuffed everything we could into the suitcases to cover every possibility. Most of it never got used but it did not really matter as we did not have to carry it very far. The most difficult bit was getting from the front door to the taxi. Women's clothes seem to take up less space but they compensate by taking more of them. Just how many bikinis do women need? Obviously quite a lot. We were in the Maldives recently and the woman in the next bungalow had a different bikini for every day. She was in her seventies but still had a figure to die for and looked fabulous, especially in the gold one. On the other hand men's clothing is much bulkier but one pair of swimmers is going to be adequate. My dad always said that he could leave for anywhere in the world almost right away, all he needed was a tooth brush, but he never did. What to take is going to depend largely on where you are going, but the golden rule from now on is to take as little as possible.

We did an overland trip recently with someone who wore the same shirt and shorts everyday for ten weeks. He did not smell or appear grubby and was always obsessive about showering. We wondered if he had several identical pairs but the reality was somewhat different. He used to undress, reverse them and put them back on again, cover them with soap and have a shower washing them at the same time. It seemed to work, it was a hot climate so his clothes always dried overnight and if they were a little damp it did not really matter. This might be unusual but one change of clothing could be sufficient if you really intend travelling light.

My youngest daughter went off travelling and took a 65 litre rucksack, but still could not get all her gear in. She asked us to help. First of all we threw out the teddy bear. Do not take anything that is unnecessary. If you bring back any item of clothing that has not been worn then that is a mistake and to be regarded as something of a failure. If you are a serious traveller and only have a rucksack then you have to physically carry it and everything it contains. This in itself should concentrate your mind and with practice you will be carrying next to nothing. I went on a three month trip round the world with a

25 litre rucksack weighing only 6.5 Kg. There was no luggage to check in at the airport as it qualified for hand luggage. All the liquids were stored at the top in a plastic bag. There was no waiting around at baggage reclaim and less chance of it going astray.

When you start to pack, begin by laying everything out on the bed. The climate you are going to will be a major influence but a practical philosophy is, if it gets cold then put on every thing that you have. You will of course be washing clothes as you go along so make sure that they are the sort that will dry over night.

There is now a huge range of quick drying, wicking and generally cool travel clothes in outdoor shops to choose from. You will be unlikely to get everything right but if you do forget something they do have shops abroad. Maybe consider just buying clothes when you get to your destination, particularly if it is the Far East where clothes are so cheap. At the end of your trip you could just give everything away to needy and grateful locals. My daughter, by the way, continued travelling for three years with very little money. She took on jobs as she went along, mainly managing back packer hostels. It is this attitude that we need to hang on to, at some stage along the line so many older people lose the confidence of youth.

www.travellinglight.co.uk
www.rohan.co.uk

The main point, to re-emphasise, is that you never need as much as you think you do on holiday. Take as little as possible and if you need something you have forgotten then you can always buy it overseas. It is useful if you are going to be in the same climate the whole time so as to avoid different changes of clothes. Multi-purpose gear is handy, long trousers that convert into shorts or a fleece that rolls up into itself that can double up as a pillow.

Choose your rucksack with care. This is going to be your most important possession. It is essential that you choose one that it is the right size. It must be well designed and right for you. If it is too small then you will not be able to fit everything in and if it is too big then the temptation will be to fill it up and you will be struggling to lift it. Make sure it is at least shower proof and it will be a good idea to buy a waterproof cover. Go to a specialist retailer, ask their advice and try on lots of different packs. Stuff it full of gear, adjust all the little straps to reposition the pack, making it just right for you and see how it feels. Walk around the shop for a while. The zippers should all come together at the top so that they can be locked. It will not stop a determined thief but may deter an opportunist. Make sure that it has lots of compartments so that you can organise your gear efficiently with all the stuff you might need on route easily accessible. I always like to have a stretchy bit to stuff in a water bottle. Rucksacks have moved on since the heavier metal framed ones that we had back in the sixties. Now I mange with a 25 litre pack and my wife with 30 litres. Mine has an internal light weight stiffened frame made from some sort of synthetic material and a padded back with an air space to allow air to circulate and reduce sweating. There should be more padding around the hip support belt and shoulder straps. When correctly adjusted and tightened these will distribute the weight around your upper body more comfortably and efficiently. It is of utmost importance that it is all really comfortable and nothing digs into you. Keep in mind that you will have to carry it sometimes for lengthy periods. Go for something that is of really good quality and a well known brand, perhaps Osprey, North Face or Deuter. My advice would be to buy a smaller pack so you will not be tempted to over pack. With a bigger pack you will sub-consciously fill all the empty spaces. There is no need to pay out a lot of money but do not skimp on it, this is a vital piece of equipment. Do plenty of research, a good rucksack will last you at your age, for ever.

Packing is an art in itself. Every precious space has to be utilised. Pack things inside anything that is hollow. Taking things to extremes I even cut away the packaging from medical tablets. Some stuff you will need instant access to and can be stored at the top or in a side pocket. Remember that you have to lug all this stuff around. If you have a light pack there will be less of a need to find accommodation immediately on arrival at your destination, you can keep your options open and spend time looking around. Travelling light gives you greater freedom to go when and how you like.

For men, shoes are bulky items so generally I try to take only one pair, those being the ones I set off in. These are usually strong waterproof multi-purpose sandals, with an enclosed toe. This is important to avoid stubbing the big toe on rocks. They are ultimately practical, good enough for general trekking, walking, wading through mud and water and cool in a hot climate. If it gets cold then put on some socks. It may be a fashion faux-pas but at least your toes will be warm. If you are going to somewhere cold or wet, then perhaps still only take one pair of boots or trail shoes.

The following clothing is a suggested list for men. Women can substitute similar corresponding items. It is intended as a general list for travel to a variety of places but nowhere too cold. All the items should be specialist travel clothes which will dry overnight. It may appear to be very short but this is the barest minimum. Even this list could be halved if you want to wash stuff more often:

- 2 x pairs of shorts
- 4 x pairs of underwear
- 2 x Short sleeved shirts
- 2 x T Shirts
- swimming trunks
- hat for sun protection

The following items are also included but you will be wearing them, particularly if you are leaving England in the autumn or winter. Do not forget though that all these may need to go into the rucksack on arrival:

- pair of long trousers
- a warm fleece, one that packs into a 'pocket' and can double up as a pillow
- long sleeved shirt
- handkerchief
- multi purpose shoes
- socks, one pair plus some flight socks
- pack away water proof
- sleeveless cargo vest/jacket with lots of pockets

Apart from all the above there are many more items that are essential or at least may be essential for you:

- camera, spare battery and charger (I take two cameras - an SLR and a compact)
- netbook, iPad or something similar? (almost essential)
- sun glasses, reading glasses etc.
- flask or water bottle
- alarm clock
- torch and head torches plus spare batteries
- books to read which we swap en route (or a Kindle)
- screw up rucksack, or something similar for extra space
- fold up umbrella (can double for sun protection)
- sewing kit
- washing line
- sink plug and small packet of detergent
- magnifying glass (one of the drawbacks to getting older)
- universal power plug (a must have for everyone)
- mobile phone - We avoid taking one but often wish that we had one and most travellers we meet always carry one. It is best to buy a really cheap phone and load it up with a local SIM card on arrival. Never take your expensive phone that will be extortionate to use and tempting for potential thieves. If you have to take it then make sure you switch off data roaming and use your phone only to text.

Toiletries can be bought abroad but take some small essentials. Make sure they are no more than 100 ml if you are to take them on the plane or they will be confiscated:

- small shampoo and conditioner
- tooth brush and paste
- shaver (I take an electric shaver and charger but a wet shave is just as good.)
- travel towel an ultra-light, quick-dry micro fibre (share one between you?)
- nail file, clippers and tweezers
- small hair brush
- small scissors but only if you are checking in your baggage

A small medical kit:

- all the tablets that you are prescribed
- malaria tablets if necessary
- first aid dressings
- antiseptic cream
- sun tan cream
- hydrocortisone cream for insect bites
- insect repellent, a Deet based one.
- aspirin or paracetamol (take an aspirin just before every long haul flight)
- ear plugs
- hand sanitizer
- water purification tablets
- pain killers
- laxatives
- antihistamines
- travel sickness tablets

In addition to all the above we occasionally take:

- travel kettle (rarely taken but sometimes an essential luxury and small items can be packed inside it.)
- food that you cannot do without such as Nutella, Marmite, marmalade etc.
- plastic poncho, if we know it is going to be really wet

Then there are some obvious things:

- passport - make sure it is valid for six months from arrival
- your bus pass, or passport is useful for proof of your age - many places throughout the world offer half price or even free entrance to senior citizens
- driving licence - if you intend hiring a car and have an international driving licence there can be no refusal, available at certain Post Offices at £5.50 for 12 months
- EHIC card - if you are travelling through the European Union

Miscellaneous items:

- safety pins
- sellotape
- rubber bands
- sticky labels
- plastic bags
- combination lock
- water proof bags

All these items need to be packed in smaller travel packs. Compression bags are useful to get more in, although they will add to the weight and some travellers find they will split if asked to do too much. They will crease some clothes although you should have abandoned such items by now. I am more in favour of rolling up clothes and only use a compression bag for a tent, fleece or down jacket.

I have omitted ladies clothes here, but for the ladies I would like to recommend a sarong. It's small and lightweight, doubles as a bath and swimming towel, skirt, dress, scarf, sun cover and sleeping sheet and essential for both men and women visiting temples in many South East Asian countries. So you need 2 sarongs!

Check that all the contents will pass through the scanning machine and are allowed on the plane. I once forgot about a much cherished penknife that was confiscated at Schiphol. I had to return to the main part of the airport, find a Post Office and mail it back to myself.

We have a list of things to take stored on the computer which we print off before each trip. It is a list that includes every conceivable possibility. By no means will everything be needed but items that are can then be ticked off as they are stored in the rucksack. That way you are less likely to forget things. You, like me at my age, may require an aid to memory. On our journeys we jot down further things that we think might have been useful and update the list when we return home although it is never intended that everything is going to be taken. I went through a worrying time in my early sixties when I thought I was getting early onset dementia. I was forgetting things, names of plants, places I had been to or sometimes going to my garage at home to get something only to arrive and have no idea what it was. I had to retrace my foot steps and start again. I was tempted to go to my GP and ask for some Arracept until I discussed it with other friends of a similar age who were all experiencing exactly the same problems. Getting back to the main point I tend to make a lot of lists and not only for travelling. Some go a bit over the top but other useful ones connected with travelling are, 'things to do before leaving the house' and a reminder about 'essential things to do upon returning'.

At your age you are probably on some sort of permanent medication, blood pressure tablets or statins. Make sure you have enough, count the days and count the tablets needed. Also you may be staying in some romantic places, even if it is a tent in the desert. This could seriously spice up your love life so don't forget the Sildanefil. At our age every little helps as we slip back into a life of sex and drugs and rock and roll.

Carry anything you cannot possibly do without, such as medication, in your hand luggage in case of bags going missing.

Keep with you a list of all your emergency contact numbers. Make copies of all your documents including your credit cards, passports, visas, bus pass, everything you can think of and email them to yourself.

If there is some room left over consider taking some luxuries. We miss things like mature cheddar, Marmite, and Earl Grey T-bags. Make sure that you are allowed to take whatever you choose into the country you are visiting. It would be bad enough to have it confiscated but you might get fined into the bargain. We landed at Cairns and they had sniffer dogs at customs. You have to put your rucksacks on the ground and let the dogs do their stuff. Never ever try to take fruit or any animal or vegetable products into Australia. A friend had saved his apple from the in-flight meal and got fined the equivalent of £90. Luxuries to some will be essentials, but not to others.

Many countries throughout the world are poor and people are desperate for things we take for granted. Try to take some gifts for children and adults. You will frequently hear children asking for a school pen and they are small items to carry. Do not, however, encourage any form of begging by handing out stuff willy-nilly. It is much better to take these items direct to a school. Any small educational stationary is ideal, pencils, rubbers and calculators. Do a bit of research and find out what is needed, there is a good website called stuffyourrucksack. In Cuba people needed soap, underwear, virtually anything. Most Cubans are too proud to ask for things but will be extremely grateful to be offered items you do not need. What we really wish we had taken were some balls for children to play with. Boys were playing baseball with a ball made from screwed up paper, string and rubber bands and nobody had a proper football.

stuffyourrucksack.com

Donating money will still be the most useful thing for poor communities but it is fraught with obvious problems. Each year we have been involved in a charity to raise money some of which goes to a deserving cause of our choosing. We look for a suitable charity in whatever country is next to be visited. That way we can be sure that the money ends up in the right place. In the poorer regions of Soweto we found a voluntary nursery school that had no funding and looked after lots of underprivileged young children. It was non profit making and the lady in charge had perfectly documented accounts. If we are not sure that the money is going to a genuine cause then it gets taken home and given to an established charity. In Malawi I spoke to an American woman who I had seen put a $50 note into a wooden collection box outside a school and was beginning to regret it. We were on the crowded and infamous Kande beach and plenty of local people had seen her do it. She asked me if I thought it was safe and I told her the truth. Just how naive can you get? We were also at one time involved in a charity to provide materials to a school in The Gambia. For the head teacher on a wage of £20 a month the temptation was just too great and he absconded with everything. Other schools will sell the donations to their pupils, so giver beware.

To sum it all up, takes as little as you can possibly get away with.

Try to get to Cuba before things change for ever

4 Backpacking Around the World

"Travel makes one modest. You see what a tiny place you occupy in the world."
Gustave Flaubert 1821-1880

If you are really serious about travel then back packing is a pretty good way to go. You will be able to tailor your trip to exactly where you want to go and what you want to see. En route there may well be times when you will begin to doubt yourself and perhaps even wish that you had not chosen this option but the rewards are worth it. Only after such an experience can you really call yourself a traveller. For some of us it will not be our first experience. Many of us have done it all before back in the sixties. We were the ones who brokered the hippy trails across Europe and Asia and on to Kathmandu. We were fresh out of school or students, we had very little money and hitch hiked our way around the world. It was our generation that made a gap year out travelling between school and going to university 'de rigueur'.

You will be at liberty to stay exactly where you want but if you choose to stay at a hostel or backpacker accommodation there are some advantages. Often when you arrive in any big city or town there will be a place where most of the hostels are situated. Wander from one to the other looking at the rooms, check out what is on offer and remember that the prices are generally negotiable. Great if you are travelling on a budget and even if you are well off it is a good option. Why pay high prices for luxury accommodation when all you really want is a bed to sleep in for the night? You will meet more people and have more fun. There will be more opportunities to share ideas and experiences so you will find out all the best places to go. Most backpackers or hostels that we have stayed in have been pretty good. Our main criterion is that it is quiet at night. If it isn't then we leave the next morning. If you get really stuck, then, as you are not a student anymore, perhaps you can afford the occasional night of luxury in a swanky hotel. Better still many countries offer home stays where you can live like the locals for a short time.

If you are not sure if backpacking is for you then test it on a shorter route. Anywhere in an English speaking country is going to be easier. Try travelling in Australia from Broome to Perth in a couple of weeks. Go by Greyhound bus or perhaps hire a car. The west coast is quite adventurous with lots of opportunities en route for hiking and snorkelling. South East Asia is easy to backpack around. It is simple to find both transport and accommodation. Booking an expensive tour is pointless, unless you have lots of money and want to have everything packaged up and sanitized for you, however, you will miss out on a lot of exciting things. Experiencing new cultures and exploring new places independently is good for the soul, and maybe the elixir of youth.

Back packing will provide a much more authentic experience and give you a greater chance to get closer to the country and its people. It is the ideal way to travel around the world and not just for younger travellers. Now is your chance to live like a hippy again, relive the past or at least revisit it.

When we were young to travel around the world used to seem like some sort of fantasy dream, but now it is a relatively cheap and practical option for most people. Travelling light will give you greater flexibility and make travelling to all those obscure places far easier.

How much time have you got? Being out of the country for more than six months will bring certain problems regarding tax, paying bills, looking after the garden and missing the grandchildren's birthdays, but you are retired so time should not be so important. Try to make your trip as long as you are able to, taking in as much as possible. Three months or so should be long enough to get a lot of travelling in and a good starting point is to buy a round the world ticket, which will last for 12 months. They are convenient and save you having to book flights en route. Booking all flights in advance will save money as well.

All the suggested routes that you will find on the internet can be modified to suit your own ideas but initially you have to decide where you want to go. List all the places then use an atlas to try and link them all together. You may have to make some compromises as most round the world trips come with certain rules. A mileage limit ticket is the most common one and this includes surface travel as well. If your total journey is between 25,000 and 30,000 miles it will cost less than the next level of 30,000 to 35.000 miles. Costs go up with the amount of miles and the more miles you get the more continents it will get you to and the more destinations. Each company has its own rules. Try to plan your trip in one continuous direction. You can back track over continents but not oceans.

The other RTW way is with a set fee provided by one operator. For each route only certain airlines along with their partners will operate it. As in the first option you can only fly around the world in one continuous direction either east or west. Once you have flown over a continent you cannot go back and there will be a limit to the amount of stops allowed within a continent. There will be a maximum amount of segments of travel allowed, including surface segments. Some companies allow up to 15 stopovers, each one being considered at least 24 hours in one destination.

Similar rules may apply to both methods. You can always work out a route for yourself and if you do not fancy booking it all up on your own then get one of the many companies out there to do it for you. In many ways it is better to have someone else to do this for you as then you will have their insurance backing if anything goes wrong. Specialist travel agents such as Trailfinders can advise on the best routes and quickly tell you what is or is not possible. They will know all the airlines, where they fly to and how they connect up. They will make a small charge but they employ experienced travellers who will provide you with valuable information. It saves a lot of hassle and later on they will email you with any changes to flight times.

The internet site Oneworld offer what they describe as the ultimate choice and flexibility when booking your fights. The Oneworld Explorer is based upon the number of continents visited and has no maximum mileage limit and up to 18 segments can be included in your ticket. A flight segment counts as one flight so that would be 16 flights. There are no overland penalties or mileage limits. It seems like an excellent idea, all flights are equal and there is no fee if you want to change the date and time of your flight. Failing that then they have a more versatile distance based fare 'Global Explorer' to create your perfect RTW trip. Another company to check out is staralliance:

    www.trailfinders.com
    www.staralliance.com
    www.oneworld.com

Prices are also based upon where you start your trip and in what month. The cheapest tickets are available in the low season from mid January to mid June and from September to November. So avoid July, August and over the Christmas period. Costs will vary depending upon the amount of stops and where they are.

Try to include some travel on the surface. You do not have to fly in and out of the same city. Fly into Cairns travel around Australia for six weeks and fly out of Sydney or wherever you wish. It will add to your adventure and give you greater freedom and allow you more time to soak up some local culture. Consider including train passes or greyhound bus passes.

Routes and times can be changed for a small administration charge, although the one time when I tried to do it the charge turned out to be a largish one.

Check the Foreign and Commonwealth website. If they recommend against going to any country or specific areas then do not go. Not only will you put yourself in danger but you will invalidate your insurance. Log on to their site anyway as there are lots of travel tips and up to date advice.

www.fco.gov.uk/travel

The only problem with a round the world ticket is that you are on a rigid timetable, not that I personally have ever found that to be a problem. When booking up it is useful if you can be flexible with your dates, avoid travelling at weekends or holiday times. If you are prepared for a little inconvenience then early morning, late night and indirect flights can be a lot cheaper. Consider booking separate budget flights for some places. For instance internal flights around Australia are better booked in Australia.

When you do book up always ask if there is a special rate or special rate for seniors, and do this for every holiday that you book. Some of these discounts are not well advertised and you have to request it, if you are going to receive it. Australians seem particularly well cared for in this respect. Every 2 years pensioners are subsidised by the government for travelling abroad.

For our first RTW trip we decided upon the major places we wanted to visit and then looked at other places on route that seemed like worth visiting. The first place we pencilled in was Easter Island. It was one of those places I had read about as a child. None of it was completely true but I had spent the last fifty or more years thinking, 'one day'. The story I remembered was that sailors had discovered the island on Easter day, the most remote place in the world, abandoned with huge statues facing out to sea built by a race of giants. Having decided upon Easter Island we found that we had to arrive from Tahiti and it was most practical to travel on to Santiago. The second dream destination was Angkor Wat, plus we were committed to visiting relatives in Australia, so our trip eventually ended up as follows, London - Dubai - Mumbai - Thailand - Cambodia - Vietnam - Australia - Tahiti - Easter Island - Santiago - Buenos Aries - London all in 92 days. With such an extensive itinerary within a relatively short time frame the trick is to get the balance right, to see as much of the world as possible without having to rush too much. Inevitably we did not explore some places in any sort of depth but had some great experiences. There are hundreds of different ready made round the world tickets available and some seem to be very good value. Ours was a great trip and briefly here it is in slightly more detail just in case you need a ready made plan.

Dubai for 3 nights was the first stop. We chose to stay in a hotel on the Deira side of the creek in amongst all the hustle and bustle of the traditional souks and markets. It was a bit of a run down area but we preferred it to the glass and steel splendour of all the skyscrapers on the other side. The dhow wharf was fascinating with Arab traders loading up ancient wooden boats. It was also Ramadan, so no drinking and eating all day. No swimming, dancing, singing, they even sealed the swimming pool off so nobody would be tempted to jump in. In this part of the world do not be tempted into anything too affectionate in public with your partner or you could end up being arrested. At sundown all the men had meals in the street leaving their women at home to look after the children. The side streets were covered with communal meals and all the men sat around cross legged eating with their hands, in silence. There were very few women to be seen after dusk and those out in the daytime were always completely covered up. Across the creek is the Bur Dubai, the glitzy bit, full of magnificent buildings and huge shopping malls. You can take a bus or cross on an Abra, a water taxi, for next to nothing. Amongst the skyscrapers you cannot easily walk anywhere, there are no pavements, nobody is expected to walk, you would be crazy to walk, as it is just too hot at 40 degrees plus every day. Unless you are a little crazy you will step from one air-conditioned taxi or shopping mall to another. We ended up feeling glad that we had stopped in Dubai but did not feel a need to visit again. Other people of course may love it and everyone should go and judge for themselves.

The second stop was Mumbai for 2 nights. It surpassed our expectations and gives visitors a chance to see some of the 'real' India. Arriving at 02.10am we had a snooze in the airport and then took a taxi at 6am. The utter squalor is fascinating in some bizarre and voyeuristic way. The streets in the early morning are relatively quiet with hundreds of people asleep everywhere. Dozens of bodies were just lying around in every conceivable spot, even in the middle of the road. We watched a heavy lorry manoeuvring around an elderly sleeping woman. She might have been dead but nobody seemed to be at all concerned. We stayed in a cheap hotel right next to the chaotic Crawford market. The market was a fascinating run down place, built by the British and now dirty, smelly and noisy, but exciting. In such places India is an assault on the senses. With careful planning quite a lot can be done in Mumbai in a short time. We took a taxi to Colabo on the sea front dominated by a huge arch marking the place where in 1911 King George V and Queen Mary arrived, the first British monarchs to set foot in India. We had just missed the small ferry to Elephant Island but after a little waving it did a u-turn and came back for us. We leapt aboard from the jetty in the style of invading pirates. Elephant Island is a world heritage site where at the top of the hill sits a huge cave that has been further excavated and the internal walls decorated with amazing carvings of Hindu deities. The one showing Shiva in all his magnificence is said to be the best in India. If you do not fancy trudging up the hill in the heat you could always opt for the decadence of a sedan chair. Another cheap taxi ride took us to Chowpatty beach. Nobody actually sunbathes there but in the evening it attracts huge crowds. We were lucky to see a Hindu ceremony. It was mostly women and children praying and chanting around a home made floral shrine. A Fakir worked himself up into frenzy as he wailed and flagellated himself with metal chains. Then in some sort of a trance he walked upon a bed of nails along with further wailing sounds and demonic laughs. All sorts of other little ceremonies took place before he finally collapsed with exhaustion onto the sand. The beach is littered with washed up bits of interesting debris from Hindu ceremonial offerings that have been sent out to sea on improvised rafts. Later a big crowd gathered around two large eels and beat them to death with sticks before a grateful old man took them home to cook. I have friends who refuse to go to India because they say they would not be able to cope with the poverty. It can be difficult to come to terms with and you will see the most appalling cases of deprivation. There are terribly deformed beggars dragging themselves around on makeshift trolleys, but that is part of what India is about. At night thousands of people will lie down again on the pavements and sometimes in the middle of the road to sleep. It is a culture shock but things are beginning to change as the Indian economy develops.

Bangkok was the next stop for 3 nights. No need to book accommodation here, just get the shuttle bus from the airport into town and then a local bus to Khosan Road where there are dozens of backpacker hostels and hotels catering for all sorts of budgets. Bangkok has changed a lot over the years and you now have to pay to get in all the temples and the Royal Palace. Everyone is trying to squeeze as much money as possible out of you but it is still very cheap and a wonderful destination. In the heart of the backpacker area there is always lots going on. The weekend market is worth a visit as it is a huge sprawling affair selling everything, a cross between Anjuna market in Goa and Camden in London. While you are there treat yourself to a Thai massage which will cost very little. Another half day was spent at the Vimanmek Mansion - the largest golden teak structure in the world. A visit to Patpong Street is an absolute must, the really seedy red-light area. There are scantily glad girls everywhere and sleazy men trying to lure tourists into clubs. We went into a bar and a girl immediately got up, she squeezed herself in between my wife and me and offered us all sorts of interesting things. The Pussy Club had an interesting 'menu' and it is amazing what the female anatomy can do. On the other side of the main road is the street for those batting for the other side. Lots of cute Thai boys in tight shorts with middle aged white men in tow. What goes on there is even more intriguing than the 'girls' side. There are also lots of 'lady boys' particularly serving in the restaurants who look absolutely stunning. Of course there is much more, according to your interests, to see in Bangkok. You can get everywhere cheaply by the wonderful tuk-tuks, but remember to negotiate a price with the driver before you get in. It depends what time of year you go but there can be massive tropical storms in and around September time. We sat under cover in a restaurant and watched the water rise alarmingly quickly. They only last 15 minutes or so but it is quite exciting.

It is very easy to travel overland throughout South East Asia. We started out early for Cambodia getting a bus to the border and then another to Siem Reap. You have to book up the day before at one of the many travel agents. It was all surprisingly easy and you even get picked up from your accommodation by minibus. At the border we were dropped off at a cafe to fill in visa forms and had to hand our passports over to a young girl, who sped off on a motorbike to get them stamped at the local consulate. Then it is a long and bizarre walk through no man's land and several check points to get visas before finally crossing into Cambodia. It was here that we encountered our first problem. Although we had booked the onward journey we had apparently 'just missed' the connecting bus, but we could get a taxi right away for an extra 300 baht. This is one of several possible scams that you have to put up with. Either wait the 3 hours for the next bus or pay up. In Cambodia the roads deteriorated and Siem Reap, at that time, resembled a frontier town. There are smart new buildings mixed with old ones and pot-holed, muddy streets. Food and accommodation is again ridiculously cheap. In SE Asia our accommodation averaged out at about 8 pounds a night! We ate really well for about 5 pounds nightly and that was with drinks included!

Beng Mealea is waiting for you to discover it

Angkor Wat was the main reason to go to Siem Rep and it is truly awesome. My camera stopped working here and I was forced to buy a new one to record the wonders of it all. Words cannot really describe it or photos do it justice. There are many 12th century temples spread over a huge area and we spent 2 days touring round them. Again a tuk-tuk for the day costs very little, and a 3 day pass for the temples at that time cost $40. Ta Prohm is one of the most interesting temples where the trees are entwined with the rocks and where part of Indiana Jones & The Temple of Doom was filmed. This is possibly the best sight of its type in the world. The only downside is that at times it was teeming with Japanese tourists, swarming over the temple like agitated ants, but they are all on coaches and will disappear quickly enough. Tourists sometimes can be a real nuisance. It gets very crowded at midday and the best times are early or late, when the sunrise or sunset is over the main temple. The following day we hired a taxi for the day to go 60km east to

Beng Mealea which was also used as a location in the filming of 'The Temple of Doom'. A taxi is the only realistic way to get there as few travellers venture that far. It is an Angkor Wat in the making, overgrown and completely un-restored. This is real 'Boys Own' adventure stuff. As we arrived the end of the monsoon hit and the rain was torrential. We took shelter on the ground under a tarpaulin along with some souvenir sellers. At the site you can clamber over the ruins as you wish, at your own risk. The stones are very slippery after the rains, but we walked and crawled through dark tunnels ankle deep in water, edged our way over roofs and along the tops of walls. Our past rock climbing experience came in very handy and you need a good head for heights. The rain brings the snakes out and the area around is apparently still land mined. Wisely we decided not stray too far away. For much of the time we were on our own in this wonderful place. Get there before the tourists.

Siem Rep has an excellent old market, an interesting night market, good value restaurants and it is easily explored by bicycle. You are supposed to ride on the right hand side of the road but that is not absolutely necessary. Sitting outside eating is a pleasant way to watch the world go by. A 'lady boy' caught our eye, long blond hair, a short skirt and a figure to die for. We booked a boat ticket to Phnom Penh and after a sort of 'rest' day took the ferry down the Tonle Sap Lake to Phnom Penh. This is one of the largest and deepest lakes in Asia and although more expensive than the bus it is far more interesting. The boat was shaped like a torpedo and sped across the lake for 3 hours at 50 odd mph. then more slowly for a further 3 hours where the lake narrows to a river. We passed some remarkable sights. There were thousands of individual houses and communities either on small floating islands or on stilts, some, several miles from land.

Arriving in Phnom Penh the tuk-tuk drivers and baggage handlers are waiting in ambush. We ignored their insistent offers and walked the short distance into town, which is easy to do with just a small rucksack to carry. As with most places on our travels we booked in for one night and then found a better place the following night. The first one turned out to be the sort that charged by the hour. It is quite easy to find your way around Phnom Penh and we spent three days there. The two major sights are those connected with the misguided Pol Pot and the Khmer Rouge. Firstly was the infamous Toul Sleng Genocide Museum. Before Pol Pot emptied the city it was the high school. It has been left as it was found and is pretty grim. Here high ranking people and anyone who was educated were tortured, sometimes for months on end until they finally confessed. The Khmer Rouge photographed and documented everything. All the victims' photos are on display there, each with the same wide-eyed terrified look, men, women, and children alike. It was a truly awful place and I cannot write down the full details of what happened. From there, the second visit is to the killing fields at Choeung Ek where the prisoners were taken to be slaughtered. Terrible atrocities took place here, entire families were wiped out and there is an informative museum to act as witness. We felt it was a visit that had to be done and came away with a thorough understanding of that dreadful time.

The bus to Ho Chi Minh City 245km away took about 6 hours and was excellent value at that time (2009) for only $9. There is a boat but bad traveller's tales were filtering back about this option. HMC is a vibrant community with friendly people. We took a trip down to the Mekong Delta for two days. On the way the bus filled with smoky fumes, we were stuck by the roadside for 3 hours and everybody refused to get back on. It was very disorganised but still quite good fun, if taken in the spirit of adventure. We spent lots of time on six different boats, going round islands, floating markets, sampling snake wine, rice wine, coconut wine and local fruits and passing through little waterways where the Vietcong once hid out.

The Mekong Delta is becoming a bit too touristy. The biggest floating market is no longer very big and now sells mostly tacky souvenirs. The transport system on the land is so much improved that floating markets have become redundant. If you continue a further twelve miles up stream you can find a smaller more genuine floating market. Back in HMC dinner outside was accompanied by a relentless stream of hawkers and beggars. The third day was spent travelling 105km north to the Cao Dai Temple to watch the midday mass. Caodaism seems like quite a sensible faith in that it embraces all religions and only worships one God. It is uniquely Vietnamese and now a minority but intriguing sect. 55km to the east are the Cu Chi tunnels, where against all the odds the ill-equipped Vietcong held out against the mighty Americans. On the way we passed the crossroads where the Americans dropped a napalm bomb on a village near a temple and the iconic 'Mai Lai' photo was taken. It was of course a 'cropped' photograph and made to look far worse than it actually appeared, if that is possible. There is absolutely nothing to see there now but easy to recall that photo. We crawled through 100 metres of tunnels on different levels. It was hot, dark and cramped but interesting, even enjoyable. This immense network of underground tunnels is where the Vietcong hid right under the noses of the American forces. Not everyone wants to do that sort of thing particularly if they suffer from claustrophobia and there are frequent escape routes as you crawl along. There were all sorts of other Vietcong buildings all camouflaged from the air. We shot 10 rounds with an M16 which was great fun but outrageously expensive. Where else can you shoot live ammunition? There is even a choice of guns. Go for the AK 47 for the full Rambo experience but it will be over in a flash.

Next it was Australia for about seven weeks and it came as a big shock. Everything seemed so expensive after South East Asia. The idea in Oz was to see as much as possible without rushing. We chose to book all the flights beforehand although it is cheaper albeit less convenient to sort them out when you get there. We flew Cairns, Darwin, Perth, Uluru, then overland to fly out of Sydney.

Cairns is a good place to arrive to for the traveller. At the airport there is a notice board with free phones for various accommodation and they will even come and pick you up. Cairns, has a beautiful esplanade, and is a great place for walking in the nearby rain forest and hills. There is plenty to do and see but we took two main trips. It is easiest to book an excursion or otherwise hire a car. Firstly it was up north to Cape Tribulation to stay overnight. Once you cross the Daintree River civilization as you know it is left behind and there are no services provided at all. No electricity, water, mobile phone coverage, nothing. The area is also quite lawless with the police not being keen to go up there. The community look after themselves and visitors can get into serious difficulties if caught misbehaving, say dropping litter. Angry residents could sweep down from the hills at any time and turn nasty. There is only one road and that turns into a track after the Cape Tribulation, if it rains hard you can be cut off for weeks on end by landslides. A nearby area had half the annual rainfall of London in half an hour! Can that really be true? The whole area is a World Heritage Site and is the longest continually developing rainforest in the world. Nothing has changed for the last 250 million years.

Secondly we took a sailing boat out to the Great Barrier Reef for the day. Seeing the largest collection of living things on the planet is a must for all travellers. This was one of the most looked forward to trips of the tour. It was fortunate that the trip we booked was under subscribed and we were bumped up to a more expensive one. You need good sea legs for this excursion as it is a rough trip out to the reef, my wife was sick and I was feeling queasy. Many others onboard were sick, some so sick that they could not do the scuba dives that they had paid so much for. Scuba divers will have a fantastic time but snorkelling is also good. We both did some snorkelling and saw thousands of amazing fish on the coral reefs. It was my first Scuba dive but being on a more expensive trip it was a longer dive than I really wanted. It was a bit scary at first trying to get the breathing right and not to panic and at one time I wondered how I had managed to get myself into such a situation. I was down there for 45 minutes or more and glad to finally get back up. We also took a trip in a glass bottomed boat which is a good way of seeing a lot quickly. This 'bumped up' trip was to a luxury boat with a banquet for lunch, champagne, cakes and coffee and I got a $100 dive for $25. Just our luck!

Darwin was hot and sticky with limited attractions in the town itself and we did a complete walking tour in 3 hours, but I am probably judging it unfairly, you have to get outside of the town and explore. It is also here that we encountered some problems. On the first night at 3am in the hostel some young Irish travellers were screaming and shouting outside our room. I found myself naked in the corridor making some pointless threats, but at least they did not laugh at me and moved away. We changed to a different hostel the next day. One of the main reasons for Darwin was to visit our daughter in Katherine so we took a Greyhound bus. This is a convenient option in Oz.

My daughter lived out in the bush in a cabin on a 6 acre plot and this was more like the real Australia. One day it was 45 degrees during the day but did cool down nicely at night. The land is difficult to cultivate but teeming with wallabies. The first day we took a UTE (Toyota Hilux 3L 4WD) and drove up to Kakadu National Park to the Jim Jim Falls and the Twin Falls. The distances in Oz are vast, 600km+ return just to see a waterfall. We were on good roads for 2 and a half hours then 45 mins on an unsealed road and hardly saw any other vehicles. After that in the park we engaged 4WD for 40mins and had a challenging off road experience up and down huge bumps, over rocks, deep sand, through water and rivers. At times the vehicle was in mid air and so was I hanging on to the steering wheel. If you do not have a 4 wheel drive they will not let you into the park. It was great fun and miles from anywhere. It is only possible to get so far before having to abandon the luxury of the air conditioned UTE to trek onwards. After 45mins we arrived at a plunge pool that was supposedly crocodile free. Entirely on your own and in the sweltering heat just strip off and dive in. That evening we tested out some Aussie specialities, crocodile, kangaroo and buffalo steaks on the BBQ.

Katherine Gorge is one of the spectacular places in this region and a 4 hour trip is the only way to see this wonderful natural creation. Nearby further south are the Edith Falls where you can swim 280 metres across the lake and into the waterfall. On our last full day we drove 100k south to the Mataranka thermal springs. It is magical sitting in the pool surrounded by trees full of flying foxes. If you do ever get to this region make sure you visit and learn about the fascinating life of the barramundi fish. You can opt to feed them which is somewhat scary and all over in a split second with a large splash and bang. The one metre fish jump up and suck in the bait from your outstretched hand along with air into their mouths, only to explode the air out again with a loud bang. The bite on your hand is quite rough but it is only a scratch at most.

We flew to Broome, a small pleasant place which owes its existence to pearl fishing. No need to get a taxi as the town is adjacent to the airport. Hiring a motor scooter for three days is a good way to get around, for sightseeing and to visit the wonderful beaches. Broome is home to the world's oldest outdoor cinema picture garden where you sit out on deck chairs. The fact that the airport is so close and a succession of small jets flew over just above the screen added immensely to the experience.

Nearby slightly north there is a wild life park containing amongst other things two and a half thousand crocodiles. It was here that we learnt for the first time exactly how dangerous crocodiles are. As we approached one pen I saw the crocodile slide slowly back into the water. Then as we came up level with it the crocodile shot out smashing into the wire fence. We were so close that the fence bent outwards just enough to touch us. The crocodile slammed into the fence so hard that its nose was bleeding. Out in the open we would have stood little chance, they are seriously dangerous. Many of the caged crocs here were renegade ones that had invaded communities and threatened lives. They had in effect been given ASBOs. The males were put in separate cages with a screen between them to stop them trying to attack each other. We no longer walk too near creeks up in Northern Australia. If you ever do get attacked by a crocodile then grab hold of its jaw when it is closed and hold on tight. All the muscles in the jaw are geared up for snapping shut quickly. That is why they lie with their mouths open, their jaws reopen far more slowly as there are fewer muscles involved.

Perth came as a bit of a shock because it was quite cool after the heat of the north. Okay, hotter than back home in England but colder than we had become used to. For such a big city Perth has not got many cultural attractions. There is the gallery of Western Australian art and a museum, other than that there are a lot of shops. One highlight was a train ride to Freemantle, from where whale watching trips can be taken and we got up close to a humpback and her calf. There is an interesting museum outlining the early history of the immigrants and the disgraceful treatment of the Aborigines.

Another flight took us to Ayres Rock known to the locals as Uluru. It certainly is an impressive big lump in the middle of nowhere. We walked the 10km around it and were upset that we could not climb up it as it was closed due to extreme hot weather. There is a climbing, moral dilemma here as the Aborigines regard it is a sacred site and they do no want people clambering all over it. You have to decide for yourself. The sunset was truly awesome and the rock does keep changing various colour shades but there is nothing much else. The flies are a constant nuisance so go prepared; try tying a few wine corks on to your hat to dangle. It was nice just being at Ayres Rock after reading so much about it.

A coach took us to Alice Springs, 275 miles away, leaving at 4am and stopping at Kings Canyon for four hours to allow travellers to do the canyon rim walk. This is a spectacular piece of landscape and a challenging walk in the heat of the day. High up on the cliff is a really good place to shout and listen to the echoes. Go for the more difficult walk to the top of the canyon rather than the one inside the canyon designed for the 'wussies'. Alice Springs is another iconic place but again there are not many attractions. Property prices are high as there is no building land. It may be in the middle of nowhere but the government has given all the surrounding land back to the Aborigines. The real plight of the Aborigine people is in evidence here. With their traditional way of life taken away many have turned to serious drinking, exhibiting all the problems that go along with excesses. Alice is a good jumping off point for other places and the Ghan railway took us down to Adelaide. The train journey is a classic trip and took 22 hours at a sedate pace through the wilderness. This is another trip worth booking up in advance.

Adelaide is a beautiful city and we extended our stay there. It has a super botanical garden, and an excellent museum and art gallery. The Sir Donald Bradman museum at the Adelaide Oval is a must for cricket lovers and we managed to blag our way into the ground where NSW were playing SA. Once inside I persuaded an official to give us a tour of the old wooden, 'heritage' scoreboard which was in use at the time. This is the original ramshackle wooden scoreboard that runs alongside a modern one operated by enthusiastic volunteers. Inside you have to climb up several storeys that all resemble a children's advanced adventure playground. They even let me change over the scores. Here in Adelaide we picked up our hire car for the next 20 days. First it was a three day road trip following the Murray and Swan River valleys sampling wine on route to Geelong to meet up with long lost relatives. They all came out as £10 Poms back in the sixties. It is believed that this word came from the early convicts who were Prisoners of Her Majesty. Geelong also has a superb botanical garden planted up, with wonderful insight, in the mid 19th century. We toured the Bellarine Peninsula before heading off down the Great Ocean Road. This is one of the great drives in the world, built by soldiers returning from the Great War in order to provide meaningful work. We passed by fabulous beaches and look out points, stopping at all the classic tourist spots, including the 12 Apostles and many other rock formations. It was here that we saw our first Koala bears high up in the trees beside the road. We would not have stopped if it had not been for another group of people standing there staring up into the trees. On the way the route cuts across a peninsula where there is a lush rain forest. An interesting walk follows a track under towering Myrtle beech trees beneath which there was a forest of 20 foot tree ferns. Turning up north we stayed two nights in the Grampians, where we did the classic 'Pinnacles' walking route, among several others, passing by quite a few waterfalls. The Grampians are wonderful with great walking opportunities and a laid back attitude. The Youth Hostel is a great place to stay where most of the clients were even older than us. Joining the YHA can be worthwhile before leaving home.

On to Melbourne for what turned out to be five days. What a fabulous place it is full of cutting edge architecture and lots to do and see. As great cities go it is one of the best and we loved it. The Eureka Tower is the highest vantage point in the southern hemisphere and the lift takes you up 300 metres in 38 seconds. Leaving Melbourne behind the classic route is to drive the Great

Alpine Highway and this took us more than 300km over the Great Dividing Range. At the top, at some 6000 feet, it was 27 degrees and yet we walked through patches of snow still left over from the winter. Then there was a long drive to Canberra. Where was everybody? For a capital city it is a very strange place. It was a very short stay, mainly for the art galleries again before heading off to the Blue Mountains; my optician had recommended them being one of the highlights of Australia. When we arrived it was hot and bush fires were raging nearby so the park was closed for walking, but the views were terrific. The next day it was cold and wet with a thick mist, the only wet day we had in Australia, but we still managed a classic 4 hour walk down a steep cliff. This was the Giants Stairway, with 900 stone steps cut into the vertical cliff face, through a rain forest and past many more waterfalls. Although the visibility was down to 50m or less it all had a magical quality about it.

In Sydney the hire car got dropped off after some 2,600 miles. Sydney is a really nice place, particularly the area around the harbour. Try to do as much as possible here including all the main things such as an essential tour of the opera house, up the Sydney tower, the virtual reality Oz experience and the Sydney Harbour Bridge climb. The bridge climb takes three and a half hours and was exciting, expensive but not very challenging. Much of the time was taken up with talking and safety requirements. The two main beaches, Manly and Bondi are fabulous. We spent one day exploring all the waterways by ferry hopping. You can buy a day pass and have a lot of fun going all over the place hopping on and off. Our backpackers was right in the middle of the red light district, so there was plenty of night life to ogle. Australia is a great destination and we will return. We found Australians to be excellent company, friendly and helpful. A good idea for next time is to buy a four wheel drive vehicle in Southern Australia, use it to do most of the touring and then sell it in the north. Garages up there are always in need of good 4WD vehicles and this is a very practical option for anyone visiting for a lengthy period.

We had to go to Tahiti for a short stay mainly to enable us to get to Easter Island. Tahiti sounds exotic but the surrounding Islands are far better and on a Sunday Tahiti is sort of closed. Crossing the International dateline gave us two Sundays in a row.

Easter Island was wonderful, slightly bohemian, lawless and also odd. There are only two main intersecting streets and the shops seem like they have been waiting for supplies to arrive for months. Hiring a

4WD Jeep to get around is almost essential, as outside of town many roads are just dirt tracks. The massive statues of the famous heads, Moais, are awesome, although many look quite sad lying face down on the ground. Some were pushed over by warring tribes or in 1960 by the earthquake and ensuing tsunami. The island is made up from three main volcanoes one of which is up with my best natural wonders of the world, Rano Kau. There is the most wonderful walk along the rugged coastline to it, rising steeply up through the woods and fields. Looking down into the calderas it resembles a giant Monet painting with floating islands of bright green vegetation. One side faces the ocean and a sea cave is undermining the structure. Geologists calculate that in roughly 45 years the sea will break through into it and this amazing sight will be lost forever.

We were disappointed to have no photos for Tahiti and Easter Island as our camera was stolen. It was the camera that I had bought in Siem Rep and I shall explain all the details later. We had some fantastic images but more importantly they still remain as wonderful memories.

In Santiago with its massive cathedral, there are lots of galleries and museums. The cemetery is particularly amazing and so vast that it has its own metro stop and dozens of roads intersect it. Perhaps not everyone's idea of a day out but if you like cemeteries it is one of the best. We travelled further north up to Valparaiso, a world heritage site for a couple of days. This is a colourful town built on the sides of lots of hills. 100 year old funicular railways take visitors up to the hill tops where there are lots of little galleries, shops and great views over the town and harbour. We spoke to several travellers about Valparaiso all of whom had had bad experiences. We also had a few bad things happened to us in Chile and they soured some good memories. Every where we went there were dozens of stray dogs that barked all night and the streets were covered in dog mess. It was here that we were mugged and our camera was stolen. See the chapter on 'Safety' for a full account.

Buenos Aries, our final destination is a fabulous city with so much going on, one of the most exciting cities in the world. We stayed in the lively San Telmo district and everywhere there were street markets, entertainers and musicians. In the main square, the balcony on the Casa Rosada is where Eva Peron, and Madonna in Evita, addressed the crowds. Also there, every Thursday afternoon at 3.30pm all the increasingly aged mothers who lost their sons in the time when the generals were in power, (they took over in 1976) make a dignified parade around the square followed by a rally. There are lots of museums and galleries including one dedicated to Eva. Her grave in the wonderful cemetery at Recoleta is easy to find, just look for the crowds. It is another one of the most interesting and architecturally unique cemeteries in the world. The cafe Tortoni is the most famous in Argentina to grab a coffee and the El Antenio book shop is one of the world's most interesting, being housed in an old theatre. The Tango is the big event in the city and we went to the theatre to see a great show. It is the nearest thing to having sex with your clothes on. Over in the La Boca district all the cafes have super tango performers in the street and outside restaurants. La Boca has become very touristy even though it is within an undesirable district. Cross over into the wrong area and you will almost certainly get mugged. Food is good value in BA and the steaks are definitely the best in the world. I had a steak six nights in a row at the same parrilla.

If you have never been on a round the world trip then I envy you because you still have that to look forward to. It is often described as a trip of a life time and it is but I would be quite happy to do one every year.

Sydney Harbour Bridge

5 Trekking

"Walking is the perfect way of moving if you want to see into the life of things. It is the one way of freedom. If you go to a place on anything but your own feet you are taken there too fast, and miss a thousand delicate joys that were waiting for you by the wayside."
Elizabeth von Arnim 1866-1941

There are plenty of really tough trekking challenges out there, but most normal people will not be climbing a Himalayan peak, only the extraordinarily fit would attempt say, the Kokoda track trek in Papua New Guinea and for some even the South Downs Way may pose a problem. If you find it hard just taking the dog for a walk then you can skip this chapter. For keen hikers there are plenty of treks to be done but for most of us at our age we have to be realistic. The joy of trekking is that it gets you to remote places, places that can only be accessed by foot. You can truly get to wonderful parts of the world where you can be alone, at one with nature.

One of the first treks I did was Mount Kinabalu. At 4095 metres this is the highest point in South East Asia. Located in Sabah, Borneo, it is a UNESCO World Heritage site. If you happen to be on holiday there then it would be rude not to attempt the trek to the summit. It is a speedy climb so you only need to devote two days to it or three at the most. There is also the problem, that in going from sea level to over 4,000 metres in 24 hours is going to cause some people medical problems. I could have booked the trek up in England for what was £300+ at the time. On arrival it would have cost £90 or so at the hotel. I got an early morning taxi to the bus station in Kota Kinabalu and took a bus to the national park gates. Once there you are obliged to hire a guide and book up accommodation in the mountain hut. The total cost at the time, a few years ago now, was about £30. At the starting point they were reluctant to allow me to begin as all the other groups had already set off. Once on the trail though, you will easily pass some of the slower hikers. It is a beautiful walk and you cannot get lost as there is only one path. For the most part the route has been cut into a series of steep steps and in other parts there are ladders. You do need to be reasonably fit but anyone can do it if they are determined. There is plenty of time to get to the over night hut and the secret is to walk slowly and steadily. The biggest difficulty may be your reaction to altitude. Altitude sickness or acute mountain sickness (AMS) is something which generally occurs above 2,400 metres. Some people are unaffected by AMS and others may suffer on one trek but not on another. You can help avoid this by spending an extra night in the national nark, becoming conditioned by sleeping at altitude and there are some lodges just outside the park gates. On this particular trip there were quite a lot of people who were affected with vomiting and debilitating headaches. They remained at the overnight hut and did not go on to the summit. Maybe some were just plain lazy as everyone has to get up at 2am for the final push to Low's Peak at the top. Setting off in the dark and cold is an exciting challenge and a head torch along with plenty of water is essential. It is not difficult, compared to many other treks, and plenty of people do it successfully with no prior hiking experience. I was walking with the employees of an Australian cosmetics firm. They had been sent there as a bonding exercise and were all different sizes and ages. Nearer to the top there is a big sloping granite slab which is possible to walk up unaided, but there is a fixed rope for safety and also to act as a guide in the fog. Up near the summit the air is thinner, walking requires more effort and it is very cold and windy. The intention is to arrive to see the sunrise but part of this idea is to make sure that everyone has plenty of time to get off the mountain. Descending is perhaps worse than going up. It is easier on the heart and lungs but much tougher on the knees and it is wise to take frequent rests. Trekking poles are very useful and save a lot of stress on the knees, back and ankles. They also help balance and reduce the likelihood of falling. A study revealed that on flat terrain a hiker with two poles would transfer 13 tons per hour away from his body, and this went up to 34 tons when descending. Even going slowly the descent will only take four or five hours. Once down just outside the park gates a bus will take you back to town. In the hotel the next day it was easy to spot those that had done the climb, they were all walking slowly and in pain with aching muscles, but this soon wore off. Anyone can do this climb with a little determination, even though it may turn out to be one of the most physically demanding things you have ever attempted.

For easier trek try Mount Toubkal in the Atlas Mountains or there are hundreds of routes in the Pyrenees and of course many more in almost every country in the world, with dozens of specialist companies offering trekking holidays. You do not even have to leave England where we have some of the most wonderful hikes through the countryside, hills and mountains. Below I am going to give a brief insight into two classic treks, Kilimanjaro and Everest Base Camp.

Kilimanjaro is, at 5,895 meters or 19,341 feet, the highest mountain in Africa and also the highest free standing mountain in the world. It is a huge dormant volcano in North West Tanzania close to the Kenyan border. Top mountaineers and adventurers aspire to climbing the highest mountain in each of the seven continents and this is one that you can bag for yourself. The others are not quite so accessible and these are, Everest in Asia, Elbrus in Europe, Vinson Massif in Antarctica, Aconcagua in South America, Denali in North America and Cartensz in Oceania. Kilimanjaro is the one that celebrities sometimes choose and many people undertake as a sponsored climb for charity. It is a classically shaped mountain rising out of the African plains in the shape of an upturned V, like a small child's drawing. The good thing about it is that it is relatively easy in that there are no technical difficulties and no specific mountaineering skills are required. Again the one thing you must have is lots of determination, walking uphill for five or six days is very hard work, and it is uphill every single part of the way, there are no flat bits. I chose to ascend by the Machame Route which is a six day ascent. The success rate is a little higher on this route, possible because it is a day longer, giving climbers a greater chance to acclimatise. On this route you will be camping and porters will be carrying all your gear. You have to book with a licensed company as there is no independent trekking. There are several other routes to choose from one of the most popular being the Marangu route nicknamed the 'coca cola' route. This is the least expensive and the main difference is that that includes the relative luxury of shared hut accommodation rather than tents.

When starting off from the park gates with the daunting prospect of all that effort ahead of you the basic mantra will be, 'pole, pole' or in English, 'slowly, slowly'. It may seem strange to tell people how to walk but it is good advice. Slow and steady is the best way to conserve energy and acclimatise. If you need walking poles, which you probably do, then do not forget them for this trek. AMS is more likely be a problem for some people at this altitude and almost everyone will suffer in some way. Certain individuals are just more sensitive to changes in atmospheric pressure. Many problems can be avoided by ascending slowly and ideally by climbing up higher only to descend lower again to sleep. You are probably going to suffer from one or maybe all of the following:

- headache
- nausea
- dizziness
- tiredness
- loss of appetite
- stomach upset
- unsteadiness
- insomnia
- shortness of breath
- raised heart rate

You have to accept that you will not quite feel yourself but would be unlucky to suffer from all these effects. These symptoms normally begin after a day or so at altitude and then gradually subside as the body acclimatises. They are also worse at night. Some people take Diamox (acetazolamide) tablets to help avoid altitude sickness. They are supposed to reduce the likelihood of AMS but are not a substitution for proper acclimatisation. They improve the pattern of breathing and thus the quality of sleep. Taking Diamox could give you a false sense of security but on the other hand may help prevent all those nasty symptoms.

For most people these symptoms will be mild and disappear quickly leaving you free to enjoy this fantastic experience. The Machame route takes climbers to the peak from the south west and is thought to be the most beautiful and best of all the routes. From the Machame gate you ascend first through the tropical forests, then heather and moorland and finally alpine dessert to the icy peak. To begin with the days will be warm and the nights cold despite being so close to the Equator. Even on the first night you cannot leave your boots outside the tent or they may freeze solid. The route takes you through some of the mountain's best places and you will have a wonderful time walking at your own pace each day. There is the cloud forest on the southern slopes, followed by the dry and dusty Shira Plateau and finally the huge glacier near to the top. The Rebmann Glacier is the nearest glacier to the sun and is gradually disappearing.

The whole trek is a challenge where you can ask yourself whether you have got what it takes, and the final day is a very tough one. We left at 11 pm in the pitch dark and already there was a zigzag line of lights from head torches wiggling its way up the mountain. Again you leave early ostensibly to watch the sunrise over the east African plains, but more importantly to get everyone off the mountain early. The wind is howling and the icy rain is driving into your face. You must be well equipped, good solid walking boots with at least one pair of thick socks, thermal underwear, lined trousers and waterproof overtrousers. Above the waist probably four or five layers with thick gloves and a full face mask and hat. All I had showing was my mouth, nostrils and eyes and I had to screw them up against the rain and sleet which was driving in horizontally. My nose was running but it was just too impractical to get out a handkerchief and wipe it, so snot icicles developed. We trudged up in a tight column with the slowest up in front. It is necessary to keep walking just to barely keep warm. I had two litres of water in a camel back but the water in the tube froze solid so I could not get to it for a much needed drink. The sensible trekkers had tubes with protective insulated covers. I carried the extra weight of a two litres block of ice to the summit. Here again I must say that anyone can do this trek. Some of our group were smokers and others not particularly fit and slightly overweight, but they were all determined to succeed. Interestingly everybody in the group of 12 gave their bags to the porters to carry except for the two eldest, me at 60 and another man who was 43. We were determined to get up there unaided. Not too far from the volcano rim one of our party dropped like a stone to the ground suffering from AMS. One minute she was trekking in line with us and then suddenly she fell to the ground like a sack of potatoes. It was surprising as she was perhaps the fittest of us all, a trainee police woman in her twenties and doing a mountain leadership course. That is the nature of AMS, it does not differentiate or discriminate. There is only one solution and that is to descend quickly to a lower altitude to recover and after a short time it is possible to ascend again. At this point on the mountain there were a number of climbers being quickly frog marched down between two porters. If you do not descend to a lower level it can lead to high altitude pulmonary oedema or high altitude cerebral oedema both of which are potentially fatal. The collapsed girl was taken downhill and did recover quickly enough to get up to the rim of the crater a little later. It was a bit of a shock at this point to find we were not actually at the top. It is another forty five minutes or so, around the crater rim, up to Uhuru peak which is the highest point in Africa. Up on top with the evil winds biting into you and sucking away any body warmth it is not the best place to hang around for long, just long enough to get your photograph taken by the sign post at the top. This is not for everybody, I can appreciate that but remember anyone is capable of doing this trek but you have to think, do I really want to do it?

Everest Base Camp is my number one favourite trek ever. It can be done independently but it is a lot less hassle with an organised group. We chose to do it during the winter, in January. It is much colder but the skies are clearer and the trail is almost deserted. There were 10 in our party and only another 4 trekkers on the trail. Do not go in June to August as it is too wet. From Kathmandu you have to fly into the tiny airstrip at Lukla. We had to wait for two days for the weather to clear enough for take off, and some of that time was spent sitting under the aircraft on the runway just waiting for the opportunity. The flight itself is wonderful with magnificent views of the Himalayas and it is at this point that you can appreciate just how big they are. There are no flat places to land at Lukla and the runway is on a steepish slope. The small fixed-wing plane sort of crash lands and taxis uphill to a quick stop. It has been rated as the most dangerous airport in the world. The trek starts at this point and is undoubtedly one of the best walks in the Himalayas. You are crossing valleys which makes the terrain up and down all the way, with the ups being bigger than the downs. In total you will be climbing up more than the height of Everest itself. Again novice trekkers can complete this easily as long as they are reasonably fit. Only one of our group of ten failed to get there and he was by his own admission unfit. You will cross exciting rope bridges strung high above the valleys and at various points glimpse the top of Everest itself. There are amazing mountain views and Buddhist monasteries to explore. Lots of little shrines are dotted along the trail adorned with prayer flags, and small structures with prayer wheels that you must approach from the left and spin around as a quick way of 'reading' the Buddhist mantras. On the way you will meet the Sherpa people, pass through tiny little villages and one big one, Namche Bazaar, the capital of the Sherpa. You will be following in the footsteps of Sir Edmund Hilary and Sherpa Tenzing when they set off in 1953. Accommodation en route is in small wooden tea houses where, if you are lucky, you will get a shower. Above the tree line there is no fuel and small stoves burn dried Yak dung as fuel. Everyone huddles around these fires in a futile attempt to get warm and in winter that is not really possible. If you only have a limited amount of underwear and clothing then washing and drying clothes is nigh on impossible. Yak trains are a common sight and pose an interesting problem if you meet one half way across a rope bridge. Stand well clear as the tips of their horns are sharp.

Everywhere along the trail there are magnificent views. We saw and heard the awesome sound of an avalanche the other side of the valley. Like distant thunder the sound travelled through the thin air accompanied by clouds of powdered snow. There is a fascinating graveyard that you pass by high up on the trail with memorials to climbers that have died. Trekkers get strung out, you can walk at your own pace, and there are plenty of flat areas where you can take it easier. When the sun gets up it becomes surprisingly warm but make sure you always have your fleece and waterproof in your back pack. The weather can change quickly and if the sun goes in the temperature will drop alarmingly quickly. At that altitude with nothing to cover up in you will lose body heat at a frightening rate.

On the Everest Base Camp trail the porters will carry all your gear

We arrived at the final tea house in the afternoon. It was already well below zero at minus 10 centigrade or more. It is nothing more than a big wooden shed but it does provide much needed shelter.

The final part of the trek is a six hour round trip that takes you right to Everest Base Camp itself, which is a flat and desolate area strewn with rocks. In winter it is deserted but in the spring climbing season becomes a hive of activity. You will probably be exhausted but try to find time to wander around this fascinating place. There are various wreckages including one of a Russian helicopter that failed to lift off in the thin air and crashed back down to earth. The Kumba Icefall marks the start of the ascent, it is clearly visible on the slopes of the Everest and it is here that many climbers are killed. In 2014, the most recent tragedy, massive blocks of ice fell, killing at least 13 Sherpas and effectively ending the climbing season. The glacier is constantly moving, albeit very slowly, causing crevasses to open up with no warning and huge blocks of ice the size of a house can fall. Climbers up on Everest who are unfortunate to perish and whose bodies cannot be recovered are gradually buried in the snow but generally appear again many years later at the foot of this glacier. Base camp is the end of the journey but there is one more adventure.

From base camp Everest itself cannot be seen, so the following morning there is the opportunity to climb Kala Patthar. This is a small peak from where Everest can be viewed. For this you have to get up at 5am, in the bitter cold. Interestingly again out of our group of ten only the three eldest decided to go. Having gone all that way I would have been disappointed with myself not to have done it. For me there was no option, but all those young men in their twenties and thirties stayed in bed.

The ascent to Kala Patthar starts at 5,164 meters and the track takes you up steeply to 5,550 meters. It is extremely hard going but interesting. Normally you would have no problem in walking upstairs at home but the equivalent at altitude is exhausting. After a dozen steps or so the heart is 'beating like a subway train' and you have to stop to try and recover before struggling on a little further. There is just not enough oxygen in the air so goodness only knows what it must be like on Everest itself. The ascent takes about 1.5 to 2 hours and is well worth the effort. The rocky top is marked with prayer flags and from this famous vantage point the world's tallest mountains are clearly visible. The views of Everest are spectacular. It looked like it was smoking with the wind blowing the snow off the peak and upwards into the thin air. The following is an account of how cold it can be at night,

'It was maybe minus 15 or 20 degrees centigrade and that was inside the tea house. I was fully dressed and had to get into my sleeping bag as quickly as possible. I had to take something off or I could not have squeezed into the bag. It was also pitch dark and I only had my torch for light. The trick is to shed some clothes as quickly as possible and to put others on, thick socks, hat and gloves.

It needs careful planning and also I wanted to leave my clothes in some sort of order to put on at 5am when it would be even colder. It took maybe all of thirty seconds. I got my head into the bag and closed the top recycling my warm breath to try to heat everything up a bit. I thought I was dying because I could not get enough oxygen into my lungs and was unable to get my breathing regulated to anywhere near normal. My chest was heaving and my body shivering and it was only later that I realised everybody else had exactly the same problem. During the night I needed to go to the toilet. Sleeping was far from easy so I hung on as long as possible, but in the end I was forced to get up. I had the foresight to leave a plastic bottle beside the bed, but getting out and in again plus having to strip down a bit to actually pee is the stuff of nightmares. You lose heat rapidly however fast you try to pee. In the morning there was a solid block of frozen yellow urine.'

The return journey to Lukla is just as thrilling with magical views. The Italians have built an unusual monument to those that have died from AMS. It is a large stainless steel pyramid engraved with the names of all the victims. It is totally out of keeping with the environment, and it can easily be missed being slightly off the trail. It is covered with hundreds and hundreds of the names of victims. AMS is a more serious condition in this region, because from the trail it is not easy to descend quickly as there are no obvious safe routes down. Moderate symptoms of altitude sickness will be more serious than the ones already described and anyone might suffer from the following:

- severe headache
- nausea and vomiting
- an increased shortness of breath
- lack of co-ordination, if anyone cannot walk in a straight line then they should descend to a lower altitude immediately

Severe altitude sickness results in a worsening of all the above plus even more extreme symptoms:

- a persistent cough
- continually out of breath
- bubbling sounds in the lungs
- coughing up fluid

- walking problems
- irrational behaviour
- double vision
- convulsions

While we were up there a trekker did get into trouble with AMS but had nowhere to descend. The only solution was to send in a helicopter, but a sudden change in the weather to fog and snow prevented a landing. He had to suffer but fortunately survived unharmed. It is wise to find out if you are likely to suffer from AMS or not before taking on this trek. A friend of mine started feeling AMS symptoms just getting off the plane in La Paz at 3,650 meters.

We arrived back in Lukla on schedule but at this point the snow came down thick and fast. The little plane could not land, we were trapped and remained there for a further six days. Food was running out because it all has to be flown in to the tiny community. Everyone had missed their flights home and some of the group were getting rather upset and emotional. It was fascinating to see how individuals reacted to such adverse circumstances. Each morning we got up to find it still snowing and the air strip covered. On the fourth day the snow stopped and with the help of the army we attempted to clear the runway. The army have a small presence at Lukla that has increased in recent years. There are machine guns, razor wire and trench positions, the perceived threat being from Maoist insurgents. We thought the army would give us all a shovel to clear the snow. The reality was far different, they went around all the houses cadging bits of wood. Each of us armed with a short plank of wood got down on our hands and knees in the snow and tried to push it all aside like mini bulldozers. After several hours we had almost got the runway clear just before it began snowing again. On the fifth day the authorities managed to get a helicopter in to evacuate those desperate to get back to their jobs. On the sixth day the snow melted away and the rest of us returned to Kathmandu. We considered ourselves to be really lucky, the next group had been waiting six days for a flight into Lukla. Their trek had to be curtailed and end at Namche Bazaar and they would not be seeing Base Camp at all.

Back in Kathmandu I was told that my plane would not be leaving until at least 10pm, so I set off in a rickshaw to do a bit of sight seeing. Unbeknown to me there was a change of plan and there had been a frantic and unsuccessful search for me. I rocked up back at the hotel at 16.50pm only to find my flight was at 17.00pm and I had not yet fully packed. Packing took three minutes. There were two motor bikes and riders standing by for me, one for most of my luggage and another for me. We hurtled off like the 'leader of the pack' weaving in and out of people, markets and cars. I was hanging on for grim death as we accelerated to suicidal speeds in crowded areas. Throngs of people parted before us like the Red Sea. Fortunately the airport at Kathmandu is fairly close and the hope was that the plane would be late taking off. However, the airport was deserted and I jumped over the check in counter, opening all the doors looking for anyone to help. Eventually I found someone sitting in front of a computer who told me that I was too late. After a bit of pleading and tapping on the computer we discovered the aircraft was still on the runway and the final passengers were just getting on. I sprinted across the tarmac to the plane and arrived on board to cheers and clapping.

I have frequently used the Adventure Company for trips such as Base Camp. Among the many firms out there, Explore also cater well for older clients.

www.adventurecompany.co.uk
www.explore.co.uk

Clearing the runway at Lukla in the Himalayas

There are thousands of trekking opportunities in every single part of the world and they do not have to be at altitude, here are just a few ideas:

Madeira - The levadas are an ingenious network of irrigation channels designed to bring water from the high mountain springs to drier areas. Many of them are cut out of the steep rocky slopes to harvest the rainfall. Developed in the 16th century they now provide great walking opportunities. Some levadas are wide and others narrow to tiny crumbling edges on the side of cliffs where a fall would result in serious injury or death. At these narrow points walkers coming in the opposite direction cause an interesting dilemma with someone having to take the dangerous 'outside' route. Most, however, provide safe and easy walking, on the flat, with wonderful scenery. There are over 1350 miles of levadas and 25 miles of tunnels, where a torch will be handy. Madeira will not disappoint you.

The levadas provide some spectacular walking

Tenerife - Mount Teide at 3718 meters is the highest point in Spanish territories. The walk starts from a lay-by on the main road. My wife did not want to walk to the top so we set out on the flat for a short ramble. It was a rocky path that gradually got steeper. I persuaded her to keep going just to see 'what was around the corner' saying that we would turn back soon. Eventually I suggested, incorrectly, that it would be further to go back than to go on to the top. She fell for it and 4 or 5 hours later we reached the Altavista refuge. To go the extra 200 metres to the crater rim requires a permit that must be obtained in advance. Descending by the cable car takes 8 minutes. We tend to avoid Playa de las Americas when in Tenerife.

Crete - Go there especially to walk the Samaria Gorge in the south west. It is 16 km long and at one point narrows to only 4 meters. Walk down from the Omalos Plateau, where there are an incredible amount of stone steps, to the sea. Here a boat takes you to a village from where you can get a bus back to Chania. Do not go to Malia unless you want to party all night.

Mallorca is surprisingly good for walking if you stay up in the North West close to all the high mountains. S'Arenal is for the tourists.

Dolomites - The Italian Lakes are a great trekking and walking destination for all grades. Travel around the lakes by ferry and use cable cars where necessary.

Naxos - We chose this island in the Cyclades as it is the largest and a paradise for hikers. It is easy to get a bus to the centre of the island where the best walks are. From the highest point on top of mount Zas at 1004 meters you can see all around the island and all the other neighbouring islands. Go out of season when it is cooler.

The Alps - Once all the snow has melted you can hike along well maintained paths in Austria, Switzerland, France and Italy. There are walks and hikes at all levels of difficulty. The classic long distance route is the Mont Blanc Trail which circumnavigates Europe's highest mountain.

The Annapurna Sanctuary - This is a high altitude trek but relatively easy as you do not have to ascend too much. Some of the most spectacular mountain scenery in the Himalayas can be seen. Be aware that you will constantly be at high altitude.

Wales, particularly the Snowdonia area offers what I consider to be some of the best walks, hikes and climbs to be had anywhere in the world and I could quite happily live there. Try the hike up Tryfan for starters. When you get to the top jump from Adam to Eve, if you dare.

The United Kingdom - Some of the best Treks in the world are on our own door step. There are well marked routes all over the kingdom. I have no need to go on too much because firstly you know already and secondly there are plenty of specialist books, but what about the following:

- South Downs Way
- Pennine Way
- Cotswold Way
- Oxfordshire Way
- Staffordshire Way
- Cumbria Way

There are lots more 'ways' and then there are the 'paths', 'trails' and 'walks'. The main thing is to get out there, make sure you do it, and squeeze as much as possible out of life. There will be some close to home where you can walk a shorter section in part of a day. If you are lucky enough to have two cars then one can be left at the finishing point to make it easy to get back, or as you have a free bus pass then use that to return. You can rediscover the joys of sitting on the top deck in the front seat unless some other old codger has got there before you. It is quite exciting seeing behind high fences and catching glimpses of things that you never noticed before.

The levadas - Go to Madeira in the spring when all the flowers are out and there are fewer tourists.

6 Overlanding

"It is good to have an end to journey toward; but it is the journey that matters, in the end."
Ernest Hemingway 1899-1961

Overlanding can best be described as travelling with a mixed group of people in a specially equipped truck or some other such, 'go anywhere' vehicle like a Land Rover. Lots of companies offer these trips through all parts of the world. Such trips will provide some of the greatest travel experiences but also each has their own unique potential problems. One of the main worries may be how you will get on with a group of strangers most of whom will be younger than you. The best advice would be not to think about your age as this sort of travel is more about where you are from and your state of mind. Maybe it will be a chance to form long lasting relationships or perhaps at the end of the trip you will be glad that you never have to see your travelling companions ever again. You could end up being some sort of wise guru who everyone turns to for advice or completely ignored with all your old fashioned ideas. Be very, very careful which company you choose to travel with and 'interrogate' them beforehand. You do not want to end up on a party bus and some of the East Africa trips are notorious for this. Make sure you ask how many people have already booked up and find out their ages. Companies should be able to give out a limited amount of information without breaching confidentiality. Get other people to phone up on your behalf and ask at least one of them to be looking for a party bus so that you can identify potential problems. If every one on the trip is in their teens or twenties then give that one a miss. Some companies do run trips only for younger age groups, but ideally a good one will want a mixture of nationalities and ages. Do not let yourself get stuck with a group of youngsters who are just out for a good time. It might be great for them but it will be utter misery for you. I have seen it happen first hand on other trucks that we have been unfortunate to park near to. Some groups of students are interested in nothing but getting totally totalled every night, and day for that matter. The focus of their trip will be to hit the local bars every night. They have just escaped from their mummies and daddies and want to let off steam. Their parents would probably be ashamed of them, as they are only interested in themselves, getting drunk, laid and making as much noise as possible. They will be rude, abusive and foul mouthed just for the sake of it. Part of it is showing off and just trying to fit in. You do not want any part of this and if you do then close this book now. Although they themselves may be having a great time, these are adolescents behaving in the worst possible way. You may be have been through something similar many years ago and hopefully do not want to repeat it. Looking at this type of travel more positively, pick the right trip and you will be sharing a unique experience with like minded people of all ages and will form some life long friendships.

So try to identify a company that will accommodate people of all ages and nationalities. Find a trip that is not aimed only at the gap year market. Every group will be different but overland travellers usually have similar expectations and are often from places like the UK, Australia, New Zealand, Canada, Scandinavia, Germany, the Netherlands and the USA. A lot of them will be travelling solo but there are generally several couples or friends together. We travelled with Africa-in-Focus through East Africa. It was not without problems and within the group of 15 there were people in their, 20's, 40', 50's and 60's. This company specialises in photography, is slightly more expensive and attracts an older clientele. They also try to cater for those wanting more personal space and comfort. For our West African trip we travelled with Dragoman who also like to have a mixed age group. With Dragoman is not just a holiday but a true travel experience. Our trips worked out well but do not commit yourself to one until you have all the details. Other good companies I have encountered are Intrepid, Journey Latin America and G Adventures. Avoid companies such as Oasis or Contiki who seem to cater for youngsters.

   www.dragoman.com
   www.intrepidtravel.com
   www.gadventures.co.uk
   www.journeylatinamerica.co.uk
   www.africa-in-focus.com

Overland trips are usually undertaken in a truck, normally a 4x4 wheel drive vehicle that can get to places that other forms of transport simply cannot reach. Each individual company truck varies slightly in its layout and will have approximately 16 to 24 seats, anymore and that will be too many people. Ideally look for a truck that is comfortable as possible with the maximum amount of room because every truck is going to feel uncomfortable after a full days travel over rough ground. There will be no air-conditioning as that will be achieved by opening a window. You will need adequate storage space for your belongings and somewhere secure for your valuables. Four wheel drive is essential if your trip is somewhere potentially muddy and remote. The truck will almost certainly get stuck, have a puncture or break down at some stage, but this is part of the fun. The best trucks have roof seats for game park viewing, a luggage locker, fresh drinking water, some sort of entertainment system, somewhere to charge up all your equipment, a library, a safe, maps, fridge and freezer. Look for a vehicle with more leg room to allow you to stretch out, and individual security and storage boxes would be a bonus. Find out exactly what is provided for camping. How big are the tents and are there any pillows or mattresses supplied?

The Kalahari Desert - overlanding will get you off the beaten track

Overlanding is all about getting off the beaten track to some of the remotest places on the planet and away from ordinary tourists. Sometimes there are long days travelling but there is plenty to see and do along the way with time to get off the truck and to explore, or go horse riding, trekking or do some cultural exploration. You are more than just a passenger, you are part of the crew and part of an adventure. You will meet people from different cultures, immerse yourself in local life and get to places that ordinary tourists never see. There are plenty of companies to choose from and journeys can range from two weeks to a year by joining trips together. Normally you will be with a mixed group of adventurous people who you have to get on with as they will be your companions for the whole trip. It is vital that you get on with them all and it can require a little patience and understanding on everyone's part. The initial meeting is important so prepare a little introduction speech in case it is needed. You really do have to get on with everyone on the trip regardless of who they are. Be nice to everybody all the time, you cannot afford to be grumpy or have too many bad days. Little things or badly phrased comments can easily give the wrong impression. Likewise never criticize anyone, be friendly, offer to help, and always be on hand to volunteer and assist in unforeseen circumstances and with difficult jobs. It is stating the obvious but listen to what the others have to say and make sure you do everything that is required of you without complaint. Similarly you will have to ignore any ill judged comments and what you may perceive as rudeness. After a week or two some people may start to annoy you as they begin to open up and after a few weeks there could be some uneasy relationships developing. For some the trip may not be turning out as they had anticipated and they start getting a little fed up and irritated.

If it is you that have some sort of a problem you could try to manipulate the group into your way of behaviour or thinking. For example we had a problem with foul language. If one person starts unnecessarily swearing in normal conversation, then somehow others do as if it is 'cool' just to use words gratuitously, or so that they will fit in with everybody. During this particular trip a few of the travellers suddenly started with bad language for no obvious reason and unaware of the impact upon the remainder of the group who were also disappointed with the way things were developing. I made a pointed comment concerning the unnecessary and ill judged nature of such language, with slightly veiled concerns, within earshot of the driver, and very soon the leader was reprimanding the offenders.

All overlanding trips require a degree of participation so make sure you know what to expect. If you are lucky one crew member will be a cook but often you will be in a group taking it in turns to cook for the rest. Other jobs will be allocated and rotated, perhaps truck cleaning, loading luggage, shopping for food, washing up, lighting fires or putting out and packing up equipment. You will also have to pitch your own tent if camping and help others as necessary.

Everyone is expected to muck in.

As you get older and hopefully wealthier there is a tendency to seek out safer holidays rather than this type of adventure trip. This attitude will greatly limit your horizons and choices. You may have already rejected the idea of overland travel, but some of this is down to pure laziness as you do have to make an effort and avoid taking the easy way out. Overlanding will be an authentic travel experience, not a distilled version. This is not going to be a holiday but more of a travel experience.

The following characteristics are given by Dragoman to define an 'Overlander':

- possesses an almost uncontrollable urge to travel
- expects more from a holiday than just a suntan
- open minded, with a great sense of humour
- considers a hot bath every day a luxury, not a necessity
- enjoys the company of others (even those who don't bath every day)
- loves to wander off the beaten track
- respects and embraces other cultures
- doesn't insist on a pocket sprung mattress to get a good nights sleep
- handy with a shovel if called upon

Your guide is of the utmost importance. Dragoman provided the most professional guide I have ever encountered. He had exactly the right attitude, diplomacy, level of friendliness and he was knowledgeable and willing to listen to everyone's viewpoint. In East Africa it was unfortunate that we had a poor guide who frequently got drunk and out of control. He had no people skills, used foul language to the group and halfway through the trip the group forced him to leave. It is a good idea to make enquiries about your potential guide before booking.

If you intend going anywhere remotely dangerous then check the FCO website and abide by it. Tours are designed for some freedom and flexibility so itineraries can be changed on a daily basis as necessary. Our trip to West Africa was supposed to go through Mali but had to be cancelled due to various militant groups causing trouble. If the FCO says not to go then do not go.

There will be a kitty that everyone has to pay into, generally on arrival. This could be quite substantial on a long trip, but essential and you will be informed about it before leaving. Basically it is a group fund which covers a range of things, accommodation, campsite fees, food and activities, unforeseen events and extras. It should be managed by the leader in conjunction with at least one of the clients in order to make sure it is properly spent. At the end of the trip the residue will be split between the group. Do not allow it to be in control of one person.

The following is an account of our trip through East Africa with a group of strangers and shows how relationships can break down. The first half of the trip was 27 days Nairobi to Victoria Falls and the second half was another 27 days continuing on to Cape Town. This route is well travelled by lots of companies and visits all the major tourist attractions. Every trip will be different but group dynamics will inevitably evolve in its own unique way. This will give you an idea of what to expect. It is not a daily account but a more general one for each country visited.

Camp sites in Eastern Africa are generally pretty good. They all have shower blocks, good toilets and often a restaurant, bar or small shop. You will not suffer too much hardship.

Getting there

Two days before we were due to depart there was a foot of snow, no trains were running and very few planes. We were worried but miraculously overnight rain swept the snows away and we arrived at Heathrow right on time only to find that our flight to Nairobi had been cancelled.

So our first day was spent at the Premier Inn, Heathrow and we caught the next day's flight out. Luckily we had allowed for an extra day, which is always advisable, and allows an extra day sight seeing. We chose not to stay in the recommended Nairobi hotel but in a much cheaper one just down the road. It was just by the Israeli embassy so security was reassuringly tight. That evening we met our fellow travellers most of whom were with us for the full 56 days. It looked encouraging and we were hopeful that everyone would get on well. It was a good mixture of ages and nationalities, five couples and five single women. There were five over sixties, two in their fifties, three in their forties and five in their twenties. Everyone knows that they are going to be with the others for a long time and realise it is important that they get on, so the sensible ones chose their words carefully and tried to appear as pleasant as possible. First impressions are the most important in how people perceive you. At this stage we paid our kitty contribution which was quite a hefty sum.

Kenya

We departed the following morning in a big overland truck with 13 others. Two of the group coming from Canada did not make it on time, however, the company made sure they caught up with the group a day later. Our seats were allocated so there were no arguments, but try to avoid being at the back where you will bounce up and down on unmade roads, it is best to be in the middle. Trucks vary from company to company but are all similar. Ours was one of the best ones with reclining seats, big windows, individual lockers and a safe. There was also a shared fridge and facilities for charging up appliances. We had a tour leader, driver and cook.

Nairobi is quite westernised but also has a reputation as being dangerous. There is a lot of scare mongering but it is best to be cautious and sensible. As we travelled out of the town, areas became very shabby and the people were obviously poor. We stopped at a big town, Nakuru, where we went for a little exploration. It was here that my wife successfully prevented a pick-pocket who deliberately bumped into us with an accomplice. As the only white Europeans we must have stood out like a sore thumb and were targeted. There were two men in the crowd walking down the street and one man banged into the left arm of my wife also distracting me. She wondered why he had done that almost deliberately and immediately thought of pick-pockets. (She watches too much Crimewatch on television) Then a second man, 'accidentally' walked into me. He had a coat over his arm concealing his other arm and hand which he put inside my jacket. Quick as a flash my wife had hold of his hand. He said, 'What?' as if nothing had happened and in seconds they were gone. We are increasingly aware of what is going on around us and all our money and valuables are always safely stashed away. Later we spent a brilliant day on safari in Nekuru National Park where we saw zebras, impalas, baboons, giraffes, white rhinos, wart hogs, various monkeys, buffalos, ostriches, plus lots of other birds, particularly flamingos and pelicans. More impressively we caught a glimpse of a rare black rhino and finally we finished up spotting 2 lions, a female and a young male resting in the crook of a tree. The truck was equipped with individual roof hatches so everybody had a grandstand view.

At dusk we found lots of tiny chameleons hidden in the bushes. One of our group told us all off for handling them because we could spread diseases. He was probably correct but it was an unnecessary thing to do and annoyed a few of the group.

So far we had been getting up at 5am as the distances we had to travel were very long and on poor roads, 200 km the first day and 456 km the second. This was a participatory holiday where we had to put up and take down tents, prepare food, clean, wash up etc, but it was all good fun and not too onerous if taken in the right spirit of adventure. We had to do this on a rotational basis with one day off, food preparation, clean truck and wash up. Cooking chores were eased considerably by having an onboard chef who also bought in all the food. With many companies you will have to source your own food and cook it for the group.

Tanzania

We crossed the border into Tanzania where an official diddled one of our party out of $50. She had left the money inside her passport and the grateful customs officer pocketed it, thanked her and handed back her passport. Five minutes later she realised her mistake but he denied everything. You always have to be on your guard, people are poor and most officials are corrupt. This same girl was an attractive young blonde and constantly flirted with every male that was nearby. She revelled in being surrounded by young black men. Tanzania was immediately different, much more authentically African, with mud huts and grass roofs. It was our turn to help to prepare dinner which we did on the bank overlooking Lake Victoria, it was idyllic. The 'blonde' had been assigned to our cooking group but after a few minutes decided that it was more important to go and tell some boys that she did not want to buy their jewellery after all, rather than help prepare the food.

Onwards another 460km to the endless plains of the Serengeti where hippos were wallowing in the water and more lions roamed around along with countless wildebeests. The Serengeti is some 14,760 square km. and forms just a small part of Tanzania which puts the vast scale of Africa into perspective. We bush camped in the middle of nowhere with our tents in a circle around a fire for safety. Hyenas and jackals were howling and circling around while lions roared in the distance. We did not go far from the tents and both boys and girls, if caught short in the night, with potentially large and hungry animals on the prowl, it was a wee behind the tent. Everyone was finding it exciting and having a good time. Nearby was the Ngorongoro crater, reputedly one of the seven natural wonders of the world. A Serengeti in miniature, just twelve miles wide and the largest inland calderas in the world, it is like a giant Noah's Ark teeming with mammals and bird life. In the centre the mirror-like Lake Magadi is ringed with throngs of flamingos. It is of a unique topographical beauty and contains a staggering concentration of wildlife. The undoubted highlight was seeing twenty lions and a confrontation between two lions and three buffalo. In a war of nerves the buffalo repeatedly charged the lions who sauntered insouciantly away. These two animals are of course part of the 'big five' and among the most dangerous, the other three being the leopard, rhinoceros and elephant. I had always thought the big five were named as such because they had no natural predators. Apparently it is because they were always considered to be the most difficult animals in Africa to hunt on foot. We camped on the rim of the crater, it was really cold and hyenas and jackals prowled between the tents at night. All around there were Masai warrior encampments, still herding their goats and cows in the traditional way. They also paid us a visit to sell trinkets.

At this point 'Blondie' was becoming isolated from the group. She was a Kiwi and the other Kiwi couple on the trip made it clear that she was not a good representative example of their country women.

On safari trips overland you will quickly learn which sort of animal poo is from what animal and how old it is. Elephant or buffalo, lion or leopard? Track marks are important in the mud beside paths and interpreted in the same way that 'Tonto' did for the 'Lone Ranger'. Lions, elephant and buffalo tracks are easily distinguishable. You may find yourself looking out of the window scrutinising lion poo, assessing how old it is and looking for fresh paw prints. When you get home you can impress your friends and grandchildren with your knowledge.

You do not have to go to Africa to encounter big cats. This is a story I related to the group around the campfire. It is always good to have something ready for such occasions.

'I grew up in the Surrey country side and my parents' house was surrounded by fields and woods on three sides. To get home quickly it was easiest to take a short cut across the fields. I was 18 and coming back from a party late at night. I was not in the least bit frightened of the dark and well accustomed to seeing foxes and other wild life. My route took me through two fields and the path followed a shallow valley just south of Kenley aerodrome. Where the two fields met, the woods converged, and at this point I heard a noise to my right coming towards me from up in the wood. I stopped still hoping that I might see some wild life. The noise approached rapidly and I saw a big cat charging towards me. All in a flash it sped right past me, so close that it brushed my trousers. It was as big as a large Alsatian dog but completely ignored me. The night air was still and I could even smell the warmth of the animal's breath. I was temporarily rooted to the ground in terror as I heard the sound fade away up the opposite hillside. I sprinted home looking back several times but nothing was chasing me. The next day I told everybody about it but nobody believed me. My parents were convinced that I had had too much to drink but I know what I saw although at that point I did not realise that it might have been a puma.

I did not dare take the short cut again for several days even though it meant a really long detour, but finally I plucked up the courage. I walked swiftly through the first field looking all around me and about halfway across I saw an animal again. It looked like a big cat on the brow of the hill. As I walked it kept pace with me keeping low in the grass and it appeared to be stalking me. I again sprinted all the way home but this time I did not look back. Soon after this I went off to university and I never encountered what might have been the Surrey puma again.'

There are without doubt, large cats living in England, in 1991 a lynx was shot in Norfolk and a leopard in 1993 on the Isle of Wight, just two examples of many. People acquire them as pets, either legally or illegally, as kittens they are cute, but a large wild cat would take a lot of looking after. Owners get fed up and not knowing what to do abandon them. It has been estimated that a large cat could survive in England on road kill alone.

The legendary Surrey puma was frequently sighted in the sixties and tracks were also found. Experts were called in from the Natural History Museum to examine them. They measured the stride length and paw prints and concluded that they could only belong to one animal, a puma.

On one occasion the Surrey puma was spotted on a local common creeping into some bushes in the middle of a field. The police were called in and they surrounded it. Slowly they moved in with an armed marksman at the ready. They crept nearer and nearer, then suddenly the beast jumped out! The police described it as the biggest tabby cat they had ever seen.

Tanzania/Zanzibar

We passed by the snowy peak of Kilimanjaro where bragging rights were afforded to several of the group who had hiked to the top. Again this is not a detailed account and we did stop at many more interesting places such as snake farms and spice plantations. Not everything always runs smoothly, we ran out of diesel and also broke down. To catch up on the lost time we all got up at 4am for the long trip to Dar es Salaam passing through small frantic towns and scrubland dotted with wattle and daub huts covered by grass roofs. It got hotter and hotter as we moved further south. At Dar es Salaam we camped right on the beach and swam in the hottest sea any of us had ever encountered before. It was sad though, to see that the coral was either dead or dying. The crossing on the fast ferry to Zanzibar takes two and a half hours, and here we had the luxury of bungalows, on a beach in the north, for 3 nights. We all chartered a dhow for a snorkelling cruise, did the obligatory spice tour and had a bit of a rest, before staying a night in the wonderful Stonetown. Not everyone liked Stonetown and its maze of narrow streets, crooked passages and crumbling houses with overhanging balconies. Intricate carved doorways are the lavish remains of former slave traders' houses. The nights were hot and sticky but much better than being at home in the English winter. Freddy Mercury was of course born there but, being an openly gay man not celebrated by the local largely Muslim population. Group dynamics were beginning to develop in an interesting way.

Two more of the group, a financial adviser and his girlfriend were detaching themselves from the main group along with 'Blondie' and our guide, forming a drinking and smoking group in the evenings wherever possible.

We were up at 4am again to journey west across Tanzania, 620 km through endless scrubby farmland and then up into the Tanzanian highlands for the night where it was cool again. The twisting road through the mountains was the most dangerous we had ever encountered, with hairpin bends and steep slopes. Several lorries were overturned or had rolled down the cliff and one had just crashed into the rock face spilling thousands of tomatoes across the road. Some of the lorry drivers had little consideration for the safety of anyone else on the road. A huge lorry overtook us on a blind hairpin bend with a sheer cliff on one side. Anything coming in the opposite direction would have been wiped out. On this occasion everything was alright and a bus full of locals was narrowly missed.

Part of the problem is that many vehicles are not roadworthy, are badly maintained, and have poor brakes. A broken fan belt on our truck held us up again for 2 hours.

A common sight on African roads

On long journeys there is plenty of time to talk and everyone moves around the truck to have a chat and pass the time. Most people quickly learnt to avoid the financial advisor, his conversation was more of a long lecture to anyone who would listen. His girlfriend seemed totally mismatched, not only to him, but everyone else.

En route expect to pay fines to the police. You will not have to pay it personally but it does come out of the group kitty. It is a scam but if they are not too greedy then it is expedient to pay up. The police will normally find a fault with the truck, on one occasion the lights were too high and on another they were at the wrong angle. Basically it is highway robbery, they might as well all wear masks.

The far west of Tanzania was much more lush and hilly. Bananas and tea were the main crops and a tour of a tea plantation was interesting.

A grumbling dissent was beginning as it became clear that the itinerary had been changed and we were going to be staying eight nights in Livingstone which most of the group thought was too long. There was a 'lively' discussion and it was obvious that the group leader did not like some of the group wanting to question and negotiate his decisions. Some group members were beginning to be openly critical of others.

Malawi/Zambia

We crossed into Malawi and turned south, down the western side of Lake Malawi, or Lake Nyasa as it was formerly known, where the Great Rift Valley comes to an end, and camped on the lakeside shores. The lake is 580km by 80km, the water was warm and situated in an idyllic setting with a background of mountains. That night our tour leader drank too much and started behaving very unprofessionally.

On route the next day several of us openly confronted our leader and asked him not to use foul language and pointed out that his responsibilities were towards the group. He promised us that it would not happen again. Travelling further down the lake we stayed at the infamous Kande beach for three days over Christmas. Several trucks from different companies stop there as all of them travel similar routes. Kande was a bit of a 'curate's egg', although we had a fabulous time. There was a spit roast pig on Christmas Day along with swimming in the warm water while our guide slept off his hangover. We were glad he was asleep as he was no use to the group. When he awoke it was yet more abusive behaviour and foul language. One of the nearby trucks was more of a 'gap' year party truck, which is okay if that is what you want, but none of us wanted to be near this group of unpleasant youngsters intent on behaving badly before having to rejoin the human race. The noise finished at 2.25am and started again at 5am. Be absolutely sure you are not booked up on a party bus. Games were organised with other trucks, during which our leader got drunk again, tried to disrupt the games and harassed several women, pressing his attentions on them when they were clearly not wanted. Relations with him and most of the group had by then broken down almost completely and we were all in the process emailing complaints to the company owners. Many of the group had serious words with him apart from the three who were more isolated from the main group who started to befriend him.

We were all swimming in Lake Malawi and the financial advisor's girlfriend recounted a story to me. She was from the North of England whereas I am from Surrey,

'Do you know I saw this accident in Dorking? This car ran off the road and hit a wall. The owner of the house, he comes running out and he's not concerned about the driver at all. All he wants to know about is who is going to pay for the damage to his wall. People from Surrey, they're all like that aren't they, all just rude? It's the same for everyone in the south isn't it?'

I swam off without answering. This all may sound unpleasant but the main part of the group had all bonded well, created their own entertainment and were having a wonderful time. The owner of the company had received our emails but seemed unconcerned.

Malawi was a wonderful lush rural country full of hills and fields, the huge lake never being far away. The people although pitifully poor were lovely and made the best of what they had. There is no rubbish because everything has a use, and is recycled. Children follow you around asking for just about everything that you have regardless of value. They will slip their hands inside your pockets and take the contents.

Back on the road we crossed into Zambia via a muddy no-man's-land. A difficult journey of 40km each way took us to the majestic South Luangwa National Park, over bumpy dirt tracks, but it is the only way in and out. Here people live along side the wild life. We chose to put our tent up on the banks of the river where hippos were grunting and we were all warned of the dangers present during the night. There was yet another four hour morning game drive as well as an evening one, but out of the big five, a leopard sighting still evaded us. We were starting to become a bit blasé about some of the more common animals.

Zambia was also a beautiful country stretched out over a high plateau covered in woods and fields. Throughout Africa there are vast tracks of wilderness and it is an overwhelmingly agricultural continent. Everyone is up early tilling their land with mattocks and sweeping the bare earth outside of their mud huts, thatched with grass for a roof. All of the people we met were very friendly and welcoming. The first half of our tour ended there in Livingstone where we had seven days to rest.

Zambia/Victoria Falls/Zimbabwe

It is difficult to describe the Victoria Falls. You can see the mist rising from 25 miles away, filling the sky like smoke. When you get there the noise is immense with ten million litres of water per second plunging over the precipice straddling Zambia and Zimbabwe, yet this was the end of the dry season with only 10% of the maximum water. The falls are 1,708 metres wide, with the smaller but more exciting section on the Zambian side. We were drenched by thick swirling mist within minutes, so it is difficult to take photos with a normal camera. You just have to accept that you will be soaked and enjoy the moment. Our truck was returning to the camp site after only two hours but we opted to stay on, firstly to walk to the bottom of the gorge. Here we had a picnic on a rock, above the churning waters, in a thunder storm and under the bridge linking Zambia to Zimbabwe, from which intrepid bungee jumpers dived. Later I made my way over the top of the falls, about 100 metres upstream. It is a possible, but dangerous route through raging water and over rocks to tiny isolate islands of calm. Other people were doing it with guides holding their hands. I foolishly attempted it on my own and in the process frightened myself to death and still have bad dreams about it. There are plenty of taxis to take you home although you have to bargain hard. To begin with they will all stand firm and quote the same price but eventually someone will break ranks, particularly if you start to walk away.

A couple of days later we decided that we really ought to go to Zimbabwe as it was so close it would be rude not to. For this privilege you get charged an exorbitant amount for a visa depending upon your nationality or whatever they want to charge on that day. The British come out of it fairly badly. However, we got to see the full length of the falls and were once again drenched with spray. Seeing is believing, sitting on the edge of the gorge watching the water plunge down 107 metres (Niagara is only 58 metres) and we had to drag ourselves away reluctantly. The following day I did an awesome and thrilling micro light flight over the falls. It is a bit like being attached to a lawn mower with wings, swooping down into the swirling spray. There are lots of activities on offer albeit quite expensive.

On our final day we chose to do the trip to the Devil's Pool. It was the final opportunity of the season as the waters were becoming too deep and the current far too fast for safety. A speed boat took us to Livingstone Island, where in 1865 Dr. David Livingstone himself first set eyes upon the falls. From there we swam, crawled and waded, hand in hand, for some 25 minutes through swirling waters, fast flowing currents and over slippery rocks, to get to the Devil's

Pool at the top of a fearsome cataract. It seemed that we could at any moment be swept to our deaths. The pool is like a large Jacuzzi situated on top the of the falls. You have to jump in and the current takes you right to the very edge. We were sitting on a rock ledge of the pool with our backs to the sheer drop, hanging on for dear life in the current. We were with a very competent guide I must stress, but it was just sheer madness. I could feel the current lifting me slightly, we were all terrified and could not believe the position we had managed to get ourselves into. There we were sitting on the edge, on the top of one of the highest waterfalls in the world, right in the middle of the falls, and in a current. One mistake and you would get washed over the top and plunge to your death. If we had known the reality we probably would not have chosen to do it.

The Devil's Pool right on the very edge of the Victoria Falls

To return we swam through rapids, again with strong currents and across the top of the falls. It seemed foolish and it would have been quite easy to get washed away. The most frightening part was where one by one we all had to swim as fast as possible across a 25 foot section with a narrow stream of water rapidly coursing down the middle. A further 60 feet away it plunged over the edge. The idea is to get up enough speed to get through the 'fast' bit quickly.

Nevertheless you are inevitably seized by the current, whisked away, and have to grab on to a fixed rope further down nearer to the edge. Miss the rope and that could be the end. There are no health and safety requirements here. All four of us in the group were frightened and shaking but it was brilliant and afterwards we could not believe we had actually done it. If you do not believe me check it out on YouTube. When we looked back at where we had been our first thoughts were that it was not possible. It was the final day for the 'swim' as the rainy season was beginning, so we did it at the most dangerous time. The fact that you could possibly die somehow added enormously to the experience. There are lots of other trips on offer but nothing can prepare you for the monumental magnificence of the falls.

The group dynamics were becoming fascinating. Our leader swore not to drink again and went to bed early on New Year's Eve. The company even sent an extra leader to 'keep an eye on him'. This did not help too much, being a fellow Afrikaner she was quickly in cahoots with him and soon became known as the 'Pit Bull'. It was such a diverse group and not everyone got on. There were five women travelling on their own and five couples, all of different ages. The filthy rich, loud mouthed financial advisor with his unpleasant girlfriend were disliked by everyone. The scatter brained blonde apparently had a boyfriend from Afghanistan who had not turned up for the trip. She continued to flirt with every male who passed by and we suspected she was sleeping with our cook. There was lovely middle aged couple from the Scottish highlands whose sole aim was to 'help'. A slightly overweight 40 year old had just been deserted by her husband but was sensible and good company. Another of the solo travellers was a wonderful German girl who has been everywhere you can possibly imagine and a young 'over the top' Canadian on her way to see her boyfriend in Cape Town, plus us and three others. Things would change as four of our party would leave and five more join at the halfway point.

A new male traveller from America arrived as a 'special surprise' for 'Blondie' who he had apparently met a few months back. The rumour mill began to work overtime. Her boyfriend in Afghanistan, who already had a wife and teenage daughter, emailed her to make it clear that either the American or she had to leave the trip. He was in the 'security' business. The cook did sleep with 'Blondie' on New Years Eve but had spent every night prior to this with the Canadian and wanted to marry her and move to Canada. The Canadian was feeling very miffed but she was by then on a flight to Cape Town to finish with her boyfriend. Meanwhile the cook had sensibly disappeared for a few days.

Botswana

We crossed the border from Zambia to Botswana over the Chobe River by ferry, where four countries converge, the other two being Namibia and Zimbabwe. It was a two hour wait to cross over whereas lorries have to wait up to three weeks. Botswana is one of the three least populated countries in the world and includes the vast Kalahari Desert. It is also quite well off since diamonds were discovered in the sixties. The famous Bushmen of the Kalahari, who were uniquely adapted to the climate and conditions, having lived there for tens of thousands of years, have been driven out and suffer a similar fate to the Australian aborigines. Those who try to return are arrested and beaten, their traditional way of life has been replaced by alcohol, boredom, depression and illness.

One evening there was a loud humming as if a helicopter was warming up. It continued for an hour or so then it begun to rain dung beetles, a few at first then thousands of them. In the evening as a snack, some of us ate larvae the size of a man's finger, but they were better fried than raw.

We did 2 game drives in the Chobe National Park, one on land in the morning and another on the water in the evening, still no leopard sighting but lots of crocs and hippos. Another gruelling 600k in the truck took us to the Okavango Delta. The Okavango River does not flow into the sea but into the Kalahari Desert to form the biggest inland delta in the world. It is well worth the expense to take a one hour flight over it on a light aircraft, a GA8 Airvan to see the wonderful patterns and colours from 500 feet up.

On the shores of the Okavango panhandle we abandoned the truck and travelled deep into the watery delta for 3 days carrying all our gear with us. First by 4x4, then speedboat and finally by mokoro, a two man Kayak type boat with a man to 'pole'. We stayed on a little island which we shared with all sorts of wildlife but there were no facilities. No running water and a hole in the ground for a toilet does not bother most people who choose overlanding. There were a lot more mokoro trips and 'nature' walks. We were 'lucky' when a huge hippo leapt out some 10 feet in front of our mokoro and splashed away. It could have been really dangerous but was certainly exciting.

Hippos kill more people than any other animal in Africa exactly in such situations.

We swam in a creek where we were assured there were no crocodiles despite the area teeming with them. Everyone was jumping around, splashing and making a lot of noise. Apparently this is enough to frighten crocodiles away but do not take my word for it, play safe and let someone else go for the first swim.

Some mornings we were held up waiting for 'Blondie' who seemed to work to her own timetable. Occasionally someone had to go and search for her. Once I found her in a hotel drinking a coffee while everyone else was on the truck ready to leave.

Namibia

We crossed the deserted border into Namibia where you could get free condoms on 'entry'. The campsite where we stayed had been voted the best in South Africa, and most are generally of an acceptable standard. Here a jackal got into our tent and dragged out a rucksack, we chased it away but always remember to zip your tent up when you are not in it. Etosha National Park is one of the biggest and best stocked in Southern Africa and we were there for three days. Sometimes the animals can be elusive, possibly more of them see you than you see of them. We saw four of the forty eight remaining black rhinos but only two of the one hundred and twenty thousand elephants, plus a white rhino, a whole family of lions along with other wildlife. Black rhinos are rare, they are still grey but with round ears. One particular male got annoyed and almost decided to charge the truck, he pawed the ground and snorted but sensibly decided against it. Still no leopard, the last of the big five to spot but we did see an African wild cat, the first of the secret seven. The other six are the serval, aardvark, pangolin, genet, civet and porcupine. There was only one more game drive left at this point, that same afternoon, but disaster struck quickly in the form of a massive thunderstorm. We raced to the tent to close the window flaps but too late to avoid an internal flood and our final game drive was cancelled. Namibia, one of the driest places on earth was flooded, we were wet and so was a lot of our gear.

The Canadian who arrived as a surprise for the flirtatious blonde was asked to leave after several days of discussion. The word 'stalker' was mentioned and he did depart, but not before going down on one knee and presenting a diamond ring.

Our unpleasant tour leader stayed with us along with the new trainee guide, an ex-park ranger who was very knowledgeable, but unfortunately had yet to develop people skills. Relations between some of the group were getting a little strained. The loudmouth and his common girlfriend were disliked by everyone.

We travelled west and stayed at a cheetah sanctuary. Injured animals were brought there and eventually rehabilitated. They had three tame ones in a compound which could be patted on the head and neck and came up to lick our hands. It is an awesome experience as their tongues are like coarse sandpaper rasping up and down your skin. They particularly liked male arms possible because the salt content in the sweat was higher. Then everyone jumps into the back of a truck to go to an open enclosure and throw raw meat to semi wild cheetahs. At this point you realise they can move very, very quickly. I have mentioned that some trucks are party trucks and we had the misfortune to have one with us at the cheetah sanctuary. They were all standing there beers in hand shouting and screaming and taking no notice of the sanctuary rules. Their leader was also out of control and trying to show off, he jumped off the truck into the enclosure where the cheetahs were and began goading them with a stick, shouting and trying to confront them. We were all secretly hoping he would get mauled or worse. Later I had a quiet and unpleasant word in his ear but he was probably too out of his mind to understand. I repeat do not get involved with a party truck.

There were quite a few trucks like ours on the road. Most act responsibly, make little noise and are considerate to others. This one particular party truck, however, was full of youngsters, noisy, foul mouthed and inconsiderate. These were the ones we had been on a camp site with for one night at the beginning of the trip, and they had kept us awake all night with loud music, and screaming. Unfortunately they were also staying at the cheetah camp with us. As we all had to get up at 5am most of our group went to bed at 9.15. The camp bar was supposed to be open from only 8.30 to 11pm, but seeing the opportunity to make some money the proprietors decided to sell alcohol all night. There we were in the middle of nowhere but the noise was intolerable. After a while I put my earplugs in and eventually went to sleep but awoke at about midnight to more constant noise. Most of our group were also awake and at 1.15am I went to look for our leader to ask him to intervene, but could not find his tent. I went to the bar and found that it was actually our leader who was making much of the noise. The bar was still serving beer and he was absolutely drunk out of his mind, along with some girls. I told him he needed to go to bed and he called me a 'fucking wanker'. I said that he had promised never to drink on the trip again and he told me that he had lied. Then rather a lot more was said, and after a lot of traded insults I screwed his beer can up and threw it on the floor telling him that he needed to act more responsibly towards the group. At this point things started to get really serious and an awful lot more insults were traded, most of his being a stream of foul language. I did keep my cool and did not swear but unhappily our leader completely lost it and went berserk. He put his nose right in my face and was shouting 'go on hit me' interspersed with more insults. He must have said this some 20 or 30 times. I went back to the tent but as the noise continued unabated I went into the truck to lie down in, hoping that it would be quieter. A little later our leader arrived back into the campsite shouting and swearing at everyone, and began verbally abusing my wife. So I was out there again with the leader who was yelling, trying to pick a fight, and screaming abuse about everyone in the group. By this time most of the group were up, remonstrating with him and trying to calm him down. He kept coming at me and had to be physically restrained. I did make several carefully worded personal comments which can be far more effective than foul language. For example there may be no better way of insulting a slightly overweight woman than earnestly asking her 'if she has put on a little weight?', or making veiled comments to a man questioning his, intelligence or virility. Everyone knew our guide's position was now untenable and that he would have to go. The new guide eventually got up and it took another 30 minutes to make him go to bed.

In the morning we put our guide in the front cab of the truck with the driver and drove 270 km north to Opuwo where he was forced out of the truck for good. Almost everyone was thoroughly glad to see the back of him, however, he was the photography expert, which left us with no advice or seminars.

In the small town of Opuwo dozens of the Himba tribe women were walking around semi-naked in their unique tribal costume, mixing freely with more westernised Namibians. Himba tribeswomen wear goat skin leather outfits which resemble an outlandish Vivian Westwood design. Layers of goat skins hang down at the back from their waists along with a crude leather bag. The whole effect is something like a Victorian bustle. They wear nothing underneath and no clothes above the waist line. We drove up into the hills towards

Angola to visit a Himba village. This is a wonderful experience and a highlight for any visitor. We took them approx 300 litres of water which they are desperate for, plus rice, flour, bread, apples, oil and other essentials.

The Himba tribeswomen are very photogenic

The women are amazing, they rub their bodies with a mixture of ochre and cow butter which smells rancid but keeps them warm and gives their brown skin a wonderful glow that blends perfectly with their clothing. Their men folk like them like this but they themselves wear western type clothing. One of the chief's wives demonstrated how they prepare themselves for their man. This involved burning incense and holding the smoking embers under each arm and up between their legs. They sang and danced for us and we danced with them.

The Himba tribeswomen all wear traditional dress

Tourists visit them, but not many, and they did seem to be genuinely enjoying themselves rather than just performing. At the end they spread their jewellery out on the ground hoping to make some sales. If you get a chance to visit the Himba tribe then do not miss out.

The 'adviser' and his girlfriend criticised us all for taking photos of the Himba tribeswomen and described the situation as being like 'a zoo'. They chose not to take much part and spent most of their time filling up the water containers.

Back in Opuwo there is another interesting group of tribal women. These are the Herero women who still dress up in long Victorian crinoline, with head dresses representing cow horns. It is good to see people hanging on to their traditional ways of life.

Turning back south through Namibia there were very few tarmac roads so it was rather bumpy in the truck. We went through the mountains to Twyfelfontein where we saw both rock engravings, and paintings, including the most famous one in Southern Africa the 'white lady of Brandberg'. Then it was on to the Cape Cross seal colony where half a million seals create an awful lot of noise and smell.

The group stopped at Swakopmund for three days, where we had the luxury of sleeping in bungalows with our own showers. This is a German town on the coast where, for a full 8 months every year, there is a sea mist everyday until late afternoon. Some of us went quad-biking in the desert racing up and down dunes in a 'wall of death' fashion. It is best to go for the more powerful bikes with gears, because you can go faster and it is safer when climbing higher up the dunes at a greater angle, if you go too slowly the bike topples over. It was two exhilarating hours very well spent.

'Blondie' left at this point with no farewells. A week later she sent an email to everyone with an opinion upon each of us. Some of us came out better than others.

Southwards through Namibia the scenery was ever changing, deserts, mountains and rugged plains. Some of the oldest rock formations on earth are there. Nothing grows and in most places nobody lives there, and the dirt track that passes as a road is deserted. If you are lucky you may see one other car in a day. The next stop was Sossusvlei where the highest sand dunes in the world are and it is one of the most spectacular sights in Namibia. Everyone climbs the famous dune 45, so named because it is at the 45th kilometre of the road that connects the Sesriem gate and Sossusvlei, and this is also one of the highest at 170m. You should start at dawn when it is cooler, the colours are strong and constantly changing. It is hard work, walking in sand uphill is never going to be easy, but once up on the ridge it does become easier and ultimately rewarding. Try to think of it in terms of getting you fitter.

Just behind the dunes is a petrified forest where the gnarled and isolated trees have stood untouched for 600 to 900 years.

Sossusvlei

It is an eerie place where lime has been washed out and baked hard on the surface. In the middle the dry crust is like a skin over a drum and underneath it sounds hollow. It is a perfect photographic location.

On another horrendous day we travelled for 8 hours in up to 45c of heat. The truck broke down with a puncture and to add to the troubles we had to make a huge diversion because a bridge had been washed away. Eventually we ended up at Fish River Canyon which is the 2nd largest canyon in the world. My wife and I did a two man canoe trip paddling 15km down the river stopping just before a waterfall. It was a bit scary at times as the river was running high and we were going somewhat faster than we would have liked.

We had to abandon the truck at the South African border because the rules had suddenly been altered, stopping GB registered trucks entering the country. The boss of our travel company came to pick us up on the other side. We had a meeting where he tried to address the problems we had encountered with the guide and he managed to handle the situation very badly. He thought that his guide had been provoked and that he also needed some 'down time' as well. It did not seem to matter to him that the guide was continually drunk, spent many days asleep and snoring on the truck with a hangover, sexually harassed some of the women and openly abused us. He could have handled it so much better, all he had to do was apologise and perhaps buy everyone a drink. The entire group got even angrier and four more people left a day early. Our kitty money was never discussed or accounted for and we received no refund. Maybe it was all used up on expenses but could quite have easily been misused.

So our trip ended in acrimony but despite the problems, just about everyone thoroughly enjoyed it. We had a great time and saw and did some wonderful things. All the African people we met were friendly, honest and often deeply religious, however, the white Afrikaner is a whole new story.

If you go on such a trip you need to be flexible, tolerant and willing to participate fully. I have only given a summary as a full account would take up another book. We visited fifteen game parks most of which were similar and saw enough wildlife to satisfy anyone's needs. Just being involved in such adventure was enough and we were happy just to be travelling and watching the scenery unfold from the relative luxury of our truck.

South Africa and Cape Town

Cape Town is a fabulous city and fully justifies its good reputation and we did all the things you have to do. Robben Island was all a bit too rushed and somewhat ruined as they have over renovated, removing all the graffiti rather than leaving it as it was when occupied by Mandella. It is easy to take the bus up to the foot of Table Mountain where we hiked up and took the cable car down. It is much more rewarding to hike up and wander around at the top, but most visitors are too lazy. The Botanical Gardens here are rated as the seventh best in the world and are so big that it has separate hiking trails of its own. Cape Town has a lot more to offer and a good way to see it is by taking the hop on hop off tour bus. There are museums, St Georges Church, Green Market Square, and the National Gallery amongst many other attractions here. Everywhere seems safe although some of the poorer black community will try to hassle you for money. There is still a massive economic disparity, communities are integrated quite well but it is still the whites that have all the wealth with the blacks working in the service industries. We spoke to many different people about these issues. Very briefly we found that the older generation who had lived through apartheid were happy enough as their lives were so vastly improved. It is the next generation who are disgruntled and many were out of work.

For the final part of the trip we hired a car. It is normally best to do this well in advance before you leave home. We drove down to Cape Point and on to the Cape of Good Hope passing through Chapman's Peak drive, apparently one of the world's top four drives.

The Garden Route

The Garden Route is also rated as one of the world's top drives. On leaving Cape Town we drove past, through, and around some of the townships. We were quite shocked at how big and sprawling they actually were. Tens of thousands of people all cramped together in squalid corrugated tin shacks. It is a little bit scary and not somewhere where unaccompanied tourists should stop. Interestingly there is also a large white township somewhere. During the Apartheid era most of the whites had jobs even if they were not up to it. In 1994 when The Government of National Unity took over many large firms were taken over by the black community and lots of ineffective white employees lost their jobs. Such people now make up this township.

The coast line is absolutely stunning but unfortunately it was February and the whales are only winter visitors, so for us the first place of real interest was the Cape Agulhas. This is the most southerly tip of Africa and where the Atlantic and Indian Oceans officially meet. We did see pods of dolphins and giant rays some two metres across. The town of Oudtshoorn is inland and the world centre for ostrich farming, a fascinating place with lots to see and do including the wonderful Cango Caves slightly further north. The 'adventure' route is far better than the standard one. Only three people opted for this, all the twenty or so others, being typical tourists, took the easier route. It turned out to be more like pot holing in parts, 2.8km of massive caverns, narrow passages and low tunnels. The crux was the 'Devil's Chimney', a tiny narrow passage twisting upwards and sideways and the 'Letterbox', only 27cm wide and a tight squeeze to wriggle through. Certainly the best tourist caves we have been down.

The Wilderness National Park had only one good hiking trail, the 'Half Collared Kingfisher' and the Tsitsikamma National Park at Storms River had another excellent hike, the 'Otter Trail'. It was a bit disappointing considering the importance of these sites. We had packed all the remaining spaces in our rucksacks with children's books and teaching aids and carefully brought them from England to the township school at Storms River, a dilapidated group of shacks where the principal was helping to build a new classroom on his Saturday off. Our last stop was in the beautiful Jeffrey's Bay before flying from Port Elizabeth to Johannesburg.

Johannesburg

Johannesburg has a bad reputation and our main goal was to do a tour of the township, Soweto, to see for ourselves the site of so many of the struggles against apartheid. Soweto was interesting but also disappointing as it has been somewhat gentrified. We saw all the main sites such as Mandela's house and museum and the place where the student uprisings began, but the area is developing fast and some of the new houses are becoming quite desirable properties. There are no problems here walking around by yourself. It was only up in Kliptown where we saw real hardship, and poverty and donated some of our 'charity' fund to a voluntary organization looking after children. Soweto is far safer than central Johannesburg which is now a no go area at most times. The big companies have relocated from the city centre and the buildings are now occupied by squatters, illegal immigrants and criminals. Nobody has any work and they are desperate. At night even in the leafy suburbs the risk of attack is so great that everybody travels by car, nobody goes out on foot. Every house is protected by electric gates, razor wire and vicious sounding dogs.

From our many discussions it appeared that not all is well in the rainbow nation and many people predict problems ahead. Go and see for yourself. We were on the plane home that night.

N.B. Going back to the question of successful insults, in a previous life I used to teach senior boys. On one occasion there was an excellent trainee student teacher who always handled a difficult class well. One particular boy tried every trick in the book to bait or annoy him, he fell off his chair, farted, slammed his desk lid and made silly noises, but nothing worked, the student handled the situation perfectly. Then this boy hit upon the answer and said,

'Sir, you will never make a good teacher.'

It was the perfect insult, the student broke down and lost his temper, becoming a good teacher was the only thing that mattered to him.

Sossusvlei

The Victoria Falls are 107 metres high

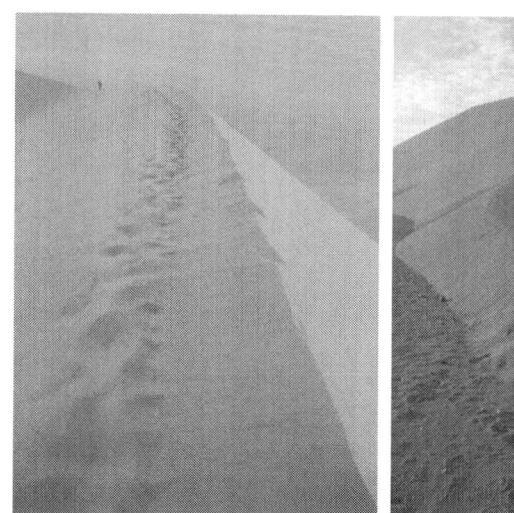

The famous dune 45 in Namibia

The Devil's Chimney   Himba tribeswomen's bag

In East Africa you will get up very close to the animals

(There is room within the 'overland' market for a company that specializes in *real* adventure travel for the fit and active over 50's or 60's.)

7 Train Journeys

"I have found out that there ain't no surer way to find out whether you like people or hate them than to travel with them."
Mark Twain 1835-1910

Trains are a great way to travel and if you can include a journey into your itinerary it will make your trip all the more interesting. There is something romantic about trains, and depending upon where you are travelling to can add an extra dimension to your holiday. Sometimes it can be quite an expensive option depending where in the world you are. We took the Ghan railway from Alice Springs down to Adelaide as part of a planned route through Australia. This train is a wonderful stately affair, the engine of which makes for a great photograph. The 600 mile journey passes by the ever changing colours of the barren outback and through historic mining towns. It takes a long time, 22 hours, partly because it goes at such a sedate pace. At 10pm the lights were switched off and we discovered that our 'red recliner seats' were not great for overnight sleeping. An Aboriginal family whose children made a continual noise kept us awake for long periods. No racial slur is intended, they were just a regular family with excited children. This is, however, Australia's most famous rail adventure and being popular has to be booked up in advance. Named after the Afghan cameleers who pioneered the route this classic journey is more expensive than flying. Don't do it if you are on a budget or want first class service, it is the experience that counts and the opportunity to see the outback for yourself. We thought we would see lots of kangaroos but we only managed to spot one. Also only one item of hand luggage is allowed, so pack your bags carefully. The full journey is 3,000 kilometres from Darwin to Adelaide via Alice Springs. Prices range according to how much comfort you want.
www.gsr.com.au
Travelling by train will appeal to some people more than others but everyone should try at least one journey. So why not start with the longest continuous journey in the world, the Trans-Siberian Railway. Crossing the world's largest country, spanning 7 time zones, it is an epic journey through the remote wilderness of Siberia, across the fringes of the Gobi Desert, to the shimmering shores of Lake Baikal. This is one of those trips that everyone talks about and has to be done sometime, it is the ultimate train journey that crosses one

third of the globe. We chose to go from Moscow to Vladivostok, which is the classic route, a distance of 9,259 kilometres or 5752 miles, although this distance varies slightly according to different sources. There are several alternative routes such as starting at St Petersburg and the Trans Mongolian route ending up at Beijing, but having been to both of these places we chose to see somewhere new. We also decided to stop in Kiev on the way; it is always worth looking for a stop over wherever you go just to see as many places as possible. Kiev is definitely worth a visit although at the time of writing the crisis in Crimea might put you off. Consider doing this trip properly by taking the train from London St Pancras overland to Moscow, flying is cheating.

There are special luxury trains that go all the way from Moscow to Vladivostok. They are far more expensive and packages still come in different classes.

www.goldeneagleluxurytrains.com
www.sundownersoverland.com

If you want to experience the real journey then take the public train, travel with the locals and speak to them. The same train does not go all the way but is a series of three, or four connecting trains if you start from St. Petersburg. You can choose to travel, first class in the relative luxury of a 2 berth compartment, or second class, in a four berth, cheaper but more cramped compartment. First class compartments are exactly the same, minus the two upper berths. En suite facilities are just a myth, these are basic trains, utilitarian and solidly built, but they do have large windows which are great for viewing the countryside. There are two WC's at either end of the wagon, where you will find a hand-basin with cold water, and occasionally warm water. Make sure you have a good meal before leaving because the restaurant food is going to be a bit iffy. Lots of companies offer this sort of trip but the train is going to pretty much the same so consider what else is on offer. This is a semi-independent way of travelling if you book with a company and they combine train journeys with stopovers which will vary in length. You are not travelling in a group, nor do you have a tour leader but you will be met on arrival and escorted to a homestay or hotel. If you book a ticket on your own without stopovers it is going to a pretty tedious seven day journey.

www.transsiberianexpress.net
www.justgorussia.co.uk
www.trans-siberian.co.uk

www.intouristuk.com

The main attraction of the whole journey is to experience the Russian landscape, the unending forests and plains. It is only when you have done this journey that you can fully understand the vastness of it. The taiga or boreal forest is largely made up of birch, pine, spruce and larch although it is mainly silver birch that is seen. This continuous panorama of emptiness is dotted with villages and in reality the landscape is monotonous. Most villages are ramshackle affairs with wooden homes and in rural areas rubbish is an eyesore as householders just dump everything just outside their own boundaries. The towns are overwhelmingly industrial and most people live in the architecturally appalling soviet style concrete apartment blocks.

Be well prepared before you take this trip:

- Food on board is going to be expensive and at best ordinary, provided by a restaurant car situated in the middle of the train. There is a samovar in each carriage providing a constant supply of free boiling water for making tea, coffee, instant soup, or pot-noodles. Any instant food that can be prepared just by adding hot water from the samovar will be invaluable. Bring any snacks that you need with you.
- Drinks on board are relatively expensive and most Russians would not contemplate paying such prices, however, nobody will stop you bringing your own beer, spirits and soft drinks. If you do buy a drink do not agree to buy one for anyone else, you could end up with all the staff having a drink on your tab.
- Bring a knife and some cutlery for slicing up the bread and vegetables that you can buy from the sellers at major stops. You will also need some plastic mugs, bowls and plates.
- Wet wipes might just make a really big difference to your personal comfort.
- Some slip-on shoes will make it easy to nip to the toilet in the night.
- You are trapped on this train for long periods at a time so bring playing cards, books and games.
- Take some photographs of your family and home to show to fellow travellers in your compartment because the language is probably going to be a barrier to communication. You could be sharing your compartment with travellers from all

over the world including Russians, Mongolians, Chinese and sometimes other intrepid westerners. Russians and Mongolians like to make themselves at home so some tactful negotiation might need to take place.
- Extra things to take may be a torch, ear plugs, folding umbrella, j-cloth, universal sink plug and t-towel.

Other things to be aware of are:

- All trains in Russia run on Moscow time and departure and arrival times given in the timetables or on the tickets are always Moscow time. You will be constantly trying to work out what time it is as there are 11 time zones in Russia and this trip goes through 7 of them.
- You will have to carry your own luggage most of the time.
- Thankfully smoking is forbidden, except in the area joining carriages together, but your days as a smoker should by now be over.
- Beds are full-length with a padded base and a thin mattress with a short ladder up to the top bunk. A pillow and a blanket are provided with a fresh laundry pack containing two sheets, pillowcase, and towel. Each bed has its own light, a shelf and some hooks. Each cabin has a table with a bottle opener underneath. Luggage goes under the bottom bed or up near the roof.
- It is unlikely that there will be a shower. Remember that the need to have a shower every single day is a relatively recent western social trend and not a basic human necessity.
- There may be an electric socket in the compartment under the table, but if not there is one in the corridor. If you are desperate to charge a camera battery up you might have to wait and watch it. Maybe you can ask to get it charged up in the service wagon. The standard voltage in Russia is 220V, 50Hz AC. Sockets require a Continental or European plug with two round pins. Pack a travel adaptor.
- Compartment doors can be locked from the inside, but this can be inconvenient if you are in a 4 berth with strangers. A universal train key, with a triangular shaped tip is really useful to lock up your compartment when it is empty.
- Carriages are mixed sex although it is mostly men travelling. Most passengers sleep in their clothes and do not change.

- This journey is perfectly safe, even for female travellers on their own.
- Toilets do have paper provided but be prepared, just in case. As the journey continues the toilet is going to get increasingly grubby and smelly. They each serve 36 passengers and as the train is rattling and jerking along not everyone's aim is accurate.
- In the winter the heating system is good and in the summer ventilation is good enough so you will not get too hot or cold. Outside of the train it is an entirely different matter.
- There is the question of safety with strangers sharing your compartment. Keep money, cameras and valuables with you at all times and never leave them unattended, when the cabin is empty lock up all your luggage.
- Get your money changed before boarding the train. Money changers will charge a lot more at each station.
- The train stops 5 to 8 times a day for anywhere between 2 and 30 minutes, so take the opportunity to get off, stretch your legs and see what food is for sale. Things are cheap but only Russian roubles are accepted. Better still on the longer stops go out of the station and look for a small shop. Just follow the Russians out and they will lead straight to somewhere selling all the necessary goodies. Do not be late back, the train will not wait for you and they are always exactly on time.
- Each carriage has one or two attendants who clean and maintain everything. Your cabin gets swept and mopped, a little bit, daily. They will definitely let you know if you do anything they do not approve of.
- There is not much space in the compartment so travel light. A large suitcase will be inconvenient.
- If you do not speak any Russian this is going to be an interesting test of your communication skills. Some Russians will strike up a conversation to practice their English.
- Souvenirs are available everywhere but of declining quality. A Russian doll is the obvious choice. Finding communist era memorabilia is increasingly more difficult.
- In Moscow and St. Petersburg everything is expensive and a dual pricing system operates for some tourist attractions and museums. You as a tourist will pay a lot more than Russian residents.

Moscow, the capital of Russia and home to the spy novel, is one of the world's most expensive, fascinating and untamed cities. Now capitalism has been embraced it is all glitz and glamour. Ladas have been replaced by Mercedes. Foreigners are less likely now to be considered so wealthy that they can be charged silly prices. Russians themselves have a taste for conspicuous consumption, but many still manage to wear tasteless clothes even if they are expensive. There is not much of an obesity problem here, some of the young women are stick thin and others drop dead gorgeous. Red Square is the essential starting point and is best approached through the beautiful arched Resurrection gate. It is not red as such, the Russian word 'krasnaya' means both 'red' and 'beautiful'. The square and the Kremlin are magnificent but heaving with tourists, Lenin and Stalin look-alikes pose for pictures and there are plenty of tacky souvenirs. Red Square is impressive, with Lenin's menacing mausoleum, where the father of communism has remained embalmed since his death in 1924 aged 53. Lenin did not want any of this, he wanted to be buried next to his mother, but Stalin decided to preserve his body ignoring the wishes of Lenin's widow. Stalin's tomb is tucked away behind it. One of the most powerful mass murderers in history is not quite so well thought of, although he did play a key role in the defeat of the Nazis. St Basil's cathedral with its golden domes looks like a fairy tale castle. The intensely coloured onion shaped domes have become an enduring symbol of Russia. It was commissioned by Ivan the Terrible in 1555 and rumour has it that he had the architect blinded so that he could never build anything so beautiful again.

The Kremlin is another 'must see' sight, an eclectic mix of cathedrals and churches. This is Russia's political powerhouse from where many infamous dictators and tyrants ruled including Stalin and Ivan the Terrible and from where Napoleon watched Moscow burn. Originally a citadel of the Tsars it is now home to the Russian president. The Armoury is where the Russian crown jewels are kept and some extraordinary treasures, unique in the world. Objet d'art are on display that even today cannot be reproduced, many things are made from solid gold and encrusted with countless diamonds and precious jewels, it is as if some of the secrets of the world lie here. This is a fortified stronghold built in the 11th century inside of which are the Russian Palaces of Congress, Assumption Cathedral, Ivan the Great Bell Tower and the Tsar Bell. The Tsar Bell at 202 tonnes is the biggest in the world but was never installed or rung as it got badly cracked when cooling.

The metro is the easiest way to travel around, cheap, efficient and well worth a tour on its own. It is easy enough to negotiate but needs a little forethought. As long as you have a map and get on the right colour line going in the right direction then you cannot go wrong. If you do then get off, cross the platform and retrace your steps. It is best to count the number of stops to your destination as stations are not well marked and generally in Cyrillic. The system is ruthlessly efficient in the rush hour and trains run as frequently as every 45 seconds or at most one minute with the doors open for only 15 seconds. Take the circle line and keep stopping to view some great works of art. The metro is full of opulent stations elaborately decorated with revolutionary mosaics and glitzy chandeliers. War is the main theme along with a portrayal of how happy, 'we', the Soviet people, are. The architecture and designs have no reference to religion and ideas were often tested out underground to eventually be constructed in the city above. This policy led to some unusual designs and each station has its own unique identity. Most are naturalistic designs from as wide a choice of materials as possible. The system was constructed by Stalin and the stations are deep down so as to double up as air raid shelters. Three levels of the metro are open but below there are apparently 2 more secret levels, but nobody knows about them.

Make a visit to the GUM department store, Russia's most famous department store. Now it is full of exclusive designer boutiques. Few people ever go in them and virtually nobody ever buys anything and they rely on making just one sale a day to pay all expenses. The Arbat is the touristy street, once a bohemian area, the off beat action has now moved on to the Kitay Gorod and Christye Prudy districts.

The Izmailovsky outdoor flea market is full of Russian souvenirs, crafts and all sorts of interesting things and you could easily spend a day just wandering around or haggling for bits of Soviet kitsch. Make sure you go at the weekend when it is in full swing and open from 9am to 6pm. Travel east out of the city on the 'dark blue' line to the Partizanskaya station. Exit the station and follow the crowds, walking left out of the station for about 300 meters. The 'Vernissage' costs 10 roubles to get in. Any taxi driver will know where tourists want to go and drop you by the entrance. Get a taxi just by putting your arm out, every car is a potential taxi if the price is right.

It is easy to change money but rates vary so shop around. The best rate maybe with the man on the street corner but take the usual care. Just get enough for your own needs as changing back is never quite so easy. All your left over change can be given to one of the many old women still sitting, begging, uncared for by the state and with a tin mug held out.

Hotels are often soulless Soviet-era monoliths and a home stay is a good option. Our homestay breakfast consisted of unlimited pancakes with jam, a slice of crumble type cake piled high with jam and potato cake with a higher specific gravity than lead, all washed down with black tea.

www.hofa.ru

Moscow is as safe as any other big city with the usual problems of pick pockets and petty theft. Do not let yourself get surrounded by groups of children who are ostensibly begging and steer well clear of any drunks. More recently there has been an increase in criminal attacks, just keep alert to your surroundings as you would anywhere else.

The police are no longer a threat as the new government has had a purge on corruption and replaced the senior police management. They have had their wages increased so have no need to supplement them by extracting fines from hapless tourists. They used to constantly stop tourists to check visa validity and the favourite location for doing this was Red Square. Russian visas were supposed to be reregistered for every 3 days spent in a different place and if you failed to comply the police could cause a lot of problems and impose a hefty fine. If something happens and they still find some imaginary fault, stand your ground and do not pay what amounts to a bribe. Ask to see their identification and write down their 7 digit number. Make copies of your passport and visa page even though Russian law demands you are meant to carry the originals at all times and try to avoid handing over original documents. However, the police are no longer the enemy.

Yaroslavsky station is one of the nine main railway stations in Moscow and is the western terminus for the Trans-Siberian Railway. Here you can convert your train vouchers into tickets at the machines. One of the staff will do it for you but check your tickets carefully as ours were all mixed up within the group. Travelling with us there were a married Indian couple in their fifties, a 78 year old from Devon, an autistic Punjabi from Derby (complete the limerick in your own words), a 32 year old Irishman beginning a years travelling and two lots of mothers and daughters. Some had arrived on the train from St. Petersburg which was apparently much nicer than the Moscow train. It was an older more comfortable train with good food and large compartments. It is the pattern of travel in that the trains get progressively worse as you get further away from Moscow. These trains are working trains and not designed for comfort. All the Russians, Chinese and Mongolians on board just want to go from one town to another, to either to work or go home. It is the handful of westerners aboard who are the real travellers. Maybe you have to be a little crazy as it is not going to be a holiday but more of an experience. The first leg is easy as it is only one night before arriving in Yekaterinburg, already 1167km from Moscow.

Yekaterinburg for three nights is long enough, the fourth largest city in Russia and closed to the world until 1991. This is the first major stop and gateway to the Ural Mountains. It is known as the city of the Romanovs because it is synonymous with the bloody murder of the Romanov family by the Bolsheviks on July 17th 1918. Other members of the Romanov family were killed at Alapayevsk the day after. You can see the Byzantine style Church of the holy Blood which reveres the Romanovs and just outside is a simple cross that marks the exact spot of the house, where in the cellar below the Russian royal family were slaughtered. The church was built in 3 years with private money and represents the repentance of the Russian people. The house itself was demolished by order of Boris Yeltsin, to prevent it from being used as a rallying location for monarchists. Standing on this spot it is easy to feel the weight of history and the events that changed it for ever. The Bolsheviks struggled to find soldiers willing to murder the royal family, women and children in cold blood. Some of the royal family had jewels strapped around their waists and the bullets glanced off them. The guards thought they had supernatural powers and finished them off with bayonets, finally ending a dynasty that lasted exactly 300 years. Many people think that the local people all look unhappy as if they still suffer from a collective guilt. Only one precious item was smuggled out of the house to safety, the priceless and favourite icon of Nicholas II which now hangs in the wooden church dedicated to him at Gamina Yama. This place is 10km out of the city at the beautiful Monastery of Martyrs. Gamina Yama translates as 'the pit', where the where the Romanov's bodies were discarded, and a cross marks the spot. The old mining pit is mostly filled in but still retains a silent poignancy. Here there are 7 wooden churches, set amongst the trees and still in the process of being built. Each church is dedicated to a member of the royal family as a reminder of the brutal and revolutionary past. In 2007 Russian archaeologists found what is thought to be the remains of the two children of Russia's last Tsar, Alexei and either Maria or Anastasia. Bullets were found where the children had been shot and nearby ceramic vessels contained traces of sulphuric acid consistent with the story that the bodies had been doused in acid to destroy all traces of them. The Tsar's remains were finally given a state funeral in July 1998.

32 km away you can stand with one foot in Europe and the other in Asia.

The next part of the trip is 3 days on the train, after which time you will most certainly know if you like this sort of travelling. It will also test out your ability to tolerate and socialise with people you have no choice over as companions. You simply have to get on with everyone in the compartment, even if it is just to negotiate where you are going to put your legs. You will be sleeping very close to others listening to them snore, fart and get up in the night. It is better than sleeping on an economy aeroplane but not as comfortable as business class. It is sort of like camping on wheels and at some stage you will ask yourself,

'Why did I want to do this trip?' and,

'What is the point of undergoing all this hardship?'

The answer probably revolves around understanding the experience. It is something that has to be done or at least endured and only when you have done it can you be afforded bragging rights back home. By the end of the 3 days the Indian couple seemed to be hating every minute and others were trying to avoid each other.

At one time there were a lot of shady looking men continually walking up and down the carriage peering in to compartments, looking at everything and maybe for an opportunity to take something. Always be on your guard, but as it so happened they were Buddhist farmers on their way to the temple at Ivolginsk. Nothing sinister, they were just looking in open-eyed wonder at western tourists.

At some stations dozens of people will be getting on laden down with bags. The train may stop for only a few minutes and if you get in the way they will take no prisoners.

As you are travelling directly from west to east you will be constantly trying to work out what time it is. All train times are in

Moscow time but on each day an hour will be lost as you cross a time zone.

The menu in the buffet car seemed quite good and reasonably priced so I ordered a meat sandwich. What arrived was a small piece of stale bread with 4 curled up pieces of salami on it, 2 dry slices of cucumber topped with a sprig of dead parsley. I could have ordered an 'open sandwich with cooking products!' We were so glad that we had stocked up with our own food, fruit and snacks because there would be no proper meal for three days or more.

The trains we may have travelled in as children are now museum exhibits

Irkutsk is the second major stop for 3 nights, surrounded by an area of outstanding natural beauty it is one of the largest cities in Siberia. It was originally populated by the exiled political prisoners that the Tsars were trying to get rid of. In the early nineteenth century many artists, nobles and officers were sent here into exile for their part in the Decembrist revolt against Tsar Nicholas 1st. They were responsible for the elaborately decorated wooden houses dotted around the city. It became the starting point for expeditions east and north, and with the discovery of gold in the 1880's it boomed.

Nearby to Irkutsk is Lake Baikal, the deepest lake in the world at 1.6 km. One of the earth's most impressive natural wonders and often called 'the pearl of Siberia'. 600km long and 80km wide it contains 20% of the world's unfrozen fresh water and the clear water contains hundreds of species found nowhere else in the world. From December to April the lake freezes over with a crust up to a metre thick. After the snow melts in May there is a tic born encephalitis to be aware of.

Listvyanka is a little village on the lakeside that most tourists go to and is dotted with traditional wooden houses. Some are collapsing, but many have beautiful and intricately carved designs especially around the windows and doors. Unfortunately the village has become a victim of its own success. Coach loads of tourists arrive to be greeted by dozens of stalls each selling exactly the same tourist souvenirs, all over-priced and for the most part 'tacky'. It is fast becoming a scruffy little town and you do not have to walk too far to find derelict buildings, discarded bottles and rubbish. Lake Baikal is not shown up at its best and a few hours here is enough unless you plan a boat trip or some serious hiking.

The final part of the journey is another 3 nights on the train going from Irkutsk to Vladivostok. If you want a shorter experience then you can fly into Irkutsk. Some passengers changed here to take the Trans-Mongolian route to Beijing and others joined including 2 Australians, who along with Kiwis are always good company. The first 180km part is the scenic highlight of the trip as the train winds its way along the cliff lined shore of Baikal.

By now the appeal of sleeping on the train will be wearing off but again it is the experience that counts and you will be paying a lot for this trip, so enjoy it. Relationships were beginning to break down particularly with the autistic Punjabi from Derby, who tested out everyone's ability to tolerate continual tedious conversation. It was his first travelling experience, he talked non-stop and was difficult to understand. He was vulnerable and did not understand 'friendship' as such. Friends were made through buying something for them which would result in them buying something in return. Breakfast in the buffet was 550 roubles and he gave the waitress 1000. She did not want it but he insisted, and she became his 'friend', his 'Auntie'. All his friends back home seemed to be people who served him in coffee shops or anyone he came into regular contact with. For these friends he took several hundred photos, mostly 'selfies', mostly taken at arms length.

The buffet car was 6 carriages down the train and 5 of these were 3rd class open dormitory types. Within each carriage there are 9 lots of bunks 3 tiers high lining the narrow side and 18 rows sideways also 3 high. So instead of 36 to a carriage there are 81. The sideways bunks are slightly too short so as you walk through lots of feet stick out with some at head height and others at knee level, with the remainder ready to kick your stomach. Passengers are in various states of undress and the whole place smells. A fierce woman is in each carriage constantly cleaning.

This is a working train and a key part of the massive Russian railway system. It is not a tourist train and carries both freight and passengers. If you are the sort of person that is excited by every moment of your train journeys in England then this trip is maybe for you, if you have been commuting into London all your life and thoroughly fed up with it then may be not. There were very few westerners on the trip and all of them enjoyed the experience but would not want to do it again. Some of these people were real travellers and part of it was wanting to tick off another box. Only after seeing Siberia do you understand just how big and empty it is. What you initially think may be a big mistake does eventually turn into a big adventure.

Ideally, if you have time, and have come so far, take the opportunity to travel on to Japan or North and South Korea.

You are going to be tired as these trains are not ideal for a good nights sleep. You maybe 'retired' but in this case it means tired yesterday and again today. It will be nice to get home to your own bed, but flying directly east to west is going to result in some serious jetlag.

Vladivostock is the end of the line, a medium size city with a commercial and naval port. Located at the head of the Golden Horn bay it is not far from the border with China and North Korea. As the train reaches the outskirts there are some seaside resorts that look like the aftermath of a bomb attack. Until recently it had the highest crime rate in Russia and the city was always associated with the 'mafia'. This has now all changed and it is as safe as anywhere else. There is enough to see to occupy a couple of days, with a museum and a submarine to explore, a super new suspension bridge, various monuments and the house where the great Yul Brynner was born. His grandson has recently had a statue erected outside in his honour.

There are lots of other great train journeys in the world so consider the following, just a few ideas out of many,

Europe - The Danube Express from Budapest travels to Vienna, Bratislava, Prague and Krakow.

www.danube-express.com

The Taurus Express travels the 1,390 kilometres from Istanbul to Aleppo over two days. In a sleeping car it is a cheap way to do it but not a safe option at the time of writing.

www.tcdd.gov.tr

The ultimate luxury of the Orient Express. This trip was launched in October 1883 and continues to be one of the most celebrated and romantic journeys in the world.

www.orient-express.com

If you are planning any rail journey, especially if you are travelling around Europe, 'The Man in Seat Sixty-One' is a good website to start with as it focuses almost exclusively on train based travel. It also deals with rail travel throughout the rest of the world which is much more like real adventure travelling. There is a book, 'The Man in Seat 61: A Guide to Taking the Train Through Europe'. This is an essential guide and full of advice and tips. More and more travellers are seeking to avoid planes and this is the only book you will need for planning.

www.seat61.com

South Africa - Cape Town to Dar-es-Salaam. Travel through South Africa, Botswana, Zimbabwe, Zambia and Tanzania over 14 days. This is luxury travel with Rovos Rail.

www.rovos.com

Try the Blue train from Cape Town to Pretoria. The ultimate luxury train journey comes at a price.

www.bluetrain.co.za

India - Travelling anywhere in India by train is a wonderful option. Book at the station by filling in a form and taking it to the station ticket office. Send the wife off to do it as women are allowed to go straight to the front of the queue. There are different classes of travel to choose, ranging from 3rd to 1st with air-conditioning. Sometimes trains are very slow and travelling on a sleeper is a good choice. If you are planning a longer journey then book up well in advance.

www.seat61.com/India.htm

www.indianrail.gov.in

The Golden Triangle takes seven days covering the best of Northern India and Rajasthan.

www.palaceonwheels-train.com

The Darjeeling Himalayan Railway is a narrow gauge steam railway taking you from Silighuri in West Bengal to Darjeeling all in one day. A spectacular eight hour journey through forests and tea plantations it is one of the worlds great engineering feats and ridiculously cheap.

www.irctc.co.in

Canada - Go from Toronto through Winnipeg and Jasper to Vancouver crossing forests, past lakes, prairies and mountains. Driving this route would be a tad tedious bearing in mind it is 2,718 miles. The Rocky Mountaineer travelling from Calgary through Jasper and Banff to Vancouver and the rugged mountains of Western Canada makes for an expensive but spectacular trip.

www.seat61,com/Canada.htm
www.canadaforvisitor.com

Australia - The Ghan will take you from Darwin to Adelaide or vice-versa.
The India Pacific Express goes from Perth to Sydney, from one ocean to the other. This epic journey takes 3 days and 3 nights and cuts through some wonderful landscapes.

www.greatsouthernrail.com/au
www.freedomaustralia.co.uk

America - The Californian Zephyr goes from Chicago to San Francisco. It takes two days but with 34 stops you can get off whenever you wish and join up again later. Recreate the classic journey out west passing through the Great Plains and up into the Rocky Mountains. The Californian Zephyr will take you through seven states and clocks up 2,438 miles.

www.amtrak.com

Burma - The Eastern and Oriental Express runs from Singapore to Bangkok. Step back in time through the Malayan peninsula past temples, mountains and forests.

www.orient-express.com

The Ghan railway was named after the Afghan camel trains

In Malta the best way to travel is on these old buses

Some of the above are holidays in themselves but could be slotted into your itinerary as part of a trip, a bit of luxury or a necessary means of getting from one place to another, just as you might do at home. You have to try at least one major train journey. 'You've gotta ticket to ride'.

We all remember the days of steam engines

Unmistakably Moscow

8 Organised Trips

"Every Englishman abroad, until it is proved to the contrary, likes to consider himself a traveller and not a tourist."
Evelyn Waugh 1903-1966

You may be an independent traveller and would not even consider an organised, package holiday but sometimes this can be a good option. It is a safe and easy introduction to travelling if you have lost the confidence to go off on your own. However, stuck on a tour bus in your allocated seat with all the sights whizzing by is not what the traveller wants. Taking pictures through the windows only captures your own reflection. You doze off to the rhythm of the road or listen to other people snore and chatter, this is not really travelling. I still book the occasional organised trip simply because they can offer such good value. A recent 12 day whirlwind trip around China with Jules Verne took us to Beijing, with its famous sights and the Great Wall, Shanghai with all the glitz, Xian for the Emperor's Army and to Chengdu for the giant pandas. Travelling around China is never going to be easy, particularly because of the language barrier. With this deal all the internal flights were taken care of and we were mollycoddled without being too restricted and there was plenty of free time to explore independently. The rest of our group were not very adventurous and opted to relax in the hotel rather than go exploring. In Beijing we took a taxi to the night market, easy to do as the hotel doorman gave the driver instructions. It was more difficult getting back as no taxi driver understood English, why should they? The language is definitely a problem so be warned. May is the best time to go for the weather on this trip.

We also went to Goa on a package tour. The deal was so good that we could have barely booked the flight for the total cost of the holiday. On arrival we stayed for a while at the resort then hired a motor scooter for £1.50 a day and just took off up north travelling around as we wished. We're explorers not package tourists. Big companies can often offer some amazing deals so keep looking.

It is sensible to check the company out first of all. Look them up on the message boards and forums to see what others are saying about them. Are they really good value for money and what extra costs are involved? Do you have to pay an entrance fee for every place that is visited? One particularly good company is G Adventures, they were originally called Gap but they had a problem with another high profile company of the same name. They offer a sort of 'assisted travel', in that they provide a guide, use local transport and authentic accommodation wherever possible. This approach ensures that all the money goes back into the local community. They try to offer adventure travel with affordable small-groups, between 10 and 18, with no single traveller supplement. Tours, safaris and expeditions are run all over the world and are an alternative to the resorts, cruises and motor coach holidays tourists are used to. The company try to attract a wide range of adventurous travellers who want to experience destinations at a grass routes level. The good thing is that there is no upper age limit and everything is conducted in English so most of the travellers are from English speaking countries. You do have to sort out your own flights, just make sure that the trip is geared to what you want.

www.gadventures.co.uk

By small boat is a good way to tour the Galapagos Islands

We used G Adventures for a trip to the Galapagos Islands and a further trip travelling around Ecuador. If you decide to go to the Galapagos the first decision is whether it is to be a land based trip or boat trip.

With the land based option you will sleep in the same place and take daily trips out. Where you go will be more limited but it is a good option if your sea-legs are weak. We opted for a sea based option which enabled us to get to more islands including the southern ones, Floreana and Espanola. On the journey overnight, between the two islands, in a small 75 foot, 16 berth boat, most of those on board felt sick or were sick. The boat continually heaved up and down in the swell. It is best just to lie flat and try and get as much rest as possible. We were told in Quito to leave all our warm gear in the hotel but take no notice and make sure that you have a fleece. The Islands may straddle the Equator but they are in the middle of the ocean and the Humboldt Current brings cold water. You will need a wet suit for snorkelling and the boats do provide them, along with masks, snorkels and flippers if required. Make sure that your snorkelling skills are up to scratch or you will be seriously missing out and bring your own mask if you have room for it. The best encounters with wild life though, are on land with the vast number of endemic species. You will not be disappointed with the giant tortoises, iguanas, frigate birds and all the other wild life that have developed no fear of humans. You will be disappointed if you choose the 5 day trip rather than the 10 day one. Two days are lost in travelling and those on the 5 day tip miss out on a lot of sights including visiting the wonderful giant tortoises in the wild. This is a dream destination and it seems a bit far fetched that you are actually there.

Marine Iguanas will take no notice of you in the Galapagos Islands

The Ecuador tour afterwards was extremely well organised and G Adventures seemed to get the perfect balance of providing local transport between destinations and leaving plenty of time for everyone to go off and do their own thing. The highlights were staying with a local family in the Amazon jungle where it rained so very hard. Think of the worst rainstorm you have ever experienced and keep it going for 6 hours. The Quechan people are desperate to keep their culture and beliefs alive but realise it is almost an impossible dream. They did try to teach us all about local remedies and their customs on jungle walks. Most of the young people leave and go to the cities so all the knowledge is no longer passed down. On the Equator you can stand with one foot in the southern hemisphere and the other in the north. At Papallacta there is plenty of time to spend soaking in the hot thermal pools. G.A. arrange plenty of outdoor activities, horse riding, cycling and trekking, there are a lot of high volcanoes to trek up in this region. Chimborrozo at 6310m is the highest point in the world if measured from the centre of the earth. Cuenza is full of old Colonial buildings, galleries,

churches and is a UNESCO site. In Cayambe the accommodation had been arranged in the oldest Hacienda in Ecuador. A fascinating place where every bedroom had its own big log fire; again it may be near the Equator but this is high up in the Andes and can be very cold especially at night. To arrange all this itinerary yourself would be difficult.

Otavalo is the famous market in Ecuador but now much more geared up to tourism. For a more authentic experience get up early at 6am and walk the 20 minutes from the centre of town to the cattle market. Here the traders come down from the Andean hills and are dressed in traditional clothes. The men in pantaloons, ponchos and some in trilby hats with almost all of them having long plaited pig tails. The women also have trilby hats and either one or two long plaited pig tails. They are in brightly coloured skirts, with embroidered white blouses and ponchos or shawls. Unfortunately the tourists are just beginning to discover it.

For all organised trips your guide is important and can make or break it. They are generally very good if they work for adventure type companies and are with the group for the duration, however, for individual locally guided tours then it is a bit of a lottery. In a large group if you are at the back it may be difficult to hear. Some guides begin speaking before the party has all gathered together and other have such a poor command of English that you may not understand what they are saying at all. I always try to speak to them privately and ask lots of questions and get as much information as possible. I also find that after this they sometimes direct their group talks towards me alone. Some guides will assume you want to visit every souvenir shop, stop at some dreadful jewellery outlet or visit their cousin's carpet store and others just want to get away with the barest minimum. In Italy we took a tour around Pompeii and were whisked around quickly, missing a lot of interesting buildings. It was all too rushed and at the end of the tour everyone was shepherded into a cafe to spend the next 30 minutes having refreshments. Everyone did except us, we looked in more detail at the baths and explored inside other buildings, discovering so much that had been missed. It is a vast site and much better to explore independently.

There are going to be lots of package holidays that true travellers really need to avoid. Paul Theroux, the American travel writer said, 'Tourists don't know where they have been, travellers don't know where they are going.' Do you really want to be on a packaged trip where every moment of the day is organised for you? Sometimes we feel so sorry for the tourists that we see being shunted around in coaches. They all pile out and are told something to the effect that they only have fifteen minutes and then they have to be back on the coach. Other groups follow the leader who holds a flag high up in the air for everyone to slavishly follow. Wherever we are in the world, when tour groups arrive, we take a seat and wait until we have the place to ourselves again. Many years ago we took an organised coach trip around Morocco. This is not what we normally do but it was a very cheap way to travel and went to all the major cities. The guide got a bit annoyed with us as we chose not to take any of his organised tours. It was so easy to take a cheap taxi or bus to the same places that the remainder of the party were going to. The guide got even more annoyed when some of the rest of the group also began making their own way around. It can be just a matter of confidence especially when the guide clearly tells you that it is dangerous, you will get lost or mugged. In Marrakech we were told it was impossible to get into town by bus even though our hotel was located just outside the town right by a bus stop. It was a simple journey of a few stops only five minutes away from Djemaa-el-Fna, the main square. We were not very popular with the guide who was out to make as much money as he could from inexperienced tourists. In such situations it is always best to listen to advice and assess the risks involved for yourself but do not fall for any scare mongering.

So decide for yourself especially on coach travel. How many are in the group? 50 people on a coach are going to take a long time to get off and on and even longer if they are - old. Try to avoid a company that is just going to pick you up from the hotel and do little more than show you the sights from a coach window. Remember you are a traveller not a tourist.

All inclusive holidays are 'dangerous', geared up to keep the tourist 'locked' up in the resort. Along with free drinks, unlimited food and plenty of entertainment all inclusive may be the dream vacation for plenty of holiday makers. Such holidays seem to predominate in certain places like the Dominican Republic and Cuba among others. First Choice specialises in 'all inclusive' claiming it will save money. This is great for young families and those on a tight budget, they will have peace of mind knowing that everything is paid for, flights, transfers, hotel accommodation, three meals a day and unlimited local drinks will all be included in the price. I can also see the attraction for hard working younger people who just want to get away, relax and have everything done for them. However, this should not be the main consideration when booking a holiday, part of the charm with any holiday is finding a back street cafe, eating with the locals and immersing yourself in their culture. Another danger is that such holidays are possibly going to attract less desirable tourists who might say,

'This holiday has cost me £700 and I am going to make sure I drink £700's worth of alcohol.'

What's the point of going to a far off place to spend it all, or most of it, sat around the hotel pool or bar, just so you get your money's worth? It is unfortunate that local communities rarely benefit from all inclusive resorts. The situation is worse in places like the Dominican Republic, where the hotel complexes are completely self-contained and the local population aren't even employed in the hotels. Although the situation has improved a little recently as tourists have discovered that there is life outside of their compound. The nature of such holidays does not encourage people to go outside of the resort at all, which is a shame. We have only been on one such holiday and did enjoy it, but we went out every single day exploring the area and meeting the locals. Are you strong willed enough or easily tempted?

Land Iguanas are closely related to marine iguanas but are more agile on land. They are also lighter coloured, somewhat larger and have a different diet.

Some people were still not popular in Cuba

9 Cruises

"Modern travelling is not travelling at all; it is merely being sent to a place, and very little different from becoming a parcel."
John Ruskin 1819-1900

We always said that we would never go on a cruise, cruises were for old people. We may be over sixty but still were not old enough. To be stuck on a ship with a lot of old fogies, no way. We also harboured certain prejudices, one of which was that they were too expensive, but then one day an email arrived offering us a ten day cruise circumnavigating Britain for £399. It was a last minute deal and too good an offer to resist. There are always a lot of fantastic last minute deals for cruises, particularly if it is going to one of the typical cruise destinations like the Mediterranean or Fjords. We had been thinking that we had somewhat neglected Great Britain and being retired we could leave at the drop of a hat. This cruise changed or at least modified our attitudes. We sailed at night and awoke each day in a different port. All of the places we stopped at, we really did want to visit, but not for any length of time so it was ideal, in fact a single day was enough in most places. It is almost impossible not to enjoy what is on offer on a cruise, it is unadulterated luxury, with a banquet for breakfast and a six or seven course evening meal in a first class restaurant. Plus you could have lunch, afternoon tea and cakes, evening snacks, in fact you could eat all your waking hours if you so wished. Cruising is dangerous, in that the food is just too good and too plentiful, you just have to put up with it.

There was a gym, table tennis, games room, sauna, Jacuzzi and swimming pool. In addition there were a number of bars and several shows to choose from each night. We learnt not sit in the front row unless you want to risk getting dragged up on the stage, as happens with some comedians and entertainers. It is true there was a majority of old people on board but many were of the adventurous type and interesting to talk to. On several nights we were tucked up in bed while the night club was full of pensioners twisting the night away.

On any cruise you will be meeting lots of older people and sometimes it is difficult to come to terms with the fact that you may also one be of them. You may have to sit down to meals and talk with whoever is at your table. Then you might discover what extraordinary lives some of them have lived. Recently one couple enthralled us with their boating stories. They had retired at 60, sold everything and bought a yacht. They then travelled the world for 26 years, finally selling the yacht in Australia for three times what they had paid for it. Cruises seem to attract 'yachties', we continually meet people who have sailed the Atlantic, worked on boats or still live on canal barges.

The first thing to do is to explore the ship and to get your bearings. Distinguish between forward and aft, and port side (left) and starboard (right). Amidships is a good place to have your cabin where there will be less ship movement. I never think it is worth the extra cost to upgrade to an expensive cabin particularly if you are only going to use it to sleep in.

Generally each day we did some serious walking. We could not believe our luck with the weather, it was warm and dry even up in Scotland and the sea was calm so there were no problems docking and at anchorage. Also in the summer Scotland has a midge problem but if you go in April the problem can be avoided. The main midge season runs roughly from June to October. They are particularly prevalent around dawn and dusk and are so small that a single midge is difficult to see. It is only the female that bites and a swarm can inflict around 3,000 bites in an hour. You will become very itchy with red patches on the skin and some people will suffer more than others.

If you have not been on a cruise before then something reasonably short such as this is an ideal introduction. On some of the longer cruises involving crossing the Atlantic more days can be spent at sea than on land, so make sure you actually enjoy being on a boat for length periods of time. Boarding the boat at Tilbury was quite exciting. The Marco Polo is a 22,000 ton vessel carrying 820 passengers. It is not a new ship, being built in 1965 but sensibly sized for the convenience of the passenger. Another nice thing is that it is for adults only, everyone has to be over 16. Briefly the itinerary was as below and what as keen walkers we managed to do:

Invergordon - It took a day to get there. We got off the boat and took a bus to Inverness where we walked down the Caledonian Canal and along the fast flowing River Ness. Unfortunately the boats to Loch Ness were not running early in the year. Invergordon itself has a series of wonderful trompe l'oeil on the sides of various buildings around the town. Overnight we sailed round Cape Wrath where the sea was slightly rougher.

Stornaway - This is largest town in the Outer Hebrides. There is a really nice walk over the river and around the headland, up the River Creed and on to Gallows Hill for spectacular views of the town. In the afternoon we took a local bus across the island to see some impressive standing stones which were 5000 years older than Stonehenge.

Tobermory - This is the capital of Mull on the Inner Hebrides. It was almost too hot for walking but we did every trail in the Aross Park which was magical, with lots of waterfalls, then around the other headland to a lighthouse. Tobermory has brightly coloured houses and is where Ballamory was filmed.

Dublin - This wonderful city seemed a bit 'down at heel' since a previous visit. We went to the lovely botanic gardens and later drank several pints of Guinness. Draft Guinness in Dublin tastes much better in Dublin than anywhere else in the world. If you have never visited previously then you need far more than a day.

The Scilly Isles - The boat docked at St. Mary's and there was time to do a quick walk before taking the ferry to the wonderful Tresco Island and the paradise which is the famous Abbey Gardens. It was warm and sunny again and for us, the highlight of the trip.

The Channel Isles - After docking at St. Peters Port, Guernsey we took the local bus around the Island stopping at the shipwreck museum and pearl centre. We managed to hitch a lift to get inland to the tiny chapel decorated with mosaics. In the afternoon we took the ferry to Herm to walk around the island, which was like stepping back in time.

Honfleur - We did not realise how beautiful it was with an unbelievable amount of art galleries in the quaint old quarter. For some reason the Germans decided not to bomb it in the war - danke schön.

For each of these stops the boat offered a choice of trips for less adventurous and less mobile people, but many of us did our own thing. One couple were playing golf at each location, another had a jeep waiting for them to go bird watching whilst others took their sketch books. We quickly left all the boat people behind us and headed for the hills. This cruise seemed a sensible and convenient way to get to all these places.

www.cruiseandmaritime.com offer no fly cruises from the UK and the Marco Polo has the added bonus of being adults only.

www.fredolsencruises.com is another company operating smaller more personal ships.

It is estimated that over 30 million people enjoys a cruise every year with few complaints. We avoided them for so long because we thought that they just for old people, which as it so happens was not to far off the mark. Other reluctant cruisers may worry about many different things such as follows:

- Getting seasick could be a justifiable concern, but some ships are so vast that normally you will not even know that you are moving. However, everyone should pack plenty of seasick tablets. Sucking crystallised ginger is also effective.
- Viruses are a potential problem and ships are very aware of such risks. Norovirus is a very contagious virus that you can get from an infected person, contaminated food or water, or by touching contaminated surfaces. They are associated with cruise ships because health officials track illness, so outbreaks are found and reported more quickly than on land. Some ships now are much more vigilant to the point of paranoia. In the gym you may be requested to wipe down each piece of equipment with a sanitized paper towel each time it is used.
- They are not as expensive as some people might think and most are all-inclusive. There are some expenses, but all of them partially avoidable, depending upon your requirements and means. Okay, alcoholic drinks and special coffees will be an extra expense but, all food is included along with most of the facilities. If you are on a budget then think positively, water is good for you. You will only have to pay extra for special beauty treatments or such optional things as health courses offered by the gym. All the entertainment is free for you to enjoy.
- You will not have to sit and dine with people that you do not know or have to dress up formally for some evenings. All these things are normally optional.
- Occasionally cruise ships may seem a little crowded particularly if you are queuing to get into the theatre for the evening show or looking for the best seats around the boat to settle down in, but generally there is plenty of space for everyone.
- You are unlikely to get bored as there is so much going on. Each day a programme of events will be posted to you under your cabin door.

- Cruise ships are not just for going to islands and beaches they now seem to go just about everywhere.
- Gratuities are added to your bill on a daily basis. If you are not happy with this then they are voluntary, you can go to customer services and say exactly how much you want to pay.

Cruises at present seem to be incredibly good value in days of austerity and offer some amazing facilities. Some days are at sea so should you wish to be sociable there is daily schedule of activities or you can bury your head in a book. We did a mixture of activities including reading, games and exercising in the gym. To us it seemed like a good opportunity to catch up with reading as we both feel a bit guilty sitting down and relaxing at home. One of the nice things about cruising is having the opportunity to dress up for a formal dinner. Dressed up in dinner jackets, suits, cummerbunds, bow ties and long evening dresses, the guests all look fabulous. There are limited opportunities in life to do that sort of thing and dressing up is fun. It carries on one of the great traditions of cruising dating back over 100 years and it would be a shame to miss out on it. The ladies dress up in all their finery, Indian ladies in saris, Japanese in kimonos and Europeans in everything from ball gowns to cocktail dresses. It makes for a great spectacle, but is not compulsory and anyone can opt for the informality of the self service restaurant. Normally in the main restaurant you will be seated on a table with others but if you are feeling a bit anti-social or just want a quiet dinner then there are tables just for two.

You will meet people on board who have been on dozens of cruises and others who always take a cruise for their vacation. The traveller's way to think about it is that a cruise is ideal to get to places that are difficult to get to by any other means. So for the serious traveller there maybe limitations until of course we too become old and want everything thought out and packaged up for us. The clientele, although almost exclusively older people, are always very mixed. Some are so old, that apparently there is often at least one death on every cruise. The average age for this particular cruise was 55-65 years, boosted by the no children policy, but according to recent research the age is dropping year on year for cruises in general.

For the 'real' traveller there remains the feeling that cruising is sort of cheating. Real travellers get to destinations under their own steam and we still feel the same way. Since that first cruise we have done several more, but only to those hard to get to places. The next itinerary visited the Norwegian Fjords. It took us to Ulvik, Eifjord, Flam, Vik, Oslo, Helsingborg, Copenhagen, a transit through the Kiel Canal and Amsterdam. This is just about the only way to see parts of this coastline so it fitted in with our philosophy. Brief extracts from my diary give an insight as what to expect.

It took us a day to get up to the Norwegian Fjords. The Hardangerfjord took us 75 miles inland to Ulvik. The fjords are amazing deep and narrow channels flanked by high granite cliffs, dotted with picturesque wooden houses and dozens of waterfalls. We were lying in a Jacuzzi on the top deck of the boat with drinks and cakes by our side watching the scenery go by, how decadent? Then it was on to Eidfjord where we did lots of walking. Further north to the Sognefjord which is the 'king' of the fjords being so long and deep. We got off at Flam with its spectacular scenery and took a trip on the mountain railway, one of Norway's major attractions. Here we had to get off the boat quick and make our way to the station before the crowds, rather than book the trip on board. It rises up to 800 metres, took 20 years to build, goes through 20 tunnels and is 20k long. On the way back get off 2 stations before the port and walk back through the splendid countryside.

The boat looped south to Oslo where we did our own walking tour. The most impressive thing here is the amount of sculpture on display everywhere. We saw 'The Scream' and in the cathedral at that time there were many floral tributes to the young people who lost their lives in the dreadful atrocity at the youth summer camp on Utoya island. Oslo has been designated the most expensive city in the world. Norway is expensive, do not believe anyone who tells you it is affordable. Just see how much a pint of beer will cost you. We were glad we have been there but have no real need to go back.

Copenhagen was an interesting stop and it is easy to see all the major sights, lots of churches, the round tower and important buildings and palaces. The Christiania district is an intriguing place to visit. This is a partially self governing area colonized originally by hippies but now seemingly by all sorts of anarchistic types of people. It is a bohemian area covered in graffiti art and junk sculptures. No cars are allowed and no photographs, particularly so in Pusher Street where stalls openly sell drugs. (Do NOT attempt to take any photographs there.) The area has no proper roads and it is partially overgrown by nature, but this is deliberate and it is relatively tidy and free from litter. We were the only people on the boat that went there, but it was worth it. The pedometer registered over 30,500 steps that day!

We crossed through Germany via the Kiel Canal. This is an extraordinary construction, 62 miles long and the busiest canal in the world. An amazing engineering feat whereby 80 million cubic metres of earth were moved and it took 9,000 workers 8 years to construct.

Amsterdam is always entertaining and we spent most of the short time here wandering around the red light district looking at all the women posing in the windows. On a previous visit in our younger days a seedy man approached me and said,

'Are you looking for a window for your woman?'

My wife took it as some sort of compliment. Others may think of it as a missed business opportunity.

This was a wonderful cruise again, even though Scandinavia is not our favourite destination.

Another trip up took us up to Spitzbergen taking in the northern coast of Norway. This really is high up in the north, an incredible 1000km inside the Arctic Circle and such a good dot to put in your world map. You can of course go the whole way right to the North Pole itself. It will take a nuclear powered ice breaker up to a week to get there pushing its way through the pack ice, but what a destination. You can even go for a dip in specially created bore holes. It will cost upwards of £14,000 though and that is a lot of travelling money.

www.princess.com The Grand Princess is a huge ship carrying 2,600 passengers but took us inside the Arctic Circle.

Other difficult places to get to that are best got to by cruise boat are Alaska, Greenland and Antarctica, cold weather seems to be the common factor. In the future we may even take a cruise across the pond and up the Amazon but we will be older by then. Places like the Mediterranean are not for us - yet, but it might work for you.

Antarctica is a terrific destination and the final one that I will describe to give you an insight into cruising and what to expect.

Our route took us from Buenos Aries down to Ushuaia and Cape Horn. Then heading south across Drake Passage and through the Schollart Channel to Paradise bay in Antarctica. Returning north we went through the Gerlache Strait and past Elephant Island. Finally it was up to Port Stanley on the Falkland Islands and back up north stopping at Puerto Madryn and Montevideo before returning to Buenos Aries.

Cruise ships can be huge, this one is about average

Cruising is like stepping into a parallel universe where everything is perfect, but there are the many dangers associated with over indulgence. The food is normally going to be superb, not a problem in itself, the problem is that there is so much of it. Everywhere on board tempting snacks, cakes, ice creams, hamburgers, pizzas and full scale meals are on offer at every time of the day. Most people just eat far too much and it requires a lot of discipline not to do so. A further danger with cruising is that you

126

might get to like it so much that your adventure travelling will come to a premature end. You never get bored, just set forth from your cabin with a purposeful aimlessness and something will turn up.

There is always plenty do on board in the way of entertainment and activities. There will be a gym and a variety of fitness and dance classes on offer plus several swimming pools, Jacuzzis, a sauna and other facilities according to the particular ship. There are often top quality lectures many of which combine knowledge and humour. This Antarctic ship had a large thalassotherapy pool whereas others have had games rooms, table tennis and even full size basketball courts. Everyday you will meet new people especially in the dining room. You may or may not get on but you do not have to see them again. One problem is that the same conversations keep occurring but at least it gives you a chance to hone your tales and big them up.

Most big cruise ships are the same in that they have a large casino where guests can gamble away their money. Some punters just sit there for hours feeding in coins even though no player ever comes out on top. Shops on board do not vary either, most of them will be selling jewellery and watches. I can only think that they still must be just catering for demand. There is often an art gallery along with art auctions and these are surprisingly good and hold informative talks. Many other interesting lectures cover topics relating to the cruise as well as other varied subjects.

Some cruisers seem to undergo a personality change for the duration of the trip and let their hair down and sometimes themselves. Many guests seem to try and enjoy themselves despite what others may think of them. Nobody is embarrassed, apart from some of the more reserved British guests. People of all different shapes and sizes happily strip off to sunbathe or waddle around in the gym and there is always an excess of fatter and clinically obese people. If you judge people by how many tattoos and piercings they have here is a chance to put your theories to the test.

So who goes on cruises? On this Antarctic cruise of the 2000 or so guests the largest group were British, even though the ship sailed from South America. The main nationalities were as follows:

- British - 655
- Americans - 608
- Canadians - 169
- Germans - 155
- Chinese - 60

- Australians - 45
- Japanese - 37
- Hong Kong - 31
- Mexico - 14
- French-12
- Argentinean - 7
- + smaller numbers from other countries

There were also a lot of Indians travelling under British passports. Most on board were senior citizens because we are the group that have the time and the money. Do take care, even though you maybe super fit, the ship can lurch around in high seas and a broken arm will seriously mess up your holiday. The Americans are ridiculously outgoing and extroverted. The compere asks for people to do a monkey impression, the British are all looking at each other, heads down a bit, but the yanks are up there jumping up and down on stage and whooping. What is more, they are really good at it. Play The Village People, 'Young Man', the same thing, mostly Americans having a good time. They do not care what other passengers think about them, and yes, some of them are typically brash, loud, vulgar and rich. Any cruise ships leaving from Great Britain will normally have an overwhelming number of British clients. Cruise ships that leave from anywhere in the Americas will be geared up towards the American market and all the dumbing down or razzamatazz that may go with it.

The Celebrity 'Infinity' is a huge boat of 91,000 tonnes holding some 2200 guests. 964 feet long and 105 feet wide it cruises at 24 knots. There are 950 crew representing over 50 nationalities. The total power output is equivalent to 900 medium sized family cars consuming 126 gallons of fuel per mile. One interesting fact, Engineer Officers wear gold stripes with 'purple' in recognition of their British colleagues on board the Titanic. When it sank, all the engineers went down with the ship, but you probably knew this already. There are a dozen decks with plenty of things to do and each evening there is a show in the theatre with an early and a late sitting. There are several bars all over the ship and most have some entertainment, a string quartet, guitarist or singer.

www.celebritycruises.com for those that want a big luxury ship

We left Buenos Aries in the heat of the summer, sitting in a Jacuzzi on the top deck and sunbathing. It takes 3 full days at sea to travel the 1,350 nautical miles to Ushuaia, through the 'roaring forties' and into the 'furious fifties'. Sitting right at the bottom of Argentina it is the southern most city in the world. The setting is dramatic, lying beneath the jagged glacial peaks of the Montes Martial. It is, however, too touristy and full of shops selling lots of over priced goods that you probably do not want. What actually is good there, are the surroundings and the hiking opportunities. The Martial Glacier is close enough to the town to walk to. A chair lift will take you a little bit further and then it is another one and a half kilometres steeply uphill to the glacier itself. Well worth it and if time is limited a taxi will take you as far as the lifts. Up near the glacier there are several trails to explore and there may be an icy blizzard one minute with hot sunshine the next, and that is at the height of summer. Ushuaia itself, looks out over the Beagle Channel which the HMS Beagle sailed through in 1832, circumnavigating the earth on its famous second voyage of discovery. On board was the British super hero Charles Darwin as the ship's naturalist.

At about latitude 50 degrees the weather undergoes a distinct change. It maybe sunny but the wind increases to gale force and the huge boat starts to heave about in the swell. One can only imagine what it was like for the sailors on wooden schooners not so many years ago. It is from Ushuaia that all the expedition ships leave. This is a more expensive option, but many people consider it an essential part of their Antarctic visit, to set foot upon the continent. The other big advantage is that you will get into Zodiacs, small inflatable dinghies, which will get up close to icebergs and the land. If the captain spots a blue whale he will stop, a big cruise boat will not. Some companies will even take you into the interior and for a price, the South Pole itself.

Cape Horn is 56 degrees south and sometimes even cruise ships cannot safely approach it. Itineraries are at the mercy of the continent's changing moods and your Captain must juggle your viewing and photo opportunities with his career prospects. At 1,357 feet high it represents the last bit of the Andes and here the weather can change quite dramatically and quickly. It may be obvious to seasoned travellers but dress in layers and do not forget hats, scarves and gloves. Do not under estimate the wind chill factor, Antarctic summers are much like cold northern winters. Here at the Cape the winds blow from the west to the east which made it a long and impossibly difficult journey for early sailors. Tacking back and forth into the wind the journey round the Horn could take 80 days or more, the quickest passage being 30 days. Some ships had to give up and 800 went down in that earlier period of exploration. It was, however, still safer than going through the Magellan Straights where the passage is so narrow that unpredictable winds could blow ships onto the rocks. Sailors who were washed overboard generally perished because turning a wooden boat around in such harsh weather was nigh on impossible. Seamen would take off their life jackets and drown themselves rather than be pecked to death by the albatrosses circling above. Nobody kills an albatross now after the fate of the 'Ancient Mariner' in Coleridge's epic poem. He who shot the albatross brought eternal bad luck and death to his colleagues and was left with the 'albatross around his neck' for life. The wandering albatross will give a particular thrill as it glides past you. Now there are no commercial routes around Cape Horn since the opening of the Panama Canal. There is a manned light house there and a weather station but essentially this is the end of the world.

It took us a mere 2 hours or so to round the Horn in relatively benign conditions against a 30 mph headwind in a 10 to 15 foot swell. Even now if the weather is too bad then cruise ships will not go to Cape Horn and sometimes cannot even make it down to the Antarctic Peninsula. With so many small islands one can only admire the navigational skills of early sailors sailing in far worse conditions often in dense fog. High up on the headland is the Albatross Memorial to all those sailors who died. In mythology the albatross embodies the souls of all the lost sailors. We moved easily from the Atlantic to the Pacific before turning south towards the white continent.

Further south is the Drake Passage, the strip of water separating South America from the Antarctic Peninsula, which can be one of the windiest places in the world. Here in the Southern Ocean the winds can increase as you move towards the 'screaming sixties'. Now is going to be the time that you find out exactly how good your sea legs are. Instead of staggering around on the boat you could try drinking the right amount of alcohol then just maybe it will rectify your balance so that you walk in a straight line. On the other hand you might just fall overboard and if you do so in the Antarctic you will die, survival time is calculated in minutes.

The ship goes right down to the Antarctic Peninsula which is another part of the Andes that has re-emerged. This trip is only possible in the summer when the sea ice has receded. Seeing the Antarctic ice sheet, acts as a reminder that it was not so long ago, in geological terms, that much of Europe was covered by ice. Ice that was up to 3 miles deep and was responsible for carving out the rounded shape to our mountains and hills. No tourists visit the Antarctic Peninsula in the winter when it is barricaded in with pack ice and has near 24 hour darkness. The season for travelling is only from November to February with each month offering something different:

- November - birds courting and mating
- December and January - penguins hatching
- February - whale watching

The Antarctic ice has built up over hundreds of thousands of years. The ice sheet is the size of Australia and is up to 4 km thick, averaging out at 2.7 km. Snow has fallen in successive layers and been compressed along with tiny pockets of air. Analysis of these layers provides a unique insight into the climate of long ago. The Russians bored down through this ice archive that represents many different climatic zones and celebrated with champagne served up with 80 thousand year old ice cubes. They were surprised when their glasses suddenly exploded. As the ice cubes melted the compressed air burst out with enough force to shatter their glasses. These ice cores have been drilled down to depths of 3,000 metres the bottom of which are over 400,000 years old and represent several glacial cycles. Chemicals and gases are dissolved in the snow and show records of a cataclysmic volcanic eruption covering the entire planet with ash and triggering the last ice age. Sulphates are blasted into the atmosphere and absorbed into the ice. They even show the effects of the industrial revolution where metallic elements have been trapped and preserved.

The ice is continually breaking off the main ice sheet creating icebergs in a process called 'calving'. It is a unique process whereby the ice is returned to the sea from where it came so many years ago. Some of the icebergs are so big that they acquire their own weather systems. Only one ninth of an iceberg is showing above the water and they are constantly tracked to avoid collisions with shipping. Antarctica is only the fifth largest continent but holds 85% of the world fresh water and if it all melted sea levels would rise by 200 feet. There are only 3 ice sheets left in the world, Antarctica, Greenland and parts of Canada.

It is still a unique experience to visit Antarctica and only about 3,000 visitors a year on expedition type trips actually set foot on the continent. Those on a cruise can only gaze in wonder from the comfort of their ship. Two things could ruin your holiday and both of them connected to the weather. Fog would be a disaster and high winds may cause seasickness. Either could bring the trip to a premature end. It is mandatory that a talk is given about keeping Antarctica pristine before the vessel enters the Antarctic waters and there are strict guidelines for tour boats. An Environmental Officer representing the International Association of Antarctic Tour Operators (IAATO) gave our talk. Below 60 degrees latitude nothing can be discharged into the sea. All heavy oil had to be removed from the ship in Montevideo and replaced with marine gas oil. The Captain has to be aware of whales to avoid any strikes and fortunately tourism is now the growth industry here and not oil drilling or mining as once feared.

Antarctica is surrounded by water and strong winds circulate around it isolating it from the warming effects of the oceans to the north. It is the highest part of the world that is at the same time the driest, coldest and windiest. Many peaks in the Transantarctic Mountain Range are over 4,000 metres high and it is a harsh and dangerous climate. Yet there is plenty of wild life remaining still unafraid of people because the continent is essentially unpopulated by humans. Very few animal species live down there, but what does is in profusion due to the abundance of food. Somewhere north of the Antarctic Circle between roughly 50 and 60 degrees south lies the Antarctic Convergence, an ever changing line where there is a dramatic change in the water temperature. This is where the cold water of the south meets the warmer northern waters bringing up essential nutrients from the seabed for small creatures to feast on. Algae proliferate in the rich water and krill feed on it. Whales and small fish feed on the krill, bigger fish eat smaller fish which in turn are eaten by seals and penguins. There are penguins, seals and various birds in great quantities. The water temperature is surprisingly stable ranging from minus 2 to plus 2 centigrade. Nobody governs the continent, it is kept as a reserve for scientific research and remains the largest wilderness in the world.

As you near the Antarctic Peninsula it is exciting to see the first iceberg and they can be alarmingly big. In February 1995 an iceberg the size of Luxemburg detached itself from the Larson ice sheet. Soon there are more icebergs, small islands and finally Antarctica itself, the white continent, the world's last great wilderness. Just being there and knowing you are there can be enough. This was the height of the southern summer and yet it is bitterly cold. The ship glides into Paradise bay where it rotates 360 degrees against the dramatic background of steep snow covered cliffs, before turning back up north through the Gerlache Strait. There were plenty of humpback whales and penguins in the water to spot. The land is surprisingly rich in subtle colours. Bright green lichens grow in patches surrounded by the snow. Penguins feed on this and krill, a kind of shrimp, which produces areas of pink poo. The ice also looks as if it has patches of azure blue and all this against the neutral background of greys, black and white.

Captain Cook was the first person to cross the Antarctic Circle on January 17th 1773, but we never quite made it across the Circle. After 64.5 degrees latitude the ship had to turn back towards the real world. Captain Cook also turned back even though he was well inside the Antarctic Circle, and against all the odds somehow managed not to find land at all. Reluctantly turning back up North a day later you come to Elephant Island, notorious for where 22 of Shackleton's men were marooned in 1915 for 135 days living under 2 upturned boats. All of them were eventually rescued due to Shackleton's heroic efforts.

After another day at sea and depending upon your itinerary you will arrive at the Falkland Islands. These are wonderful on a nice day but miserable in the rain. Dr. Samuel Johnson wrote regarding the British military garrison stationed there,

'They must be in a state that contemplates with envy the exiles of Siberia.'

The people, numbering 2,478, are warm and welcoming. They are vastly out-numbered by over half a million sheep but this is where they make most of their living, along with fishing. Port Stanley is the Southernmost, most remote and smallest capital in the world and with its pubs and red telephone boxes it is thoroughly British. It also has the southernmost Anglican Church and other southernmost things. It is more British than Britain with lots of Union flags on show in windows. There is virtually no crime, the most serious being perhaps an over due library book and people leave their doors unlocked. Ownership is again in dispute as the current Argentinean government tries to increase their popularity with some sabre rattling.

Public billboard notices in Ushuaia state,

'We inform our visitors that by the Argentine National Law No 26.552, The Malvinas, South Georgias, South Sandwich Islands and the surrounding maritime area as well as the Argentine Antarctic

Territory have been included in the jurisdiction of the province of Tierra del Fuego. At the same time we should remember that the Malvinas, South Georgia, South Sandwich Islands and the surrounding maritime areas, are since 1883, under the illegal occupation of the United Kingdom of Great Britain and Northern Ireland'.

The memorial to the Falklands War in Stanley simply states,

'In memory of those who liberated us'.

Prior to the Falklands War in 1982 the British Government was considering returning the territory to Argentina. The process was too slow for the military government of General Galtieri. Troops invaded the islands, briefly making Galtieri a hero. He did not, however, count on the reaction from Margaret Thatcher who also sought to increase her popularity. It was a humiliating defeat for Argentina and ironic that Britain became involved in a fight for a territory that they were trying to give away. Now the Falklanders want nothing to do with Argentina and it remains a colonial anachronism that costs the British government a billion pounds a year to maintain. Dr. Johnson also wrote of the Falklands over 200 years ago,

'Claims that have remained doubtful for ages cannot be settled in a day'.

If you are on a cruise boat then you will always have the same problem arriving at small destinations. You will be unlikely to experience the isolation of the place, but sometimes you only have to walk out of town a little way and you will soon be on your own. It is well worth considering a longer holiday in the Falklands if you are prepared to risk the weather. Most places are linked by dirt roads and islands by ferry and it is a great place for wild life watching, photography and battlefield tours, if that is your thing. Everywhere there are signs of a past military presence. If you are there for a day then a walk up to Gypsy Cove is a 4 mile return journey from the visitors centre by the jetty down Ross Road East. Only the 'twitchers' will be there before you. You will pass by the Lady Elizabeth shipwreck, an iron clad ship that has been there since 1913 and there are nice white sandy beaches, although unfortunately the water is just a tad cold. There are plenty more hiking opportunities in the hills but beware of the 17 minefields remaining from the war, although they are all well fenced in. There are no native trees, the landscape is utterly glacial, and much of it is barren and isolated. Unique glacial features are the 'stone runs'. Spot some and you can go home happy or better still spot a blue whale, that really would make the trip worthwhile.

Puerto Madryn is a further 633 nautical miles away and much maligned as the place to get out of as soon as possible. There is a long beach but no litter, bins are placed every 25 metres or so and locals can be seen to pick up any tiny bits of plastic and rubbish. It is though, a deadly dull place and excursions out to see Magellan penguins and sea lions are a good option. There are one million Magellanic penguins at Punta Tombo. If you were to judge a place by how many photos you took well, I took none. Beware of getting too close to the Llamas, if they have their ears up they are relaxed and everything is cool. If they put their ears down then they are agitated and they will spit at you.

In 1865 153 Welsh settlers arrived encouraged by the Argentine government who wanted to populate the land. They were promised cultural independence in exchange for loyalty. They were enticed by the offer of a green and fertile land and they also wanted to escape the growing influence of the English. They were disheartened that their ancient and much cherished way of life was being eroded away. The voyage took two months during which time the Captain did not allow them up on the deck. With no fresh air or day light five children and one new born infant died. Just about their first act in their new homeland on July 28th 1865 was to conduct a church service and bury their dead. They must have been courageous as this is Patagonia, the dry Steppes where the Andes has sucked all the moisture out of the westerly winds. None of them were farmers, they were cobblers, miners, housewives and blacksmiths, plus three God fearing preachers. The outlying lands were dry and desiccated and they did suffer for several years, but now 5,000 Welsh speakers live there, speaking what is considered a more perfect form of Welsh than in Wales itself.

One of the best things you may do is to hire a guide with a car when the ship stops at a port of call that has little to offer. The boat often charges far too much for organised trips for all the cruise passengers. You can whiz off away from all the tourist traps and explore the real area.

Montevideo, the final stop on this cruise, has a classic and inviting European charm and elegance. In the old town there are lots of wonky pavements plus a lot of dog mess, almost as much as Santiago, so it is a careful compromise as to watching where you are going and looking up at the wonderful architecture. Many of the buildings are crumbling and speak of a former glory, reminiscent of

Havana. Some are ear-marked to be turned into fine apartments but others look beyond saving. There are gaps where buildings once were looking like some sort of reverse Rachel Whiteread sculpture. It is a pleasant city full of broad boulevards, parks, plazas, fountains and imposing monuments. It is easy to walk round in a day with an aimless purposefulness. There is a daily flea market but nothing there is cheap. I watched as some Americans cheerfully handed over $55 for some little polished stones worth perhaps $10. The vendor gave me a knowing smile. We were told that the main scam here is for someone to surreptitiously flick some imitation bird poo on an unsuspecting tourist, and then look up at the birds in the sky to distract them and finally produce a tissue to clean the mess up for them. Work the rest out for yourself. Do not listen to my scare mongering or anyone else's, Montevideo is one of the safest cities in South America. The locals, as in Argentina walk around with thermos flask under their arms and leather clad cups with straws in their hands. This contains 'mate' a sort of bitter green tea infused with herbs. It is a health thing that they do just as we might carry around a bottle of water.

Back to Buenos Aries, if you have never been there it is one of the great cities of the world. Make time to get there and stay for a week. The tango reigns supreme, so make sure you see a show if nothing else. People are literally dancing in the streets, the tango is a national institution, it is sex without the consequences. San Telmo is the best area for culture, the Recoleta is the famous cemetery and go to a local parrilla where you eat what will be the best steak in the world. If you have a spare day then one undoubted highlight are the Iguazu Falls. At more than a mile and a half wide and 270 feet tall it has been named as one of the 7 wonders of the natural world. All the areas of the falls are linked by metal walkways which give exceptional views and get you really close up and into the cataracts. The highlight is the 'Devil's Throat' which is a 300° or so circular cliff where huge torrents of water plunge down. A speed boat will take you right under sections of the falls and finish your trip off with a spectacular helicopter ride from the Brazilian side. The flight is only 10 minutes but you will not forget it.

This particular cruise took us 4,466 nautical miles, with one nautical mile equal to 1.15 land miles. Bear in mind sometimes cruise ships do not even make it down to Antarctica and have to turn back due to fog or approaching storms. Also Drake Passage may sometimes be impassable due to rough seas.

One further thing I find annoying about cruising is having to respond to every member of staff, who says,

'Good morning sir, how are you today?'

They are programmed to say this and we are duty bound to respond with,

'Fine, thank you.'

Now on a cruise ship the client to staff ratio is about 2 to 1. On a big ship that could be 1000 or more staff all wanting to ask you the same question. At first I found it okay, then after a while it becomes tedious. At some stage I am going to run out of 'fine' and 'thank yous', or perhaps I might just tell them exactly how I am feeling. I did this once in Covent Garden after being in too many shops, much to the embarrassment of my wife. Having gone into a dozen shops and been forced to answer the same question concerning my well being I did launch into the longer version. It began when I decided on one occasion just to ignore the 'Good morning' etc. and the assistant chose to quietly say,

'Okay, ignore me then.' I began by saying,

'Do you realise just how many people have asked me the exact same question this morning already?' and so I went on. Maybe it was the teeny bit of Asperger syndrome that might be within me that many men seem to have. Not everyone of course feels this way and my wife left the shop quickly. A simple 'Good morning' on board would be enough rather than a question as to someone's feelings.

We tend to avoid any of the organised trips and just disembark at ports of call to do our own thing. The excursions will be full of less mobile clients and older people who will take a long time getting on and off the coach. If you are a 'young' old person you are going to be better off making your own arrangements at most stops. One day perhaps you and I will be old enough to join in.

Remember cruising is cheating, it is not really travelling, but certain cruises are acceptable. If you cannot really get to a place satisfactorily by any other way then do not feel that you have let yourself down. Anywhere cold, as already suggested, the Arctic, Antarctic and Alaska are good cruise options. There will always be a lot of older people on board, many with a walking stick and some in wheel chairs. Cruises are ideal for disabled passengers where they are always well catered for. Most of the elderly people we have encountered have been surprisingly fit and lively, and they are quiet, polite and sociable. Be aware that food is generally superb and there is an awful lot of it available just about all day long. Statistically the average person on an average cruise will put on between seven and fourteen pounds in weight. You will need an enormous amount of self discipline to eat healthily.

Some people seem to have their own set of prejudices about cruising as we did. If that applies to you then take my advice and try it. You may yet end up as a cruise bunny and so might we too when we get old.

It is often a good policy to wait until the very last minute to book your cruise. There are dozens of good sites such as:

www.iglucruise.com which is good for special offers

www.cruisecritic.co.uk a sort of ultimate cruise guide

Prices can be slashed dramatically as operators become desperate to fill spaces. This does not always hold true, some, like the Antarctic cruise sell out quickly. Here, new stricter regulations are probably going to put prices up, bigger boats will be banned and all ships will have to use marine gas oil rather than heavy oil. That will stop all the Russian ice breakers and prices will be governed by supply and demand.

Ever wondered what store supplies a cruise ship takes?
This list is for the Celebrity Infinity catering for 2200 guests for 2 weeks:

- 24,236 pounds of beef
- 5,040 pounds of lamb
- 7,216 pounds of pork
- 4,600 pounds of veal
- 1,680 pounds of sausage
- 10,211 pounds of chicken
- 3,156 pounds of turkey
- 13,851 pounds of fish
- 350 pounds of crab
- 2,100 pounds of lobster
- 25,736 pounds of fresh vegetables
- 15,150 pounds of potatoes
- 20,003 pounds of fresh fruit
- 3,260 gallons of milk
- 1976 quarts of cream
- 600 gallons of ice cream
- 9,235 dozen eggs

- 3,800 pounds of rice
- 5,750 pounds of sugar
- 1,750 pounds of cereal
- 450 pounds of jelly
- 2,450 tea bags
- 2,458 pounds of coffee
- 1,936 pounds of cookies
- 120 pounds of herbs and spices
- 3,400 bottles of assorted wines
- 200 bottle of champagne
- 200 bottles of gin
- 290 bottles of vodka
- 350 bottles of whisky
- 150 bottles of rum
- 45 bottles of sherry
- 600 bottles of assorted liqueurs
- 10,100 bottles/cans of beer

Finally, a further word of warning, cruises are not always the safe travelling option for older people and there is a long history of cruise disasters. The idea of gathering some of society's most vulnerable, elderly people together in a confined area and exposing them to what could be an unstable environment is fraught with disaster. In 2014 the 'Explorer of the Seas' was on a 10 day cruise when 700 passengers and crew were struck down with a fast moving bug causing vomiting and diarrhoea. In January 2012 the cruise ship Costa Concordia struck a rock and turned on its side off the Italian island of Giglio and 32 people died. In February 2013 the 'Carnival Triumph' suffered a fire in the engine room resulting in flooded cabins, sewage in the hallways and a lack of food. Several boats have been attacked by pirates but the most common danger is the sea itself. There are numerous incidents of violent storms and giant waves hitting boats, injuring and even killing people. Boats will rock from side to side flinging vulnerable passengers around.

This following incident happened in 2014 while we were on the Marco Polo returning from a 42 day trip to the Amazon and West Indies. (It was too good an offer to resist) The first part of the journey was rough going through the English Channel and across the Bay of Biscay. Elderly passengers were falling over, some were badly bruised, a few seriously hurt and many people were seasick. In Lisbon one passenger was taken off after suffering a heart attack.

Three weeks into the trip norovirus struck down a number of passengers accompanied by a degree of paranoia. From then on the ship had to be sterilized regularly from top to bottom causing extra work for an already overworked crew. Well used areas like reception had to be wiped down every 15 minutes. The unfortunate passengers affected by the virus were confined to their cabins for 2 days. Rumours abounded and all the talk was about the virus, nobody knew exactly how many passengers were affected but I counted at least 26 cabins with a red bag outside for infected towels and bed linen. Also it was rumoured that several people had died, albeit of natural causes. The outbreak continued to get worse, the self-service restaurant, gym, library, games room and table tennis facilities were all closed down. Some passengers were starting to complain and about 10 passengers flew back from Barbados saying,

'We are not going through all that again.'

It was only after 16 days that the boat returned to normal.

On the way back to the Azores the captain had to speed up to avoid an approaching storm. Two days later and back at sea the boat was heading to Tilbury but still just outside the English Channel. The sea was rough and again a storm was chasing the boat. This turned out to be a force 11 gale and disaster struck when it caught up with us. The sea had been very rough in the morning, but when the gale hit, the waves became mountainous and chaos ensued. The first violent lurch was at 11.30 am and caught passengers unawares, many fell out of their seats and were left lying on the floor and again some were injured. At lunchtime in the dining room a huge wave hit the starboard side and 4 windows caved in, some passengers were lacerated by flying glass and drenched with sea water. Furniture was thrown around and everything was swept off the tables. Tragically one diner sitting next to the window died when a shard of glass embedded into his head. The broken glass flew across the room cutting many other diners. Passengers were soaked with sea water and some ended up on the floor lying in water and glass. There was blood everywhere, people screamed and some panicked running to the exit, but after the initial shock everyone was well behaved and helped each other. As the boat heaved from side to side the water swept across the room in a mini tidal wave. Several people were seen crawling up the stairs covered in blood. White faced passengers were evacuated and few actually got to eat. Following this many passengers stayed in their rooms and everyone was advised to sit on the floor. We chose to watch the sea and mountainous waves from a higher deck window. Sudden lurches throughout the day caused furniture to roll around and more people were injured. Even people in their cabins were thrown around from side to side along with all their possessions and furniture getting themselves injured in the process. The emergency medical helicopter arrived at 3pm and a critically ill passenger was winched off. The captain had to stop the ship and manoeuvre it sideways causing even more chaos. Lots of passengers decided to stay in the public areas and the crew produced an impromptu sing along. Another passenger was wheeled through the lounge all wrapped up and seemingly dead. Later the helicopter returned for a second injured woman. By 6.30pm we were all confined to our cabins and dinner that night in our room was a miserable affair for St. Valentine's Day.

All this must sound awful but many passengers I spoke to still had a wonderful time and enjoyed what was good value for money for such an interesting itinerary. The crew were fantastic and most of the passengers adopted that typical Dunkirk spirit.

A cruise is the best way to see the Norwegian Fjords

The Falkland Islands are uniquely British

Antarctica is easily reached aboard a cruise ship

Travelling by cargo ship is another possibility that can get you to most places, although it can be more expensive than flying simply because it takes longer. If you can't or won't fly then maybe this is for you, but only if you like spending long days at sea and have plenty of time. You may only have a dozen or so fellow passengers and facilities will be limited. You will stop at scheduled ports of call but only for as long as it takes for the ship's business to be carried out. It could be good option just for crossing an ocean or sea and maybe the only option for crossing say, the Caspian Sea. There are plenty of websites to trawl through and they make fascinating research. Include 'tramp voyage' or 'steamer' in your internet search. This is real travelling and not cruising.

www.freightervoyages.eu
www.strandtravelltd.co.uk

Metal walkways take you right to the edge of the Iguazu Falls

10 How tough can it get?

"When you travel, remember that a foreign country is not designed to make you comfortable. It is designed to make its own people comfortable."
Clifton Fadiman 1904-1999

Every country poses its own problems. In Russia and China for most people it will be the language barrier and in India there is the dilemma of how to deal with the abject poverty. Throughout much of Africa the lack of infrastructure will stop you getting to some places whilst other countries are just too dangerous. Apart from such obvious examples you may have to cope with extreme heat, cold, diseases, insects, hustlers, pick pockets, strange food and unhygienic accommodation, the list goes on and on. It is possible to travel in most parts of the world independently but if you want to go to remote places where few tourists venture it may be wise to go with a group. Even camping is going to be tough for some of you. The very idea of a hole in the ground for a toilet may put you off. You may even lose internet coverage!

West Africa is just about the hardest overland trip left in the world. Only a specially designed four wheel drive truck is going to make it. The infrastructure is poor and you will spend many days just being thrown around in your seat. There are other overland trips that will be similar in the amount of hardship you will have to face but this one is not for the faint hearted. As it is at the moment, there are few options left to you if you are desperate to see West Africa. It does not have the major sights like East Africa, but is perhaps one of the last real overland experiences. There will be many delays due to break downs and getting stuck in the mud. Again this will not be a holiday but will be a memorable experience and an adventure. Similarly your guide is one of the most important factors. Throughout West Africa the military police have no purpose other than to make money for themselves by taking it from you. Our guide was brilliant at handling such officials, mainly by being super friendly and along with all the travellers pretending only to speak English. Everyone on the truck ended up waving and smiling at the police and on most occasions we were generally waved onwards.

Many of the other over land trips have become too popular. In East Africa all the trucks follow the same route and stay at the same camp sites so there is a diminished feeling of isolation. Facilities are improving and hotels and shops are being built to accommodate tourists. The experiences are continually being devalued, but not so West Africa. There will be lots of nice bits but in some regions you will be the only tourists and will have that rare genuine encounter with people and places untainted by tourism. Below is a brief account of what to expect but emphasising some of the hardships encountered.

Travelling through Sub-Saharan West Africa it took 70 days overland from Dakar in Senegal to Douala in the Cameroon, passing through 10 countries. The worst bit, to begin with is getting the visas, six in England, with a further two on route. We had to make five trips to London and got the final one two days prior to departure. Some visas for West African countries can be difficult to get and they do not come cheap. Including train fares, visas cost us about £600 for each of us. Travellers from other countries can face even more difficulties. There are companies that will do it all for you but at a hefty cost.

We met our fellow travellers, only eight of us, plus our guide and driver. My wife and I, four single women in their 20's and 30's and two Austrian doctors in their 30's, who were engaged and testing the strength of their relationship. There were supposed to be a further eight but they had dropped out following recent troubles in some of the countries that were on the original itinerary. The route had been changed to avoid Mali, so therefore we could not go on to Burkino Faso. Militant Islamic groups were causing trouble and as it stood at that time we were advised not to go through Nigeria and there were also doubts about Cote d'Ivoire. A further member of our group, a lady in her sixties from New Zealand had to withdraw. Arriving at Dakar airport late at night she made a terrible mistake. In arrivals someone offered her a taxi and led her around the back of the airport to a car. On the way to her hotel the driver stopped the car, turned around and attacked her, she put up a fight but was no match for a young man. The circumstances were terrible, he ripped her bag from her neck leaving ugly red wheals, beat her unconscious, and threw her into the road. She lay there for several hours before someone stopped. Fortunately she could still remember the name of her hotel but all her possessions had been taken including her passport with all the necessary visas and she had nothing but the clothes she stood in. It was a very sad start to the trip. Do not make mistakes like that, always get into a proper taxi, in that case a yellow taxi with the proper licence plate and number. Always negotiate a price before getting in and never get into a taxi that has another male passenger. I know single female travellers that will text the cab number to a friend before even getting in. Do not get paranoid about such things though, most people throughout the world are honest citizens trying to make a decent living.

Dakar airport was a bit chaotic with hundreds of taxi drivers all asking far too much. It took us about twenty minutes of serious haggling to select a driver, but at least we got to the hotel safely. Dakar itself had very little to offer, we were pleased to have visited but do not want to return. There are plenty of tourists there and sometimes they are seen as an easy target. We had to leave a local market quickly when too many dangerous looking touts 'were closing in'. As we neared the market tough and nasty looking men were making unpleasant comments. We suddenly became aware of six or so such aggressive looking men, all walking towards us from different directions. Always be aware of your surroundings and what is happening and when in doubt get out.

It probably sounds a bit grim so far, but this was West Africa and we were not expecting a 'holiday' as such. The overland company that we were with had not done this exact route before and few other companies operate in the area. They were running the trip at a loss just to keep it open. So it was more 'expedition' status and the itinerary changed from day to day.

A week into the journey and at times the weather had been stifling, occasionally relieved by a massive downpour. Away from Dakar and the cooler resorts of the Atlantic coast the people in the country had a different attitude to tourists and were genuinely friendly. In the Gambia this was even more so, sometimes we had dozens of children hanging off each arm. Tourists on their package holidays in their beach hotels will not encounter the real Africa.

In both Senegal and The Gambia we did a lot of boat trips mainly for bird watching, The Gambia being one of the best places in the world for 'twitchers'. Inland in this part of the world the sun is relentless and everyone needs to take precautions, lots of sun screen and a hat are essential and light long sleeved clothing to cover up. Some days are long and tough, it took us six hours just to get across the Senegalese/Gambian border and river.

Everybody was put into three groups cooking alternately for the others. This suited us fine and we loved it, but we already knew what to expect from previous experiences. The whole group was becoming like one big happy family, everyone else was in their 20's & 30's but although we were old enough to be their parents we seemed to fit in well enough. Additionally we were all assigned different jobs on a rotational basis, cleaning the truck, washing up, getting out equipment etc.

Further down the Senegalese coast we stayed in Cape Skiring for the weekend and enjoyed some of the best beaches in Senegal. It was just before the season started so we had a huge deserted beach to ourselves. This was the easy bit of the trip, there was no camping yet, but we had stayed in some run down but interesting rooms & ramshackle lodges.

The luxury part of the trip was over and Guinea Bissau the next country was one of the poorest countries in the world with a male life expectancy of just 47. The war of independence and the recent terrible civil war caused havoc and almost all the country remains land mined. At the border crossing we were possibly the first truck load of tourists ever to cross. Nobody visits here so there is no tourist industry or important sights to see. We were crossing areas of political, social and religious unrest. Our leader was in touch with home base on a daily basis to update us on current problems. So our route changed daily and from then on the adventure really began. There were dozens of military police check points where sometimes we had no option but to pay the obligatory fine (bribe). Photographs in sensitive areas such as borders, government buildings and military posts could have resulted in a few days imprisonment. The whole area was unstable and in Bissau, the capital people were shouting out excitedly what translated as, 'whites', and for the most part they seemed genuinely friendly.

There were no proper camp sites and we had to 'bush camp' wherever there was a suitable space. One night on sloping uneven ground there was a massive storm. Luckily we were on slightly higher ground and our tent was the only one left dry, but everyone else's was flooded out and many of their clothes were soaked.

We did not always camp but some of what passed for hotel rooms are simply dreadful. If we could have done so we would have upgraded back to our tent. The rooms in most 'hotels' are squalid affairs with paint peeling off the walls and filthy beds. Any bed linen will be equally as dirty as will the floor, sink and toilet. You may be lucky enough to have running water and electricity is likely to be on and off at best. Remember not to touch the electric wires that will be sticking out of the walls, especially not those in the bathroom. Finally learn to like insects, you will have to live with them.

'I was walking alone in the Central Guinea Highlands, through remote settlements, tiny little villages and isolated communities. Some people just stopped and gawped, some waved and others took one look and ran away in terror'.

It is experiences like this that make it all worthwhile.

Sometimes we were hot, wet, tired, dirty and hungry after a full days travel over roads that were nothing more than a rutted cart track. After one particularly difficult day we were so exhausted that we all too tired to even eat. It was hard work and often there was no shower to look forward to at the end of the day. It was the end of the rainy season so it was easy to get stuck in the mud, and we did, several times. The money was silly at 112,000 Guinean Francs to the pound. I had a wad of cash the size of a brick. We spent a long time in Guinea and it was one of my favourite West African countries, mainly because there were no tourists there, nobody was pestering you for money or trying to rip you off.

One evening we could find nowhere to stay or camp and late in the evening we drove onto a local village football pitch. It was raining and we had nowhere else to go. The locals began arriving ending up with about 70 or so just standing there in the pouring rain watching our every move. We requested permission to camp and they agreed but would not accept any payment. They stood there watching intently, mostly in silence and they remained long after we had gone to bed. For them this was a unique experience not to be missed.

At this point we noticed that one of the pretty Australian girls had 'copped off' with the driver/mechanic. (They did make a nice couple though.)

Border crossings in West Africa tend to be a piece of string across the dirt road or muddy track, with a few pieces of rag hanging from it. Guinea Conakry was another poor country ravaged from recent troubles. It should be rich as it contains half the world's bauxite plus diamonds and gold. The people are frustrated, they can see what everyone else has on TV and yet they have nothing, however, it is a beautiful, wooded and mountainous country with patches of open savannah.

In Alabi, a small town in the Guinea Highlands, we managed to rent the entire floor of a large private house. Our mechanic and one member of the group had to make the difficult 2 day return journey by local bus to Conakry, the capital, to obtain a visa for the Cote d'Ivoire. Two of the group stayed to rest in the house while the other six of us went out in the truck searching for a legendary waterfall. Our notes described it as 30 km to Dittan, then a further 5 km up a track and finally a 20 minute walk. We did not leave until 2.30pm and after one hour over bumpy roads arrived in Dittan. The tiny track was really too small for our truck as we squeezed past trees and through deep muddy pools. We could see the waterfall high up in the distance, a huge spout cascading out of a cliff, however, these things tend to look nearer than they actually are. The track deteriorated rapidly, there were tiny make-shift bridges to cross the small rivers, not really built for big trucks. It was getting late and we should have turned back but dogged and foolish determination drove us on. Disaster struck suddenly and without much warning. We knew immediately we were in trouble when the driver said,

'We're fucked.'

The truck had hit a patch of quicksand and one side began sinking into the mud. It was not far off tipping point and may have done so but it had come to rest on its axles. It was the worst case of getting stuck in the mud our driver had ever encountered. Villagers appeared from nowhere to help and together we spent 2 or 3 hours digging, packing wood under the wheels, along with special metal sand mats, but it was hopeless. The axles were still resting on the mud, it was already dusk and we needed to consider our options. There was no mobile reception so we had no way of letting the other two know about our situation, and one of them was my wife. After much discussion we told our driver/guide that he should go for help, although the first rule for any guide must be 'never leave your group alone in the middle of nowhere'. Reluctantly he went off on the back of a local motor bike. Thus the group was effectively split into four and we were left isolated in the dark, in the middle of nowhere. Five elder villagers stayed to 'protect' us overnight for which we paid them 10 euros each. The truck was listing badly and the hole it was in filled with water. Luckily the tents being stored in the truck were put up in the dark, and we pooled our resources. Between the five of us there was very little, four small beers and some bread and cheese. With no sleeping equipment we all slept badly and fully clothed as it was cold. Unknown at that time to us, our guide had made it back to the house for 10pm, to inform the other two.

In the morning a big lorry came from Dalabi, a nearby town, along with some big guys who were used to such problems. They wanted 200 euros, cheap at European prices, but the price went up went up when they saw the situation. The first attempt to tow the truck out failed, the cable tensed but the truck only rocked a bit. The big guys shovelled several tons of soil into their lorry to make it heavier for pulling. They dug down and created a stable platform of wood and jacked up the side of the truck. Men were crawling under the truck almost totally immersed in muddy water. Dangerous work as the ground was very unstable but they needed to squeeze more wood underneath the wheels. It was slow progress and we were all caked in mud. Black and white people begin to look alike when coated with mud.

As the morning went on people arrived from seemingly nowhere, wandering out of woods and scrubland. Mainly brightly clad, elegant women on their way to market, with goods balanced on their heads, sashaying slowly along the path to the village, returning later in the afternoon. Old and young alike were all intrigued to see such an unusual sight in their quiet community. Very few of them were fat and the older women were positively skinny. Some had the sort of curvaceous figures that only a black girl can have.

By 2.30pm the men had dug deep down to free the axles. The truck was stabilised and huge planks were rammed under the back wheels. The lorry was hitched up to the tow cable again and in one long slow tug, amid clouds of black exhaust fumes and loud cheers, pulled the truck free.

This was not the only incident involving a waterfall, there are plenty of them and most in this part of the world are rarely visited. We knew roughly where this next particular one was but not quite sure how to get there. After a one hour trek following the river we came to a rickety suspension bridge. The way ahead seemed to be blocked and crossing the bridge looked like the correct way. It spanned some 200 feet over fast flowing water and was held together with bits of wire, string, metal plates and wood all haphazardly joined together. There were some wide gaps where rungs had dropped out, it did not look safe but had to be crossed. Nobody wanted to be first and it was one of the girls who eventually volunteered. She negotiated the crossing painfully slowly and most of us followed on in turn. Some of the group had more commonsense and refused. We then discovered that the route was not over the bridge but indeed straight on. One or two people expressed anger at putting their lives at risk unnecessarily. The waterfall itself was another 30 minutes along forest tracks and well worth the effort.

The route from Guinea to the Cote d'Ivoire was tortuous. The remote northern route being the only safe option; further south special permission and an armed guard is required. Just before the border we stopped to do some food shopping in a small town. My wife and I were only a few minutes late back but there was no truck. We waited 40 minutes becoming increasingly concerned before taking two motor bike taxis to make a search. Everyone in the town knew where the truck had gone, a group of white tourists is an unknown event. We eventually found the others at the police station, crammed into a hot, tiny and dirty little room, looking somewhat subdued. Islamic extremists had started shouting at them and forced the police to take them all into custody. These guys with their flowing robes and long beards were really aggressive and we too were duly 'arrested'. The extremists were outside our 'cell' still shouting, probably wanting to have us tortured to extract a confession. The problem was that they had never seen tourists before, did not really understand the concept of tourism and thought we were there for another purpose. The police too were shouting at each other, particularly at the junior one who had made the arrest as they had no idea what to do with us. After three sweaty hours and a lot of shouting they let us go. Where else can you have such an interesting holiday experience?

Further down the road, where at times there was no road, only muddy tracks, we emerged from the jungle to the border crossing comprising of a mud hut with a grass roof. The sole official was confused by our sudden appearance and unsure what he needed to do. He had no exit stamp, without which, we could encounter entrance problems on the other side of the border. He said that there was a man, an hour or so away that might have a stamp but we decided to risk it and if necessary blag our way through. There were several more check points but nobody really examined the passports thoroughly enough to spot the error. Officially we never left Guinea. The border guards were just so surprised to see us and being asked to actually do some work was probably too much to cope with. These guys spend most of the day sleeping in the shade. There were no other vehicles on the route and for a long way after the crossing, nothing at all. The drive through the forest tracks was long and uncomfortable, it was late and we had very little food. The Cote d'Ivoire was a much richer country in comparison to Guinea and we found a small hotel at 1.30am after 20 hours on the road. It had water, a hot shower, electricity and the internet. St Christopher, the patron saint of travellers must have been with us that night.

A day later on appalling muddy roads again in the middle of nowhere the police stopped us and refused to let the truck continue. What they said translated as,

'There are mines on the road ahead and it is too dangerous to continue.'

An hour later I set off on foot with the driver to investigate. The road conditions were almost impassable and the only traffic coming the other way was the occasional motor bike. At times we waded knee deep through mud and water keeping away from the verges, just in case of land mines. After 3 kilometres we came to the problem, it was the mining company Rio Tinto. They were an advance party exploring the area for resources and astonished upon seeing us said,

'Where the fuck did you come from?'

There was no real problem, the police had been informed by the 'mining' company that they were surveying land and to warn motorists. Something had been lost in translation. I stayed up there while the driver went back to get the truck. Our 4x4 vehicle was the only one capable of coping with these conditions and on other occasions we pulled lorries out of the mud. That day we were on the road again for 20 hours and it was another one without proper food.

Cote d'Ivoire is a fairly well developed country but the FCO only recommends all but essential travel. Yamoussoukro is the uninspiring capital with the tallest basilica in the world. It is a totally outrageous and grand gesture, but magnificent. We moved south to the coast for two days rest and relaxation on the beach. Before the civil war this had been a big tourist destination and only now are people slowly drifting back. Just smatterings of Europeans are there but lots of rich Ivorians.

The truck had a major breakdown and we were forced to continue by numerous bush taxis, basically along the coast and across the border to Ghana. Here we stopped to help out at a school, mainly building a classroom wall or at least buying the materials for the 'brickie'. Some of us helped out working with the children in the classroom but the 'brickie' made it clear that he did not want our help regardless of our individual skills. Ghana is also better developed as

West African countries go and has over 500km of unspoilt beach. There is, however, a ferocious rip current and each year many people drown. The truck caught us up two days later.

Two wonderful nights were spent deep in the primary rainforest, sleeping fifty feet up in a tree house, listening to the forest sounds. It took 45 minutes trekking along tiny slippery jungle paths in the dark to get there. There were no facilities but a hole in the ground, you have to suffer a little with such unique experiences. Some of us then went on a night time walk searching for wildlife. In the dark you do not see the ants that cross the paths in columns of tens of thousands. They were nasty biting types but thankfully not stinging. Very unpleasant though and had everyone jumping around like lunatics trying to shake them off. Also there, you can experience Africa's only canopy walk.

Fortunately the group were all getting on well together, but some were suffering badly, with upset stomachs headaches and heatstroke. The two Austrian doctors in the party suffered worst, they were ill and wanted to go home. When they did go home a few days later, one of them was so bad that he had to spend a week in a hospital specialising in tropical diseases, but he did make a full recovery.

In Accra, all except one other member of our group left as it was the end of their trip. For us it was the halfway point and seven new travellers joined us. It doesn't matter who they are, you just have to get on with them. We try to see the best in people regardless of what we may perceive as their faults.

The next group was completely different, four girls and six guys. Most seemed affluent and were aged in their 30's, 40's and another was 62. One of them, a forty seven year old Canadian/Pole was clearly going to be a problem. His opening line was,

'I am millionaire, all my friends are millionaire or almost millionaire. I do not want to sleep in tent I want to upgrade whenever I can. I not care how much it cost.'

This was not the best opening line. He also went on to try and change the route, even suggesting going to another country and consequently other travellers tended to avoid him. Go with the flow and select your words carefully at first.

He did nothing to help to begin with and would talk non-stop, often about himself. On the first night one of the Germans told him to keep quiet or he would have to get his ear plugs out. We, or rather my wife as a former head of an autistic unit, quickly diagnosed him as being on the Autistic spectrum, certainly Asperger syndrome. He would talk for hours solely for example about flight connections,

'If you get the 6.50am flight from LHR to Paris it will arrive at 8.10am then get the 9am to Munich from where you can pick up the 12.10 to Istanbul then catch a bus to the station from where you can get the 18.30 train to Ankara.'

And so it went on and on. Okay, I made all this up, but he didn't, he knew all the correct flight times and connections throughout the world. If you got fed up with that you could ask him about different editions of guide books. His main aim on the trip was to find an internet connection. My favourite comment that he made to me was when I was feeling really ill with a pain in the kidneys, he said,

'My father had a pain just like that before he died.'

There was also another slightly Asperger traveller with us. What are the chances of that in a group of twelve? He was knowledgeable about almost everything but at thirty one desperate to get a girl friend. His problem was that he was too honest, devoid of certain feelings and less able to empathise than normal people. On a small boat he said to one of the girls who was just a little overweight,

'I will have to move over to accommodate those child bearing hips.'

Two nights on the beach in Ghana was almost like a holiday, before heading up north again and crossing into Togo. Togo was instantly likeable with lots of lush forests and hills. It also has wonderful beaches and fetish markets but it is unfortunately becoming a little too touristy. There is a constant cry from the locals of, 'cadeau, cadeau'. The fetish market near Lome is a bizarre place and according to your taste, tasteless or exciting. Sometimes you just have to roll with it. The stalls are piled high with the dismembered parts of almost every African animal and the sweet smell of death is all pervasive. It is fascinating but also horrific, some of our group did not want to look and others had to be dragged away. There were rows upon rows of sad looking dried song birds, skulls of everything from monkeys to hippos along with dried snakes, lizards, bird heads, and perhaps worst of all, the foot of a gorilla. A 'living' nightmare of lifeless faces, monkeys testicles, jars of eyes, bat wings, severed heads of baboons, leopards, buffaloes, cheetahs, bears, chameleons, and crocodiles. Who are we to judge, Animism and Voodoo are an essential part of the culture here and animal parts are used as offerings in Voodoo ceremonies. Voodoo still has a place, particularly in Benin where locals will attend a Christian church in the morning and then go on to a Voodoo ceremony later. Voodoo is still practised with other religions and works alongside them. This is the part of Africa where Voodoo originated. It is not about zombies and sticking pins into dolls, but an animist belief system with a creator God and the attribution of a soul to all other things including trees, waterfalls and rivers. The smell of the fetish market at Lome will meet you before you actually see it and remain with you long after leaving.

The Fetish Market

In Togo and more so Benin there will be plenty of opportunities to encounter Voodoo close up and witness ceremonies. Many villages and individual houses will have a sacrificial rock covered in blood and gore as if an animal has exploded.

We took a boat across Lake Togo to Togoville but had to turn back when it began to sink. The old wooden boat always looked inadequate to take twelve heavy people, water was pouring in through the gaps faster than we could bale it out. We weren't worried about getting wet, more about our expensive cameras. Four of us transferred to another boat which still only just made it across, again with a lot of bailing out. We all took a bigger boat for the return journey. Togoville sounded lovely in the guide book but turned out to be just another dirty little village. It is incredible that we had to pay a guide to walk us around to see almost nothing. He insisted that the first stop was the bar and ordered beers on our behalf despite the fact that we did not need them at 10 o'clock in the morning. Not only that, he charged us more than the bar price, which my wife confronted him about. There was an area by the lake side where all the rubbish was thrown over the church wall into what passed as the main street. The village had no idea about how to present itself and was perhaps a victim of past success. There were other pathetic places to visit but only for an extra payment. The modern church was the only place really worth looking at and here our guide tried to rush everybody in and out. He had more gullible tourists arriving and already knew by then that he had blown his chances of a tip.

Our trip took us right up to the north of Togo and crossed over into Benin close to the border with Burkina Faso. Our accommodation was in a remote national park for two nights bush camping many miles from even a small village. There were lions, hippos and buffalo but they were few and far between, possibly all chopped up in the fetish market. If you want to see wild life go to East Africa. We spent two hot and dusty days on bumpy roads without much to show for it. With no facilities for several days, everyone was becoming very grubby but at least we all smelt the same. Benin is the home of Voodoo and Animism and the markets are fascinating, with fruit and vegetable stalls alongside Voodoo supplies. Many of these markets are chaotic but with very little variety of food for sale. You could, however, buy a whole cow chopped up into pieces all ready to take away in a wheel barrow with the head tastefully displayed on top.

Ouidah is the spiritual home of Voodoo and former major slave trading post. Slavery is still big business and tourism in this area trades on its slaving history, but it is still a humbling experience. The Place Chacha in Ouidah is where the slave market was. Once sold, the slaves walked 3 miles to the sea past the site where the Tree of Forgetfulness once stood. The slaves were forced to walk around it to erase all memories of their homeland and you can follow in their footsteps.

Unfortunately it appeared to us, that Islam is sweeping down from the north in many West African countries. Even the smallest villages had mosques being built, buildings that were rather too big and grandiose for the communities they would serve. Many things seem set to change as traditional ways of life disappear. We have often stayed near to mosques and the Muezzin wailing and calling the faithful to prayer at 4.45am is pretty inconsiderate for those wanting a lie in. I thank God every day that I am an atheist and that I can think for myself.

The group was holding together well considering their differences. Some of the men were not pulling their weight and several had no idea how to cook. By then a few words had been said particularly to the two men with Asperger syndrome. If you tell them clearly what to do it does work, they will follow orders but do not seem to have any initiative. They will stand and look at the potatoes and the potato peeler whilst everyone else is working, but will only actually peel them if told to do so. Another of the German men, aged 46, had never cooked a hot meal in his life and asked that a special photograph of him cooking should be taken to show his mother.

'My mother will not believe this, I buy take away food every evening or eat cold food, I go to my mother's each weekend and she cooks for me. My mother and I we buy a bottle of wine every Sunday.'

That guy really knew how to enjoy himself, his life sounded boring but the real story can be different. He had escaped from East Germany as a boy, in the time of the wall, swimming over a river in Romania only to end up in prison in the then Yugoslavia. He was a carpenter, flew light aircraft, acted as a life guard and could drink an awful lot of beer.

Down to the south of Benin we stayed overnight on the island of Ganvie. This is a remarkable village on stilts constructed in the middle of Lake Nokoue and built by the Tofinu people fleeing from the slavers. Established in the sixteenth or seventeenth centuries, the Dahomey, who were a slave trading tribe, were forbidden by their religion from entering the water. Now it is a thriving and fascinating community and with a population of around 200,000 people. It is probably the largest lake village in Africa and much more authentic than others around the world such as those on the Mekong Delta. Every building is on stilts amongst a labyrinth of canals. All transport and business is conducted by pirogue, a wooden boat similar to a gondola. Even the tiniest children paddle around, some just on a make shift raft constructed from water containers lashed together. The problem here is that it is a tourist hotspot and the locals are all getting a bit fed up with cameras intruding into their daily lives. Nevertheless, it is a fabulous place to see.

Throughout this journey there were several scary moments. We stopped in what we thought was a quiet spot for lunch beside the road and set everything up for preparing our meal. Several locals stopped to look at the unusual sight, word got around and quickly we were surrounded by villagers. Technically we were on their land. They all became very excited and noisy, some were aggressive, others had machetes and several tried to secretly break into the back of the truck. Part of the problem was that we had food and they claimed to have none. One of the men was the village chief and wanted to make this clear to us, as well proving a point to the villagers that he was in control. I had already asked for his permission to stop for thirty minutes or so but now he wanted to know what we would give to him and the situation was quickly getting out of control. We retrieved our fold up chairs that were now in amongst the villagers, and put them down as a deliberate barrier between us and them. The situation could have turned out badly as the villagers began pushing forward and becoming more belligerent. The secret in such circumstances is to remain calm, show no fear and try to appear friendly, and this strategy just about worked. Lunch was a desperate and quick affair and everything was thrown into the truck for a quick getaway. The chief was shouting and pointing to a tiny slice of cucumber on the ground. My wife gave him a withering look and stooped down to pick it up; the chief had humbled the white people. The truck sped away from the jeering villagers and we were relieved to escape unscathed.

On another occasion we stopped at a small town to draw out cash. Everybody in the town had seen us doing it, a whole queue of white people in a line taking out wads of wonga. A little way out of town we missed our turning but before going back we found somewhere nice, beside the road to have lunch. As we ate a man came walking up the road with his hand behind his back, he looked suspicious. At the same time a motor bike screeched to a halt and two masked men dismounted and walked towards us. You could tell just by looking at them and the way that they walked that they were trouble. We acted really friendly but each and every one of us had the same bad feeling. Our guide moved nearer to his machete and I checked out where the bread knife was. The two guys looked at all of us and claimed that they were the military police. It was pretty obvious that they were checking us out and wondering if they could take us on, four men and six girls. Whatever their intention they left without incident but all our party realised that it could have been potential danger although it might have all just been our imagination. Luckily we had to turn the truck around to get back on the right route so avoiding any potential trouble, if there was to be an ambush further down the road. The man with his hand behind his back kept on walking, apparently lots of Africans walk that way. We drove for a long time without stopping after that incident just to make sure. It is always essential to have your wits about you at all times.

Nigeria was a big worry on this trip, we were supposed to spend ten days there but the political situation at this time was deteriorating. Reports were coming back to us from other travellers warning us not to go, other travellers were saying that they would never consider going and there was talk of an armed bodyguard. The FCO only had one potentially safe strip showing in the middle of the country as terrorist groups were active in both the north and the south. Consequently we intended to race across in three days and avoid any unnecessary stops. Boko Haram in the north is an Islamic fundamentalist group and in the oil rich south militant groups are kidnapping white workers for ransom. It would be particularly unpleasant to be caught by Boko Haram, whose name means 'western education is forbidden'. At present they target and strike fear into only the local population but remain a dangerous threat to the political stability of Nigeria as a whole. We chose the border crossing which supposedly had the least corruption and problems and briefly this is how it went,

8.55am. Arrived at the border between Benin and Nigeria. The border crossing took two and three quarter hours. Two hours of this was an interrogation by the chief official. We had chosen this point on the road from Ikom to Ekok as the police were supposed to be the least corrupt there. They mainly wanted to know how we were all going to support ourselves financially. We all had to show our credit cards and state how much our credit limit was. We all stated really low credit limits except for the two men with Asperger syndrome who could not understand why all our credit ratings were so low. It was all very pedantic and in the end we were asked to pay $50 essentially for making them do some work. Eventually they settled for a bottle of wine which they then shared with us.

11.45 Departed.

11.52 Stopped briefly.

11.56 Stopped again to visit four different offices.

The first shed was the Board of Health Commission. Yellow fever check. All the details written down.

We walked to the next shed which was a quarantine check. We had to declare that we did not carry any fresh food over the border.

The third shed was National Security and a woman made it very clear to us that she was in charge.

The conversation went as follows,

'We are the secret police. What are you doing here?'

'We are tourists.'

'What is the purpose of your visit?'

'We want to look at the countryside and meet the people.'

'But what is the real purpose of your visit.'

'We want to see your wonderful country.'

'Are you spies?'

'No.'

'We have many spies here trying to steal our secrets.'

So it went on and on.

The fourth shed was a further passport control and all our details were copied down again.

1.25pm. Departed.

1.47 Stopped for a truck inspection.

'What have you brought for us?'

'Nothing.'

1.52 Departed.

1.54 Upturned plank with nails in on the road. Wanted to see customs papers.

1.56 Departed.

1.56 and 30 seconds. Check point for truck papers and driver's licence.

2.07 Departed.

2.08 Waved through a check point.

2.10. Another check point but the guards were sleeping and ran out to stop us but it was too late.

2.10 Thirty seconds later. Stopped briefly.
'Where are you going?'
2.14. Waved on at check point.
2.24 Stopped by two police lounging on a bed. They wanted a passenger list and were annoyed that we had run out of copies.
2.34 Departed.
2.35. Waved through a check point.
2.36 Waved through a check point.
2.37. The manifesto was required again plus all passports. We had to take them over to a man relaxing on a bed in the shade.
2.45 Departed.
2.47 Waved through a check point.
2.51 Waved through a check point.
2.51 Thirty seconds later, stopped briefly.
2.55 Stopped and asked for the manifesto again and the passports.
3.05 Departed.
3.08 Waved through a check point.
3.14 Unofficially stopped by drunken people wanting money and alcohol.
3.52 Check point, lots of questions and truck papers.
3.55 Departed.
4.02 Immigration control. Manifest and passports wanted. We gave them an old passenger list which kept them happy.
4.29 Military check point who only wanted to know where we were going.
4.45 Stopped by federal officers to check all the truck documents. They told us that driving a right hand vehicle was illegal in Nigeria as they were too dangerous. They wanted the equivalent of £200 or the truck would be impounded and we would have to have it converted into a left hand drive. After a long discussion they dropped the amount to £40. We refused and they said we would all have to come down to the police station. We called their bluff and agreed to follow them. They quickly settled for £4 and a can of Coca Cola.
5.08 Departed.

All in all it took us some eight hours to travel only 100 km. This is what travelling in Africa can be like.

After all the worry Nigeria came as a pleasant surprise and it got much better the next day, as there were fewer check points away from the border. It is mainly the police in Nigeria who are corrupt and it is they who will rob you with unnecessary fines. Most local people were friendly and really pleased to see us, several of them made an effort to come up to us and welcome us to their country. They do not want any trouble or political and religious unrest but do want to see tourists returning. We drove for three days to the Afi Drill Monkey National Park where there were no facilities for the next three days, not even a mountain stream. If you must have a shower every day, then this is not for you. This was the rainforest and the last fifteen miles accessible only by dirt tracks. The drill monkey is the most endangered primate in the world and western volunteers are trying to increase their numbers and release them back into the wild. There were 157 of them in a huge enclosure just about ready to be returned to the wild. The danger is that the locals will shoot them and they will end up as bush meat in the markets. This is illegal and they are protected but there is nobody to enforce the laws. Some of the local villagers do not understand that the sanctuary is a nonprofit making organisation and are aggrieved that they themselves see no financial benefits. At night they came out with their guns, shooting around the edges of the compound, as a sort of challenge and terrifying the animals. The main attraction here was supposed to be the chance to go trekking for lowland gorillas. We had been led to believe that there was a one in three chance of an encounter and it would have been a lot cheaper than in say Uganda or Rwanda. The reality was that there had been only five gorilla sightings in the last 10 years.

Our group of travellers was the most diverse group we had ever travelled with but it seemed to work. We were generally first up in the morning and saw another of our girls sneaking out of the leader's tent, the driver having already teamed up with the 22 year old Aussie. The guides are not well paid but apart from free travel there are these other perks. There was a six foot seven German giant who was in a tent with another German of a 'different persuasion', and he had been seen in the close company of young African men. There were the two high functioning Aspergers, an out of work student and a well off Canadian dental implant surgeon. We were all of different nationalities and ages.

Cameroon was the final destination and here in the North the roads disappeared into huge rutted pits. Impassable during the rainy season and only just passable in the dry season even with a four wheel drive vehicle. Things are set to improve dramatically as huge swathes of forest are being swept away in a massive road building scheme. It will make travelling so much easier but less fun, as part of the experience is to get stuck in the mud and to break down. Our first night was the most unpleasant imaginable, the night was closing in quickly and there was no obvious place to bush camp. We had to camp by the side of the road on bumpy ground covered with rocks and thorny plants that could and did lacerate your legs. Despite using no lights the tent was full of thousands of flying insects. It was unbearably hot and the sweat was pouring off us, insects of all kinds were crawling over our skin, getting in our eyes and hair, we were even inhaling the tiny ones. It did gradually get better after spraying Deet into the air which killed most of the bugs. Everything got better after that, the roads improved and we made our way down to the coast and back to the fabulous beaches. This was right in the south at Kribi where we visited the pygmy tribes. Tourism quickly destroys so many meaningful experiences and a steady stream of tourists go upstream by boat to visit the pygmies who now do very little, except lie around posing for tourists, who in turn bring them gifts. Their way of life is not totally destroyed and as yet they only expect small gifts. We brought clothes and essential food but I saw someone from another group handing out bubble gum. What chance have they got? They have also interbred with other tribes so are gradually becoming bigger. How inconsiderate?

In all we travelled about 9,300 to 9,500 km, this definitely was not a holiday but was an enjoyable experience. I can quite understand that many people are not going to want to put themselves through all the associated hardship. This book is supposed to be encouraging older people to travel but I can quite imagine many readers thinking,

'I am not doing that.'

Returning to the poor accommodation in these countries, there is very little tourism and standards are pitifully low. Some of the rooms we stayed in were absolutely filthy, with bed clothes that may not have been washed for months. The floors, walls, sinks and toilets would be grimy and it would be a bucket of water for washing. Also perhaps you will have bed bugs, cock roaches, ants and other creepy crawlies. As I mentioned before if we had had the chance on some occasions we would have upgraded to our tent.

On such overland trips there is also going to be a ceaseless round of cooking, washing up, shopping and the putting up of tents. You have to do all this with good will. On many days there will be an early start, often as early as 4.45am, especially if there had been a hold up with a breakdown. There is still a schedule to adhere to and planes to catch at the end of the trip.

Finally travelling on African roads can be dangerous, or for that matter roads in many other parts of the world. The chances of getting involved in some sort of accident are high and we adopted a policy of not stopping. This is not the natural or acceptable thing to do but in Africa it is the sensible strategy. If you hit and kill someone the locals will quite rightly be angry and have an unwritten right to exact revenge. It is quite possible, in some areas, that they will justifiably kill you or detain you until you pay them a lot of blood money. So the best policy is to drive to the nearest police station and report the incident. On this journey there were two incidents, we did not kill anyone but events could have turned nasty. Firstly our driver inadvertently ran a motor cyclist and his passenger off the road. It wasn't entirely our fault but the cyclist went off the road, into the mud and after struggling to maintain balance for twenty metres lost control and crashed. They were carrying cartons of yoghurt which exploded into a creamy white mass. A few miles further down the road we were stopped by a police check. Other locals on motor bikes caught us up and later the unfortunate victims. They were all very angry and after a lot of shouting we agreed to meet them at the local hospital. There were no serious injuries and eventually they happily accepted twenty euros. They even found us a hotel and negotiated a cheaper rate for us.

In the second incident a local was standing in the road giving us directions. As we pulled away he stepped back and was hit full on by a car. The car did not stop and he flew up into the air landing some distance away. He was still alive but we drove away even though it was obvious that we had seen the incident. Our camping spot was nearby and I fully expected the lynch mob to arrive, but perhaps we pre-empted the situation by going straight to the police station.

Standards of driving can be appalling. In Africa the roads are littered with crashed, overturned and broken down lorries. There will be several such accidents daily and it is not uncommon in some areas to see thirty or more wrecked lorries beside the road or even in the middle of it with their cargos strewn everywhere. There is no MOT test and lorries are driven regardless of their condition, if you are the biggest vehicle on the road then you have the right of way.

This was the real Africa, the Africa which few Westerners will encounter, far away from the sanitised tourist areas. If you decide to take an overland trip there will be unexpected problems and this is the nature of such travel. However, most trips will be easier than West Africa and in the future even this route will become a tourist trail.

Is this bridge safe enough?

The roads can be very bad in West Africa

And you will get stuck

Going to school on Lake Ganvie in an improvised boat

Children will definitely be interested in your photographs

How to use a toilet in West Africa

Local sculptures get right to the point

Ganvie, in Benin where everyone lives in the middle of Lake Nokoue

Even our favourite overland company, Dragoman, let us down in the end. There were 9 of us travelling across Brazil, Sometimes there just is an unfortunate combination of travellers along with an inexperienced guide.

Our group consisted of 3 older travellers ages 70, 66 and 64 plus 6 in the younger group. All began well enough until the first night's camping in the Chapada dos Guimaries. Some of the younger group decided to stay up talking loudly, shouting, playing music and swearing. The conversation was sort of,

'It was fucking awesome man.'

'Yeah fucking awesome.'

You can probably get the drift. They were right next to other people trying to sleep and we all had to get up early to leave at 5.30am. We had been lying in our tent along with other campers listening to every word. Soon after midnight my wife restrained me from going over but got up, 'shushed' them herself and they went to bed soon afterwards. The next morning, at our prompting, the leader gave a half-hearted admonishment and I voiced my concerns.

Following that we were partly marginalised from the group for the rest of the trip.

The foul language and shouting continued in general conversation and in public places. I asked the deputy leader to say something, but nothing was done. The whole trip degenerated into a bit of a party trip, exactly what we try to avoid. I had spoken to the company personally about this fear before leaving and following my own advice asked about the ages of everyone travelling in each group. They assured me this was not a 'party truck' company, but as mentioned before there is always a risk with overlanding.

Several times I just had to walk away from the group to avoid saying something. On the truck first thing in the morning it was generally quiet whilst they slept off their hangovers before the shouting and screaming began again.

Our needs and feelings were not considered. We were told by the leader that they were just young people out to enjoy themselves. We appreciated that, but there has to be some sort of balance. If a company are looking to be all inclusive, with people of different ages and nationalities then they all have to be catered for. Leaders need to address this issue, we wanted to enjoy ourselves as well. It is not necessarily the individual travellers job to have to sort any such issues out. The correct procedure is always to voice your concerns to the leader but unfortunately in this case it was a younger female who was quite happy to let a 'party truck' develop.

Matters came to an unfortunate head later in the trip. The 70 year old did not want to go on a night walk because of the noise and bad language. My wife mentioned this to the leader who passed this information on. Later she approached us on this and feelings on both sides were vented. Our leader made it clear that she thought it was not her job to intervene and I should have done something myself. Basically I told her that it was part of her job and she was not doing it properly. Ideally at the camp site she should have got up, say at 11pm and told the group to either go to bed or to the bar around the corner. I apologized the next morning for some of the things I said but received no apology in return.

Having said all that, little changed, the party truck continued aided and abetted by those in charge and we continued to suffer. To add insult to injury they flooded to truck with loud music for the final 2 days. I love music, but I would never be so inconsiderate to force it upon others. We had to put our earplugs in. You have been warned.

It is difficult when a group of diverse people are all thrown in together. Sometimes you will find that you will have nothing in common with any of them, but normally everyone is aware that they have to get on with each other and do so. With the above trip we were just unlucky, further trips with Dragoman have been perfect and they remain my overland company of choice.

11 Flights

"To move, to breathe, to fly, to float,
To gain all while you give,
To roam the roads of lands remote,
To travel is to live."
Hans Christian Andersen 1805-1875

You have got to book up flights but when is the best time? How do you get the best price? Book up too early and you may pay over the odds, leave it too late and the plane may be full. Do you do it yourself on line or let an agent do it all for you? Everyone wants to find cheap flights but if you type it into Google you'll get 114 million hits, so where do you begin? As long as you have an internet connection and know when and where you are going you just need to log on and get searching.

If you are only looking for a short haul flight and are travelling light then the budget airlines are cheapest. The flights on their own are very cheap, however, be aware that there are extra fees that could turn it into an expensive flight. Requirements and fees keep changing so it is important to keep up to date. Checking in luggage is going to be expensive; this is how they make a lot of their money, so avoid taking too much. It is by far and away best to travel light, with just hand luggage if you are able to, and as an added bonus you can get off the plane and not waste extra time waiting around the baggage carousel. You are probably going to be limited to 10kg, so make sure you weigh your bag before leaving home. One good way to take more clothes is to wear the heaviest items and shoes, then stow your coat under the seat. Checking in luggage online will be cheaper than over the phone or at the airport. Stowing luggage in the hold could be anywhere from £20 to £100 or much more, return. A second bag weighing up to 15kg is going to even more expensive. If all the members of your party have cases weighing 20kg then British Airways may well be cheaper. Prices will also vary according to the time of the year. CheapAir.com did some research in America, searching through 560 million air fares, and found the optimal time to book a domestic flight was 49 days in advance. It may well be different in the UK but it acts as a rough guide. The main budget airlines are:

   www.ryanair.com
   www.easyjet.com

www.flybe.com

Charter flights are operated by companies especially for their own clients but it is worth searching for any spare capacity if you are travelling to a package holiday destination:

www.avro.co.uk

www.cheapflights.co.uk

It may still be worth phoning or asking a high street booking agent, just to make sure, sometimes they will know something that you don't. Screenscraper websites do not actually sell you a flight but will direct you to the cheapest options, generally as a list in order of price. Once you have found your flight then check it against at least two other sites, three good ones are:

www.kayak.com

www.kelkoo.co.uk

www.skyscanner.com

A package holiday may not be what you are looking for but if you intend going to a popular destination where companies buy up in bulk massive savings can be made.

Finally once you have got your booking and if seats are unassigned, turn up early to get the best positions. If like us you have already booked your seats in advance, then you may prefer to sit in the comfort of the lounge and wait until the very last moment before boarding rather than standing in a long queue. Bring some sandwiches if it is a no frills service. Check in on line the night before and print off your boarding pass before you arrive if you are able to.

www.seatguru.com will provide airline seating plans.

For long haul flights budget airlines do not operate a service, so check out all the major airlines. If at all possible book up online early and be flexible with your departure dates. Just by searching using the 'plus or minus a few days' can come up with a better deal. It is always going to be more expensive at weekends, bank holidays and school holidays. Flying mid week will be cheaper and as you are retired you should be able to go at anytime, so find out when it is cheapest during the day, week or month. Slightly out of season in May and September are good times when resorts are less crowded. With continually rising airfares it is wise to book up early and some people advise booking up as soon as you know where you are going. Flights come online 12 months in advance and they think that this is the best time to book, but most research suggests that booking too early is a mistake. However, for any really popular destination, when it is the only time you can go, then perhaps book up right away. 'CheapAir' in their research, as above, found the optimal time for booking a long haul flight to be 81 days. They also found that prices began to rise dramatically 2 weeks before departure and become really expensive 2 days before. Among other factors, business men often book up at the last minute because the price does not matter too much as the company is paying. As a general rule do not book up too early or too late.

Timing is crucial and it is almost impossible to judge it perfectly, everyone on your flight will probably have paid a different price. You have to judge for yourself what you think is a good deal and go for it. These are general rules that have been outlined, booking a year in advance is normally not the cheapest and leaving it until the last minute is a mistake, but there are occasional giveaway last minute deals. You could be lucky, airlines would rather not fly with empty seats. Check on SeatGuru how many empty seats are on the plane 10 weeks or so before departure, do this by starting to book a seat. If there are plenty of seats available then maybe it is overpriced and will eventually be reduced. It will depend upon how desperate you are to confirm your seat, but you can keep checking back every week.

The Bing Travel Price Predictor can advise you whether fares are rising, holding steady, or dropping, and whether you should buy right away or wait. It has a sliding scale and if fares are predicted to rise, you're likely to pay more by waiting. If fares are predicted to drop, you may save money by waiting. It is integrated into the main search engine and pops up when a search is made. The site claims to have a 75% accuracy and can be used for hotel rooms as well. Kayak has also introduced a price predictor which they claim to be better.

Cost may not be the most important consideration. Direct flights are always going to be more expensive than those with a stop over. You have to decide if the inconvenience is worth it. If the stop over is somewhere interesting then use it as an opportunity for a few days city break. Prices can vary if you are prepared to fly into a different airport. If a city is served by several airports then taxes and levies imposed by the airport can be different. You may have to travel further to your destination but the saving could be significant.

Check what time your plane leaves. If it is early in the morning and you have to check in 2 or 3 hours ahead then make sure you can get to the airport on time. If you are only on a short vacation and using airport parking facilities, never arrive without having made a reservation, it is always cheaper to pre-book parking.

Look at all the obvious websites to compare and see what they have to offer. With these and other companies, deals can be packaged up if you book a hotel or car hire with them:

www.ebookers.com
www.lastminute.com
www.moneysavingexpert.com/flightchecker
www.expedia.com

If you do not mind where you go or just want some ideas then kayak offers an 'explore' tool that is interesting:

kayak.co.uk/explore
www.whichbudget.com will search from a chosen destination to 'anywhere'.

Round the world flights have previously been detailed and the tickets do not appear in seat sales. The cheapest time is to set off is in April, May or June, again avoiding all the holiday times. If you want to get a good deal and make sure that you can book up seats on your chosen route then it is best to book up as far in advance as possible.

Getting an upgrade is the dream of many travellers. It is always worth asking if there are any free upgrades when you check in. It will help if you are looking really smart but the answer will normally be - no, but if you do not ask you will not get. You have much more chance if your seat is double booked. If so always insist that the other person sits there, the steward may look kindly upon you and escort you up front, somewhere nice.

Now you are a seasoned traveller make sure that you claim your air miles. Register with a frequent fliers programmes and you will soon have enough points for a free flight. Join an airline alliance and your points can be used on any of their member airlines:

www.staralliance.com
www.skyteam.com
www.oneworld.com

Although most airlines do not require you to reconfirm your flight it is best to check the airline at least 24 hours prior to departure to confirm the schedule has not changed. Airlines have the right to change flight times and dates without notice.

Make sure that you have some sort of protection in case the company goes bust. Most package companies are ATOL or ABTA protected but stand alone flights are not. Booking through an agent will provide cover and paying by credit card will give extra protection. Your own travel insurance should also be designed to cover most things.

One in ten people have an intense fear of flying but this form of travel is one of the safest. Statistically there is a one in seven million chance in being involved in a fatal accident. If you flew every single day of your life it would take 19,000 years before you succumbed. It is 19 times safer than driving.

It is always a little alarming when the plane hits some turbulence, the seat belt sign comes on and the planes get buffeted around. The worst flight I have been involved in was on a trip to Sicily. We were coming in to land at Catania when a severe thunder storm hit the plane. It was pitch dark outside and the rain was torrential. We were very close to landing and could feel that 'rushing' sensation of intense speed as we neared the ground. Several bolts of lightening hit us with a massive force jolting the passengers in their seats and every light in the plane went out. I fully expected people to start screaming, but they didn't, there was absolute silence, perhaps they were praying. Just as we were about to touch down the pilot pulled out of it, back up into the sky and on to Palermo on the other side of the island.

www.airlineratings.com to check out the safest aircraft in the skies.

The little plane that flies from Kathmandu to Lukla

12 Accommodation - Where are you going to stay?

"No one realizes how beautiful it is to travel until he comes home and rests his head on his old, familiar pillow."
Lin Yutang 1895-1976

Accommodation is going to be one of the biggest expenses on your holiday. If you only have a limited amount of money then the best philosophy is to try to use it as efficiently as possible. There is no point in booking into an expensive hotel if all you are going to do is sleep there for one night. Most people are going to be looking for the best value they can find. However, as we are all getting older a little bit of comfort will be appreciated. Personally I prefer not to book up in advance but just rock up and find somewhere on arrival, unless it is a very popular destination. If you are standing there right in front a hotel counter offering to fill a room in an otherwise empty hotel, your bargaining power will increase dramatically. The only place in the world I have not been able to find a place to stay was in Worcester, England. It was 'heritage weekend', Worcester races and the cricket, everywhere was booked up and in the end we had to give up and drive home. Quite often in many parts of the world accommodation will come looking for you. For example if you have been Greek Island hopping there will be plenty of people waiting for the ferry to arrive offering rooms to rent. In Goa we got a taxi from the airport and asked to be taken to a particular hotel, but did not get there until after the driver had insisted on taking us to several others. Wherever you are heading for, it is sensible to have at least a few hotels or hostels in your price range written down. In your research try to identify an area where there is a lot of accommodation, so there is plenty of choice when you get there. Once we were wandering around at 11 pm having arrived late and just had to accept second best until we could find a better place in the morning. Sometimes life sucks and you have to roll with it.

Hotels

A hotel may be the obvious choice for most people and they will vary greatly in price depending where in the world you are and how upmarket the place is. If you are staying for a week then a good hotel is worth paying out for, if it is just an overnight stop then it is not worth the expense. I would rather go for basic accommodation and spend the money I save on a nice meal or more travelling. Booking a hotel together with your flights can mean a discount along with some insurance security. As we age, then comfortable accommodation may become more of a priority, as may the location. You may prefer to spend some of your budget on a hotel close to the action.

www.expedia.co.uk
www.travelsupermarket.com
www.booking.com
www.hotelshopuk.com

Hostels

If you have never stayed in a hostel then you may well have an unfavourable idea of them. They are an excellent option for those travelling on a budget. They are no longer just for younger people as more and more baby boomers are travelling, and are much more pleasant places to stay because of it. There are still 'party' hostels but most guide books will give you a warning. Plenty of families are now travelling the world and staying at hostels and you can too. Most still have dormitory rooms but also provide en-suite singles and doubles. Many have excellent facilities, good food, a bar and perhaps other things like a swimming pool. Generally they are clean and comfortable and just like a normal budget hotel. Things are changing out there. What I really like about them is the opportunity to meet other travellers and to swap ideas.

If booking online, in advance, for any accommodation always pay a deposit only and never pay the full amount for the room up front. If you are asked to pay in full then check if you are on the correct internet site, there is only a minor difference in hostelbookers and hostelsbooker but one of them might be cloned. Several times I have arrived at a hostel to find it is overbooked but as long as you have a reservation you will get accommodated somewhere which may or may not be nicer.

www.hostelworld.com
www.hostelbookers.com
www.booking.com

Youth hostels

We all remember them from way back in the past, basic dormitory accommodation, situated in difficult places to get to. In the morning you were allocated a job to do before leaving, such as sweeping out the dorm. Now, grown-ups are welcomed and private en-suite rooms are available alongside the cheaper bunk beds in a shared dormitory.

If you take out a year's membership there are over 4,000 affiliated hostels worldwide where you will get a discount. They are going to be safe, clean and often well situated.
www.yha.org.uk
www.hihostels.com

Couchsurfing

This organisation, couchsurfing, puts you in touch with others throughout the world who are prepared to offer you a free place to stay. You will be sleeping on whatever space is available, on a couch or maybe the floor. Normally it is free but apparently some hosts are starting to charge for the accommodation. It is an organisation that my daughter used when she was travelling and it does seem that it is more suitable for younger people, the average age of participants being 28 years. She met local people, got to know all the best places to go and saved herself a lot of money. If you still fancy it also check out globalfree-loaders or if you are more adventurous and energetic try helpx.
www.couchsurfing.com
www.globalfreeloaders.com
www.wwoof.org

SERVAS

SERVAS seems to be the organisation that is for older more discerning travellers of our age. I know several people who use the organisation and love it. Basically it involves a network of hosts throughout the world who are interested in opening their doors to like minded travellers. The idea is that you will have the opportunity to get to know the country from within. Your hosts will provide comfortable accommodation and possibly some food. You are likely to meet interesting people who will be keen to show you all the local sites or at least point you in the right direction. In return you will be expected to offer a similar service with your own home.

It was founded in 1949 by Bob Luitweiler and his friends as a peace movement. It is a non profit making, cultural exchange organisation designed to bring people together to promote understanding, tolerance, mutual-respect and world peace. It is non-governmental, interracial, present in over 125 countries and run mostly by volunteers. Hosts are scattered throughout the world but mainly in the more wealthy countries. An Italian survey found the average age of members to be 52 years old with slightly more women members than men.

Travellers and hosts are usually interviewed when they apply to join the organisation depending upon their branch or member country practice, there is also a small joining fee. Applicants have to write a self-introduction on a special form which is valid for one year and is shown to hosts upon arrival.

There are certain criteria for joining and you must be:

- 18 years of age or older
- responsible and trustworthy
- open minded and flexible
- someone who enjoys meeting new people

To apply you will need to contact your local Servas representative to be interviewed and approved. This takes a minimum of 4 weeks but once approved you can start contacting potential hosts.

You are also required produce a letter of introduction to the host and write a travel report which has to be submitted to the National Secretary when you return home. Host lists are provided for the countries a traveller is visiting. A deposit is required for host lists, and this is refunded when returned, together with the travel report.

www.servasbritain.org
www.servas.org

Airbnb

Airbnb was founded in 2008 and has quickly become one of the world's largest hospitality brands. The system allows you to search for all types of accommodation virtually anywhere in the world at any price point. You can rent almost anything from a someone's spare room to an entire castle, a boat to a private island or an igloo to a tree house and much more. They operate in over 33,000 cities and 192 countries where 500,000 homes or so are being shared. London, for example has over 1,000 listings. As a traveller you can find somewhere just perfect for you or you could become a host and earn some extra cash.

It is really simple to find the type of accommodation you are looking for. Just log onto the airbnb website and enter where you want to go to, for how many guests and the dates. You will then be given options for what type of room, a shared room, a private room or the entire place. There is also a sliding scale that can be dragged along to suit your budget, from £6 to £500. A filter allows you to narrow your search and there is a map to find the right location.

Before doing all this it would be best to register with the company and create a profile for yourself with some photos. The more information you can supply will increase your chances of being accepted by the host who will also have a profile including recommendations by other users. This can all be done by connecting your Facebook account.

Once into the system you can only book through airbnb and they will charge around 10%. We use airbnb, it works for travellers of all ages and it is a brilliant system. A good host will go out of their way to make you welcome and your stay enjoyable.

airbnb.co.uk

Helpx

You may find that because so much of your time is spent travelling that there is less time to do all those essential jobs such as spring cleaning, decorating or looking after the garden. All the normal jobs that are carried out throughout the year get condensed into that part of the year you are actually at home and it can end up becoming quite stressful. It will not worry those of you in say a high rise flat or my friend in gated accommodation but there are people out there willing to help. Help Exchange is an online organisation begun back in 2001 by Rob Prince from England. Briefly someone comes to stay with you for a specified time and they help with whatever jobs need doing in return for accommodation which usually includes food. Hosts vary from farms to sailing boats but plenty are ordinary people like us just needing a helping hand.

www.helpx.net

Helpx has grown rapidly so check out who is in your area or throughout the world and maybe register as a host. You could of course travel the world with free accommodation wherever you go if you yourself wish to volunteer your skills. There are plenty of older people out there operating. Hosts are looking for help with every sort of job imaginable and in a typical arrangement the helper works 4 hours per day. You will get to stay with local people, have an interesting cultural exchange and benefit from local knowledge. Before entering into an agreement both parties need to make clear their expectations and exactly what sort of jobs need to be done. Maybe you could work an 8 hour day and take the next day off or work only 2 hours but provide your own food. My daughter has both worked as a helper and acted a host over many years. Her advice is to keep agreements short, say one week, particularly at first. Some hosts might expect too much or there maybe some sort of personality clash. Helpers will also vary greatly in their skills and motivation.

Home Exchange

If you are over 60 then you probably own your own home. House-swapping is a great way to go to another country and live really cheaply. There is the issue of security but remember that the other family will be putting the same trust in you. It can be just for a couple of days or months and the financial rewards are obvious as you are only paying for your flight and there are no hotel bills. Before the deal is done you can contact the other party, exchange a lot of information, get to know them and build up some trust. You can live like a local and stay in a home that is as comfortable as your own. There will be someone who could look after your plants, pets and if your house is occupied there is less chance of a burglary. Most companies charge an annual membership fee, but this cost will be quickly offset after just one exchange.

You can even swap cars, just phone up your agent and arrange cover for the necessary period of time, it is not expensive providing there have been no convictions, endorsements, fines or claims within the last five years. My insurance company charged a little more than £1 per day for this service.

www.homebase-hols.com
www.homelink.org.uk
www.lovehomeswap.com

Camper vans

This is a good option in some countries, not necessarily cheap, but allows you to travel as you please. Some holiday companies will set it all out for you, flights and campervan hire included with campsites, an itinerary and route all set up. A much more flexible option is to do it all yourself, booking up your campervan before you leave home. New Zealand is one of the best countries set up for motor home holidays along with, Australia, USA, Canada, South Africa and Europe. You can go to designated camping sites and some of the sites in national parks are free. Bigger more commercial sites charge but do provide kitchens and hot showers. In New Zealand the local law allows you to free camp as long as you are 15km from the nearest large town and off the road. In the USA this form of travelling is a way of life and the parks will be full during the high season. Petrol is still much cheaper in the USA than in England but is steadily rising.

There are other charges to take into consideration. Many of the insurance costs will be the same as for hiring a car. (See chapter 23) If you do not take out their full insurance which will be charged daily at anywhere between £10 and £20, then a bond will be required. If the standard excess on the insurance is £1500 this will be the amount of the bond. It will vary between countries and companies and is refundable if the vehicle is returned undamaged. An extra charge will be made for dropping off in a different location or on a Sunday. Generally a mileage allowance is included in the price but sometimes a limit is imposed and if you exceed it there will be a further charge. All this begins to add up plus the cost of diesel and parking in campsites. Cut down costs where you can by wild camping and live like a hippie again.

Camper vans come fully equipped for cooking, eating, sleeping and general everyday living. There will be some sort of a toilet, water tank and shower, along with a fridge, sink, utensils and crockery. Charge up all your gadgets as you drive along or plug into the mains power at a camp site. You will always have a comfortable bed to look forward to every night and there may even be a TV, DVD player, air conditioning and heating. Cooking for yourself means you will not have to search for a suitable restaurant, endure McDonalds, suffer expensive cafes or any other ghastly fast food outlets. I must add that I have been reliably informed that McDonalds salads can be quite good, but you will have the freedom to stop anywhere pleasant and rustle up a coffee and a snack.

Make sure you have some sort of vehicle assistance in case of a breakdown. Choose a van that is the right size for the number travelling in your group and a 4 wheel drive if you plan to go on dirt or gravel roads.

The advantage of travelling in this way is that you can stop when and where you like and not be stuck to the schedule of an organised tour. Campervans will go anywhere a car can go, although in a city it may be best to park and use public transport.

When booking it is best to book early and avoid peak holiday times. As for other types of holiday all inclusive deals will offer the best value. Bear in mind that some companies only allow rentals up to the age of 75. Usually the longer the hire period, the cheaper the daily rate becomes and if you book 120 days in advance further reductions are made.

www.cruiseamerica.com
www.cruisecanada.com
www.motorhomeroadtrip.com
www.unbeatablehire.com
www.wickedcampers.com
www.hippiecamper.com
www.juicyrentals.com

If you have it in mind to travel for a long time then why not buy a campervan and sell it at the end of the trip. It may be possible to agree that the garage will buy it back at a reduced cost.

If you have a camper van already then travelling throughout Europe is no problem and it could be shipped anywhere in the world for something in excess of £1,000. Try swapping it as you would swap your house.

www.motorhomeholidayswap.com

Camping

Tents have come on a long way since the chunky ridge tents which we used as children, to spend an exciting night under canvas in our parents' back gardens. Today's tents are light weight and could easily be stowed on top of a rucksack and sleeping bags compress down to tiny little cushions. A full scale camping holiday will need a lot of gear but if you are abroad somewhere with a car hire then you can operate much as you would with a campervan. Tents are also great for going to really remote places and getting closer to nature. You will be surrounded by trees and fields, breathing in all that fresh and healthy air, far away from the noise of the city. If you do not want to lug a tent around with you then they are cheap enough to buy when you get to your destination.

Property Bonds

Property Bonds do not figure in my ideas for travelling but I know several people who are very happy with them. Basically you invest a certain amount and points are allocated to you based upon this. The more money you invest the more points you get. These points can then be exchanged for a period of stay in a property. Essentially you become a part owner of properties throughout the world and you gain the right to holiday in any of these properties rent-free, year after year, for your life time and also your children for their lifetimes, without any of the maintenance and managerial complications. A small quarterly fee is levied to enable bond holders to book properties. There are no restrictions on where and when you can go on holiday or type of property as long as you have enough points. No rent is charged but there is a user charge to cover all the overheads. The examples given are £365 for a week for two in Scotland and £550 for a week in a villa for eight in Turkey. Consider the following points:

- Unused holiday points can be rolled over for up to a year or passed on to friends or family members.
- The investment takes the form of an insurance policy and can be cashed in any time after two years at a value linked to the related properties and securities, but only long term holders are likely to realise a profit.
- It is a very respectable and legitimate organisation and you will get high quality accommodation, although perhaps a tad expensive. This will suit older people who want a guaranteed standard.
- There is also no guarantee that your chosen property will be available, the best will be booked up well in advance.

One advantage is that the properties are in fairly remote places and give you an excellent base for discovering the local area. Property Bonds seem to attract middle class people who like walking. It must be better than a package holiday every year and plenty of people use this system for all their holidays, but it is not really 'travelling'.
www.hpb.co.uk
There are all sorts of organisations around catering for older and retired people who want something safe which will guarantee them a holiday for the rest of their lives. Personally I am not interested but you may be. Golden Years Holidays offer such a service, you pay a one off fee that diminishes the older you are and for that you are offered a range of holidays for life. There are three options Gold, Silver and Bronze and all require a sizeable investment. It operates on a points system similar to the above and the only extra cost is a relatively small annual administration fee. It targets retired people and it is going to be safe and dependable.
www.sherpareport.com/destination-clubs/golden-years-holidays.html

Time Share

Time shares have acquired a bad name over the years. At some time you have probably been relentlessly pursued at some Spanish and Mediterranean resorts by touts wanting you to invest. Normally you will be buying a week each year to stay in a property for as long as you want and that might sound appealing. Make sure you do like it because that is it, the same resort and the same fixed week each year, although some schemes have expanded to include a season on a first come first served basis. Time share units can work out expensive and annual maintenance fees are high. Even if you never visit your timeshare you will still have to pay ever rising annual costs. When you decide you have had enough and want to sell, then as a private owner it will be nigh on impossible. Do not be tempted in the first place, with age should come wisdom.

You will have to put up your own tent on overland trips

13 Health

"Roam abroad in the world, and take thy fill of its enjoyments before the day shall come when thou must quit it for good."
Saadi 13th century

If you go to certain places in the world, particularly if you are backpacking you will probably be ill at some stage, commonly with an upset stomach. This is one of the hazards of travelling in remote and third world countries, but the risk can be minimised with obvious precautions. Be scrupulous about washing your hands, either with soap and water, Dettol or with an antibacterial hand gel. Do this regularly, always before eating, after the toilet and following contact with people. Get into the habit of carrying and using some wet wipes for extra cleansing, wherever you might be. This is the single most important advice.

Illness and diarrhoea can ruin a few days of your holiday so be scrupulous in your hygiene. On one visit to India I was badly affected and forced to seek help at the pharmacy. They sold a tablet over the counter that had an amazing effect. From being bound to my room I became blocked up for 5 days and after that, perfect poo! These tablets affect everyone in different ways but for me it was the ultimate solution, although it would probably not be approved back home in England. It is a little worrying not to have to make a visit to the toilet for a number 2 for 5 days, and that was with a single tablet. So effective are they that we always travel with them and on a further visit to India made sure that we purchased some more. They are labelled as Norfloxacin but cannot be safely recommended.

Never drink the local water unless it is treated first, either by boiling for 10 minutes or adding purification tablets. If in doubt buy bottled water and make sure the seal is unbroken.

Street food is wonderful and usually cheap but make sure it is cooked well. A further problem may be with how it is served, with utensils and plates that have been cleaned in grubby water. It is probably wise to wait a few days to get used to a change of diet before tucking in. There is some risk with all food, especially things that are washed in water such as salads or ice cubes in drinks.

Once you have decided where you are going the first stop is the travel clinic at your local health centre, ideally at least eight weeks before departure. What injections are you going to need? If you cannot remember what you have had and how long ago they should have a record of what you have had in the past.

Like many people I hate injections. It is not the actual pain that affects me, but the thought about what is going to happen, and the waiting is the worst bit. It is knowing that a needle will slide gently in to your arm and press in a fluid or even worse suck some out, I will lose sleep. My wife organises all the necessary injections and does not tell me about it. So we go off shopping and then suddenly we turn left for the surgery and before I know it I am in with the nurse. My wife comes in with me and helps the nurse to straighten my arm out, get me to relax and get it over and done with quickly. It is all in the mind because there is no real pain. I do not have injections at the dentists, not even for root fillings. This is not because I am brave but because I am terrified of the injection. I find that I am able to block out most of the pain.

I do not have a flu jab, because of fear again, but recommend everyone should take up the offer every year. Now you are perhaps old enough, at 65, you will be offered it free during the winter months.

So what nasty complaints can you catch abroad? Here are some brief details of the main culprits:

Malaria as everyone knows it is transmitted by mosquitoes in tropical areas. It is the female that spreads the disease as only the female bites. If there is a risk where you are going then take anti-malaria tablets. Mosquitoes feed from dawn to dusk so cover up as much as possible, sleep under a mosquito net and use an insect repellent. Having to take Malaria tablets is a nuisance but absolutely necessary if you visit a malaria infected area. The main decision is which tablets are best for you. All of them can have certain side effects, but to avoid feeling sick take them directly after eating breakfast.

Chloroquine and Proguanil are for places such as parts of India where the mosquitoes have not yet become resistant to it. They work out a bit cheaper but you have to take them for the week before you go and four weeks afterwards.

Doxycycline are more effective tablets for places like Africa where mosquitoes have become resistant to C & P. You pay per tablet and costs can vary a lot. The most expensive place is going to be your high street chemist so have a search online. Again you have to take them one week before and four weeks after travelling. There are also problems with an increased risk of sun-burn, and nausea unless taken with food.

Larium - some people are allergic to it and these tablets are more expensive but you only have to take them once a week, beginning 2/3 weeks before entering an infected area and for up to four weeks after returning. They can also cause hallucinations. Your travel clinic will advise you upon when to start and finish as recommendations seem to vary.

Malarone is a lot more expensive and has to be taken daily, but only for one week after returning home. They also can have more side effects.

Half the world's population is at risk from malaria and this killer disease is responsible for 600,000 deaths every year. Do not take the risk.

Rabies is an acute viral infection caught from being bitten by an infected animal. You must get treatment as soon as possible, if not, the outcome is usually fatal. It is safest not touch any animals and get yourself a rabies vaccination before leaving home.

HIV/AIDS - There is no cure or vaccine so avoid any possibility of infection, not just through sex but think about any other ways that you can come into contact with infected blood or bodily fluids. Do not have a tattoo, piercing, acupuncture or electrolysis unless you are absolutely sure the equipment is sterile. It is the same advice with any medical treatment you might need. I wanted a wet shave in India but ultimately decided against it.

Hepatitis. A, B & C causes a liver infection that can lead to jaundice. 'A' is caught through consuming contaminated water or food. It is also present in faeces so take care over what you eat and be vigilant about washing your hands. There is a vaccine for A and also one for B which is spread in the same way as HIV/AIDS. C is also spread in the same way as HIV/AIDS but there is no vaccine so the same precautions apply.

Tetanus is a potentially serious disease that gets into the body via cuts and wounds, resulting in lockjaw, a painful tightening of the muscles all over the body. Get a booster shot if you have not had one for 10 years.

Dengue Fever is transmitted by the Aedes mosquito but during the daytime. There is no vaccine and it is advisable to cover up again but this is not so easy during the heat of the day. Use insect repellent if you feel at risk. Dengue usually clears up in one or two weeks but a few people develop more serious complications.

Yellow fever is caused by yet another mosquito that feeds during the daytime in the rain forests of South America and Central Africa. Make sure you get a vaccination as some countries will not let you in unless you have a certificate.

Diarrhoea is the big problem in places such as India and the illness you are at most risk from. In some parts of the world if you are trekking or backpacking then it is almost inevitable you will succumb. You are most likely to get it from eating or drinking something contaminated. If you do get diarrhoea then make sure you have a rehydration kit and some tablets and drink loads of water. In an emergency make your own rehydration recipe with 6 level teaspoons of sugar, one level teaspoon of salt and one litre of water. New remedies are coming on to the market all the time so see what the best rehydration is for you.

Typhoid is also caught from eating contaminated food and drink in countries with poor public health and sanitation. Typhoid is present throughout the world but particularly in Africa, Central America, the Indian subcontinent, the Middle East, South America and South and Southeast Asia. If you are staying with local people then consider getting your free vaccination on the NHS.

Tuberculosis - the incidence of tuberculosis is on the increase. If you are going away for a long time and mixing and living with the locals then get a BCG immunisation.

Meningitis A & C - Meningococcal disease is spread through direct contact with an infected person or through their coughs and sneezes. It occurs all over the world with the highest infection rates occurring in sub-Saharan Africa. Consider a vaccination if you are going to be in contact with local people in remote and epidemic areas.

Tick Borne Encephalitis is caused by the bite of a parasite known as a tick that looks like a small black or dark brown spider. Some infected people will have symptoms similar to flu that will pass within eight days, but others could be affected much more seriously. Ticks are mainly found in areas of central, eastern and northern Europe. They live in forests, woods, grasslands, riverside meadows, marshes, brushwood and shrub lands. They usually live in the undergrowth, where they can easily get onto the clothes or skin of passers-by. TBE is a seasonal disease peaking in May/June and September/October, but in fact most cases of TBE occur during summer months as this is when people are most likely to go hiking, camping and so on. There is a vaccine but protect yourself by covering up your body and applying an insect repellent. You probably do not have to worry about this unless you are walking and camping in an area of high infection.

There are almost 900 different species of ticks carrying a variety of diseases. In the UK 3,000 people are affected with Lyme disease every year, some by coming into contact with deer.
www.fitfortravel.nhs.uk

Take a first aid kit with you and make sure it is appropriate to the conditions in the countries that you are visiting. Go through it regularly and throw out anything that is out of date. Sun tan cream needs replacing every year and Elastoplasts degrade with time. Compeed plasters, for putting on blisters are useful if you are trekking. Make sure you have adequate supplies of all the basics: pain killers, diarrhoea tablets, constipation tablets, antacid and antiseptic cream.

Pack an adequate supply of any medicines you are prescribed and check that your medicine is legal in the country you are travelling to. Photocopy your prescription and take it with you along with a note from your doctor if necessary.

Some people swear by vitamins and although I am not a great believer in taking supplements I have an open mind about Glucosamine. This is a dietary supplement that is supposed to keep your joints more supple and to help people live longer. If you believe enough that they are going to work then they probably will. Not many people say anything bad about Glucosamine, but as always do your own research. If you are interested buy the high strength tablets, Glucosamine, Chrondroitin, MSM and Vitamin C. Once on a cruise ship we sat down to breakfast with an elderly couple. They had a long line of supplementary pills to take covering just about every aspect of their health that was almost a meal in itself. Maybe there is something in it as they were well into their eighties and looked in pretty good shape. The Woolston Institute recommends that everybody over the age of 55 takes statins and blood pressure tablets to prevent heart attacks and strokes and they are particularly effective when taken together.

If you are due to see the dentist go before travelling rather than when you get back. I developed a raging toothache in Santa Marie, the smallest island in the Azores. There was only one street with a handful of shops, so what chance of a dentist? As it turned out there were three and the one I chose had a sophisticated surgery with a range of equipment far superior to my own dentist in England. The dentist himself was from Lisbon and first class. In some African countries you may not be so lucky and will be sent into the jungle to chew some acmella oleracea leaves. Alternatively take some clove oil or whole cloves in your medical kit. Cloves have been used to treat toothaches since medieval times and are a really effective home remedy.

Avoid the sun as much as possible and always between 11am and 3pm. Years ago we would all lie out getting baked and sometimes burnt. Our mothers rubbed Calamine lotion into our red skin to ease the pain. The tan faded very quickly after returning home and all we had done was increase our chances of acquiring skin cancer. All of us now know better and should always apply a high factor sunscreen, and never sit out in the heat of the day. Too much sun will prematurely age your skin, sunburn is painful and can ruin your holiday:

- if you are going to be out in the sun use a sunscreen with a high enough factor - at least SPF30+
- make sure your sunscreen protects you against two types of radiation, UVA rays are the ones that age the skin and UVB are the ones that burn
- apply generously all over before going out and at regular intervals
- apply after swimming or use a waterproof product
- wear a wide-brimmed hat
- drink plenty of water

- too much sun is dangerous but some exposure is needed to produce vitamin D and just being outside should be enough for this
- a tanned skin may look good but all you have done is damage the skin (it is much healthier to remain white and avoid the sun as much as possible)
- many older people have to wear glasses so consider buying some 'fitovers' (These are affordable sunglasses designed to fit over your normal prescription glasses and you will get ultimate protection without having to purchase any special sunglasses.)

Do not try anything too strenuous that you are not used to doing regularly at home, such as running, hiking, swimming, bungee jumping. If you pull a hamstring then your holiday is wrecked.

You need a good insurance policy, one that will cover you for long periods away from home and maybe for unusual activities. Read your insurance policy line by line and understand what you are covered for, what situations and for how much money. (See chapter 18 for further information)

Do not neglect your health when you are on the aeroplane. Reduce the possibility of deep vein thrombosis during your long haul flight by keeping as active as possible. DVT can occur from sitting in a restricted space for long periods of time. With little limb movement the blood flow is impeded in the legs and can cause clotting. A clot can move to the lungs with serious consequences. Wiggle your legs around regularly, get up and walk around the plane, drinks lots of non alcoholic drinks and wear some flight socks. Also an aspirin taken directly before flying is thought to be of benefit. If you have any breathing difficulties it is recommended by health experts that you sit as near the front as possible. The effects could be worse if you are a smoker.

If you suffer from breathlessness or have chest pain when at rest, or have had a heart attack within 2 weeks of travel, a stroke within 6 weeks, have had a stomach or gut bleed within 3 weeks or undergone a surgical operation within 12 days of travelling, you may encounter problems on a long flight and your insurance may not cover you. Seek medical advice for all heart problems. Jet lag is caused by the rapid movement from one part of the world to another. Generally it is going to cause a feeling of tiredness as your body tries to adjust to another time zone. The more time zones that are crossed the longer it will take to adjust. It can also affect hunger, digestion, bowel habits, urine production, blood pressure and sleeping patterns. Travelling from west to east has the worst effect and from north to south the least. Try and minimise the effects with the following suggestions:

- fly westwards if at all practical
- fly during the daytime starting early in the morning
- on board the plane try to adapt to the local time at your destination
- eat and go to sleep at your normal time when you arrive at your destination
- sleeping as much as possible on the flight is beneficial
- as a rough guide allow one day for each time zone crossed for your body to adjust

Do you consider yourself to be elderly? If so then you will have a reduced lung, heart and kidney function which can make you more vulnerable to travel related illness. I tend to think that I look younger and am fitter than most people of my age. Maybe this is just wishful thinking but some people do age badly, life can be a bitch sometimes. How old is elderly? The insurance companies will tell you when they increase your premium as you reach a certain age. You need to conduct your own risk assessment before booking an adventurous trip and discuss it with your doctor beforehand. If old age is creeping up on you causing a loss of agility, poor vision and diminished hearing then you will not be 'adventure' travelling as such and the cruise ship awaits you.

I am not a medical expert and the above can at best only make you more aware of potential health issues. A lot of it is commonsense but it is best to consult your GP and pick up a little booklet on 'Health and Safety Abroad'.

14 Safety

*"All that is gold does not glitter,
Not all those who wander are lost."*
J.R.R. Tolkien 1892-1973

I was on my way up the steep steps on the southern edge of Quito leading up to the huge statue of Christ. Glancing up I saw a figure just disappearing and at that point I should have turned back. I was twenty metres or so ahead of my wife when I reached a small flat area. Suddenly two youths appeared out of nowhere, one circled around behind me and the other in front. One of them produced a huge knife which he held up in the air behind his head. It looked something like the shower scene from Psycho, and he was shouting, in Spanish, in a threatening way. It is amazing how much information the brain can process in a split second. Firstly I suppressed the impulse to ask him if he could repeat his threat in English. Secondly I could see that they were only about sixteen or seventeen at the most, and one of them was nervous. Thirdly the guy with the knife was an amateur. Even I knew that you did not hold a knife like that but closer to your own body, blade pointing outwards. It was the beginning of our journey, I had $2500 strapped around my waist in a money belt, expensive sunglasses, camera and a nice watch. I decided that the best form of defence was attack, so I went for him. We came together and at that precise moment my leg went down a large pothole causing us both to fall over. Meanwhile my wife was running up the steps towards me and could see it all this happening, until I disappeared from her view after falling over. She started screaming in order to attract attention. The nervous youth started shouting to his mate saying words to the effect of, 'hurry up'. Grappling on the ground I flailed away with my fists and landed a few kicks. Within seconds it was all over and they ran off further up the steps. I am not sure why, because nobody was going to come and help us anyway. Maybe because it was drizzling with rain and that I had a rain cape on, they thought I was a fat tourist and an easy target. You just do not know how you might react in such a situation, it could have had a tragic outcome and I was lucky. I do not want to put anyone off travelling because this need not happen to you. We were stupid, the steps in Quito are notorious, even the locals do not venture up there. What were we thinking? We were aware about some of the dangers in

Quito beforehand but the statue on top of the hill looked so near and it was so close to the busy streets. Nothing like this will happen to you unless you do get isolated in a dangerous area, so do your research and do not take unnecessary risks. We decided that that statue of Christ was not such a good idea and made our way back down to the town.

Do not attempt to walk up to this cross

When we reached the busy street my wife heard a whistle, as if it was a warning. As she turned around she saw my camera skimming across the ground. Someone had seen the strap trailing from my pocket and snatched at it breaking the strap and jerking the camera out. The camera stopped exactly between her and the mugger. For a split second they looked at each other and then the camera. My wife got there first and put her foot over it. He raised his fist to threaten her but by then I was upon him and landed a well timed kick. So off he ran, and all of this in a fairly busy street where nobody intervened. The police were only twenty metres or so away, did not see anything, but were very concerned. They wanted us to come to the station and make a statement to add to their statistics. We declined because we intended continuing sightseeing, but we really should have cooperated.

As the adrenalin began to wear off, I could feel that my leg was damaged. On inspection my thigh was badly bruised and was beginning to seize up. Having played rugby for years it was nothing more than muscle damage that with the correct treatment would get me fit for next Saturday's match. We got back to our hotel, bought some ice packs, pain killers and a cream to reduce the swelling. It took a few days and some painful exercises, but it did not in any way ruin our plans. Eventually my leg became black and blue provoking a lot of questions from fellow travellers.

I have given this account because it raises a lot of safety issues. We sit down periodically and review our security and safety. After this incident it was a long session and here are a few safety suggestions to start thinking about:

- Carry a whistle in areas that you are not sure about. A few loud bursts will put off a lot of potential muggers.
- Always have your money and credit card well hidden. Use a zipped pocket which is as inaccessible as possible. Choose your travel clothing with that in mind. Rohan make excellent travel clothing with zipped pockets some of which are secretly hidden away.
- If you have a lot of cash use a money belt. Wherever possible leave cash in your hotel safe along with passports and travel documents. Bear in mind that thieves know all about money belts so consider wearing it elsewhere. There are some variations and also some that can be worn around your neck, but they are pretty cumbersome.

- Take a cheap watch to use when abroad. It is also sensible to buy a cheap pair of sunglasses and other accessories.
- Carry two wallets. If you get threatened throw down the empty one and make a run for it. Better still put some obsolete credit cards in it and some worthless foreign currency. You can then run off while the mugger is grovelling for it. Resist turning around to shout, 'Sucker'.
- Keep your camera and phone well hidden along with any other valuables.
- Leave all your expensive jewellery at home. Gold is like a magnet to thieves.

After the above incident we became temporarily a little bit paranoid. We are extremely concerned about the rise in knife crime back home in England. I simply could not understand why young people felt the need to carry a knife to protect themselves, but I was beginning to empathise. I found myself looking in shop windows at big, nasty, dangerous looking knives. With one of those to brandish then the muggers might have run off and it took a while to get rid of those thoughts. As it was at this time, I had a penknife with a bottle opener and corkscrew attached that I sometimes gripped in my pocket with the corkscrew sticking outwards. My wife carried a pair of nail scissors in her pocket for a while.

This is not the only time we have been attacked in some way and this next incident concerns my camera.

Only once have we actually lost something through a mugging. It sounds as though mugging is a regular occurrence but this is our only other more serious incident and can be easily avoided if you have more commonsense than us. We were in Valparaiso, a world heritage site north of Santiago. Again we had strayed away from the tourist area high up on the hill but it did not seem like a dangerous area, just more of a residential area with fewer people around. I spotted an interesting building and took my camera out holding it high above my head for the best shot. Just behind and unbeknown to me my wife had seen three youths come out from a path by some houses and had stood aside to let them pass. They were perhaps about 18, 16, and 14. The eldest one jumped up, snatched the camera and raced off up the hill. Again you do not know how you are going to react in such circumstances but I did not think twice and sprinted after him, caught him up and knocked him to the ground with a rugby tackle. All sorts of things flashed through my mind but before I could do anything else the second youth jumped on my back forcing me to lose my grip. Meanwhile my wife was looking elsewhere and had not realised that the camera had been snatched. By the time she reacted I was already struggling with the thief. When the second youth jumped on my back she ran up and kicked him twice between the legs. He then smashed a bottle on the ground and raised it threateningly before all three ran off up the hill. I swung around, fist raised, but it was my wife who was standing in front of me. The outcome was that they all got away with our camera. That loss did not unduly bother us or getting mugged, but the loss of the camera card did, we had just arrived from Easter Island and it contained some wonderful photos. Local residents were on the scene immediately but not quickly enough to see anything, or so they said. All of this had happened within the space of barely 30 seconds. The locals phoned the police on our behalf who arrived after about 15 minutes, initially two on foot, followed by two more on motor bikes and then two in a patrol car. We were taken to the police station by car and it was during this ride that we really got frightened. As we sat in the back of the squad car the police received a phone call about another incident and set off at breakneck speed. Seventy mph on steep, narrow cobbled streets squealing round blind bends. They were responding to some sort of violent disturbance. Screeching to a halt they caught the culprit, knocked him around a bit, threw him into the back of a van and we carried on to the police station. Meanwhile the police motor cyclists did pick up what seemed to be the youngest boy, who had actually done nothing. He had been 'roughed up' a bit and was terrified, however, we were unable to make a positive identification so the police had to let him go. We made a statement and received a copy in Spanish, for insurance purposes.

    Cameras are replaceable but the loss of the memory card was annoying, however, we still had our own personal memories which cannot be taken away. We put it down to experience, with all our travelling it really should not count as inexperience, and we had another big review of our security. After the struggle I still had my Oakley sunglasses on, my wallet was in my pocket and even my bag containing our passports was still on my shoulder, it could have been a lot worse.

    Again although incidents like this occur everywhere in the world on a regular basis it is still unlikely to happen to you. If you do have something stolen then it is of no real consequence. If all you suffer is the loss of a camera then put it down to an unfortunate travel experience. Do not get paranoid but learn from it and consider how you can prevent it happening again. In our case one of us is careful to take more notice of the surroundings and be on guard when the other is taking a picture and even more so when putting away the wallet after visiting a cash machine. If you do lose something then go to the police, report it and get a statement, then when you get home your insurance company should reimburse you.

I might as well continue and relate the other minor incidents that have occurred so that you will be more aware of some other dangers. Again in Quito we took the local bus from the airport to town. Notice a pattern emerging here in that most of these incidents took place in South America? Buses are notorious for pick pockets and I could see this man inching towards me, I also knew that all my valuables were secure. He was just not very good at his job. I watched out of the corner of my eye as he began to move up the bus to get up right next to me and attempt to get his hand into the side pocket of my jacket. He failed, but he did get his Velcro stuck to my Velcro so that I had to rip his arm off me. He gave me a sheepish look and slid away.

Almost every travel book has a section, such as dangers and annoyances, and pickpockets always figure prominently, such as the incident previously described in Tanzania. Pick pockets are working the whole world over and this crime is on the increase. Take the same precautions at home as you would abroad, any crowded tourist spot in England will have pick pockets operating. My father lost his wallet at a local jumble sale. Tripadvisor have researched the problem and give the following cities as the most likely places to be pick-pocketed:

1. Barcelona
2. Rome
3. Prague
4. Madrid
5. Paris
6. Florence
7. Buenos Aries
8. Amsterdam
9. Athens
10. Hanoi.

The above incidents really brought it home to us just how careful you have to be. As a tourist you will be a prime target just as any foreigner would be in London.

The Spanish leader of one of our overland trips had his wallet taken in Madrid by an eastern European woman with a coat draped over her arm. He felt something and looked down to see his wallet on the ground. The money was already gone and it was too late to make any accusations. These thieves are good at what they do.

A ex colleague of mine was getting on to a train in Spain. As he got on he bumped into another person trying to get off. He politely backed out but only into someone else trying to get on the train. It was all too easy and he never discovered his wallet had gone until much later. Criminals have devised many devious ways to rob you so you will not know a thing about it at the time.

- Always be alert and aware of what is going on around you. Take note of any unattended items or suspicious activities by individuals. Beware if you see anyone looking intently at you or moving directly towards you. Situational awareness is possibly the most important safety advice.
- Never keep your wallet or valuables in your rear pocket, even if it buttons up as it's by far the easiest target.
- Beware of distraction tactics such as dropping any item near to you, squirting something on you, or simply jostling you. Especially be on guard when in crowds, and secure your belongings.
- Pickpockets often work in pairs or groups and it's not just the usual suspects. Be cautious with any strangers, sometimes people who don't look like they'd be a threat, such as children or the elderly can be part of larger operations.
- Pickpockets often have an accomplice who will, jostle you, ask you for directions or the time, point to something spilled on your clothing or distract you in some way.
- Stay alert in confined spaces and near passageways. Try to avoid standing near the doorways of trains as groups of pickpockets can rush out at you when the doors open.
- Before you set off on a trip, limit the contents of your purse or wallet as the smaller the bulge, the less likely pickpockets are to notice it.

- You need to be on your guard at all times and with practise this will come naturally, even when you are enjoying some of the world's greatest attractions.

I repeat here do not go anywhere that is not recommended by the FCO. For starters your insurance will be invalidated and there are plenty of seriously dangerous places in the world. While we were travelling through West Africa we heard of a German tourist who was determined to see Timbuktu. This was at a time of unrest, he would not listen to advice and ended up being shot and killed. Always follow the FCO advice and you should be safe enough.

It seems that most cities have an area where tourists should not go. Before you set out always do some research, read the guide books and ask the advice of other travellers. The La Boca area in Buenos Aries has recently been gentrified with smart new galleries, cafes and restaurants. Right alongside it, however is a run down area where muggings are common place. All we did was try to cross over the street from the chic cafes, cars stopped and warned us not to go any further, we had not intended to do so but were grateful for their concern.

Further safety measure to consider:

- Keep your backpack on your back at all times when standing on buses, trains or just waiting in hotel lobbies. If you put your bag down it immediately becomes vulnerable. Never leave it unattended anywhere, not even a hotel lobby. If you leave your luggage unsupervised your insurance will not cover you.
- Lock your luggage and clip all the zips on your rucksack together with a padlock to deter an opportunist theft.
- Use the same padlock to lock doors in hostels.
- Never venture into any areas which you are not sure about.
- Avoid carrying large amounts of cash.
- Pay for purchases with a credit card when possible so you will have some protection.
- Always keep cash in your front pocket close to your body.
- Notify the credit card issuer immediately if your credit card is lost, stolen or misused.

- Keep a record of all of your credit card numbers in a safe place at home and email all the details to yourself for easy access.
- Be extra careful if you do carry a wallet or purse. They are the prime targets of criminals in crowded shopping areas, transportation terminals, bus stops, on buses and trains. A clever thief will know where you keep it, never drop it into your bag even if you are rushed for time.
- At the airport, watch for your suitcase as it appears on the carousel. Don't hang back and wait for the crowds to disperse - you might find that someone else has already taken your bag in the meantime.
- Beware of strangers approaching you for any reason. Con-artists may try various methods of distracting you with the intention of taking your money or belongings. After a lot of travelling you will develop a natural scepticism. We are all really nice people but do not let strangers use that as a weakness against us.
- Try to avoid carrying your passport, birth certificate, social security cards, bank details or any other items containing personal details. Only carry what is absolutely necessary.
- Tell your family and friends where you are going and give them some contact details. Leave details of your itinerary and 24 hour emergency contact numbers.
- At some stage you are going to be using an ATM where you need to be extra cautious.
- Always be observant when making a withdrawal with your ATM card and keep looking around for any suspicious activity. Ideally there will be two of you and one can just watch the surrounding area. If there is something suspicious then go to another machine.
- Have your card out ready before you arrive at the machine so that there is no need to fiddle around with a wallet or purse and the transaction can be finished quickly.
- Always hide the ATM keyboard so nobody else can see you entering your PIN.
- Do not forget to take your receipt.
- Put your cash away out of sight immediately, it can be counted later.

- If you really have to use an ATM at night then get someone else to go with you. Do not use any machine that is not lit up or seems isolated.
- Never carry written copies of your PIN with you.
- Never let go of your wallet. Always make sure your hand is on it. For example if you are in a shop do not lay your wallet or purse down by the cash register.
- When you are travelling on public transport there will always be a greater risk from criminals especially pick pockets.
- Taxis - always make sure it is a genuine taxi with official markings. Never get in a taxi that is unmarked or with someone else in it already. Single women travellers need to be particularly cautious. Sit behind the driver so that you can see him and he cannot see you. Pay the driver upon arriving at your destination and while you are still sitting in the vehicle.
- Trains - all sorts of things can happen but they probably won't. Organised gangs have been known to target trains, particularly at night. There is a certain amount of safety in numbers and useful if there is another person to guard your luggage when you nip to the toilet or buffet car. Again be aware if someone seems to be blocking your way and another person is close behind you. Wherever possible lock up your compartment.
- Buses - all the same problems could occur, they probably will not. On rare occasions whole bus loads of people have been held up and robbed by well organised gangs.
- When you are out and about walking around the streets common sense is the best precaution. Be more vigilant in crowded areas and tourist spots, or anywhere that you can be distracted. For example whilst watching a street performer in a city centre.
- Don't use short cuts, narrow alleys or poorly lit streets.
- Try not to travel alone at night.
- Avoid public demonstrations and other civil disturbances.
- Keep a low profile and avoid loud conversations or arguments.
- Do not discuss travel plans or other personal matters with strangers.

- Avoid scam artists by being wary of strangers who approach you and offer to be your guide or sell you something at bargain prices.
- Beware of groups of vagrant children who could create a distraction to pick your pocket.
- Wear the shoulder strap of your bag across your chest and walk with the bag away from the curb to avoid drive-by bag-snatchers. I sometimes attach mine to my belt with a metal karabiner.
- Do not try to dress like an affluent tourist with expensive accessories and designer clothes. Try to blend in and dress as the locals do and avoid looking obviously like a tourist.
- Try to travel light so that you always have one hand free.
- Try to seem purposeful when you move about. Even if you are lost, act as if you know where you are going. If possible ask for directions only from individuals in authority. Always say to people that you have been there before. Sometimes lying is the safest option.
- Know how to use a pay telephone and have the proper change or token on hand.
- Learn a few phrases in the local language or have them handy in written form so that you can signal your need for the police or medical help.
- Make a note of emergency telephone numbers you may need, police, fire, your hotel, and the nearest British embassy or consulate.
- If you are confronted and find yourself in a really serious situation the safest option is to give up your valuables, or hand over your dummy wallet. If the muggers fall for it then at a safe distance away you can feel a little pleased with yourself and again think, 'sucker'.

There are a lot of safety measures to consider in the above, most of them amount to commonsense and I am sure that all of you already employ them. There are, however plenty more suggestions which I shall list just to make sure:

- Make two photocopies of your passport identification page, airline tickets, driver's license, credit cards that you plan to bring with you along with any other documents. Leave one

photocopy of this data with family or friends at home, pack the other in a place separate from where you carry the originals and email scans of everything to yourself. You may not even need to carry any photocopies at all.
- Get in the habit of looking back when you get up to leave somewhere. Travelling can be very distracting, and it is very easy to leave things behind. Check the hotel room twice, thoroughly before checking out, look back at the restaurant table you have been eating at or where you have sat down for a rest.
- Try not to keep your bank cards and documents all in the same place.
- Be wary of accepting food and drink from strangers particularly if they do not consume it with you. It is easy to slip sedative drugs into your food or drink. This is particularly important for female travellers.
- Do not put too much trust in local people who you have just met and even less in those who approach you.
- Try to avoid travelling at night on public transport.
- Do not hitch hike, even though you hitch hiked all over the place back in the sixties.
- Ask at your accommodation where the safe and unsafe areas are.
- If the streets have women, families and children in them generally they are going to be safe enough for you.
- Sometimes thieves will pose as a police officer and ask to check your money for counterfeit notes. Always ask for identification and never let anyone check your money, not even the real police, unless in the safety of a police station.
- You will sometimes be approached by people posing as a tour guide. I always ignore them, although some tourists have found them really useful, but occasionally they will have an altogether less pleasant motive.
- Carry a small torch as you never know when you may find yourself in the dark in unfamiliar surroundings. Take it out with you in the evenings and keep it beside your bed.
- If your cell phone does not work outside of the country, consider buying one that does for the duration of your trip.

- If detained for whatever reason by an official, ask for identification. If in doubt, tell them that you want to see their superior. Keep your emotions in check.
- Do not discuss travel plans, your room number or any other personal information in public within earshot of strangers.
- Familiarize yourself with train and bus schedules before travelling. Have an alternative plan in place in the event your transportation plans change.
- Consider purchasing a portable alarm that emits a loud sound.
- Never write your home address on the luggage tag so that it can be seen. Use a covered luggage tag or just put the minimum of information, such as a phone number.
- Try to stay in a hotel that uses cards to open room doors and if your room has a peephole and a deadbolt lock all the better.
- A room near a stairwell is safest. Take note of emergency exits, stairwells, fire escapes and emergency plans, just in case. Never take the elevator if a fire or smoke is detected. Try to stay in a hotel where the doors enter the hallway and not directly from the outside.
- Always lock your hotel door when retiring for the night. If there is a chain included, use it. I know someone who caries a small rubber wedge for keeping doors closed tight from the inside.
- If possible, choose accommodation that has unmarked 'swipe cards' rather than numbered keys for each room. If you lose your swipe card or if it is stolen, the thief won't know which room to rob.
- When arranging to meet people you've never met before wait for them in the lobby, never ask them to come up to your room.

There is another aspect of safety concerning your own personal well being wherever you may be. If you do have a mishap on any organised tour then you would hope that someone would be there help. We were in the sauna on the safety of a cruise ship, just my wife and I plus a Japanese woman, who did not look comfortable. As she slumped down more her robe began to slip into an embarrassing position. My wife went over, fixed her robe and gently shook her but got no response. In the extreme heat the poor woman had become totally dehydrated, had passed out and looked dreadful. We pressed the emergency button and waited but nobody came. We wedged the door open and phoned reception, waited, but nothing happened. At this point my wife ran to the reception in the gym and got a female instructor to come. She understood the gravity of the situation immediately and phoned for the Doctor. Even then it was far too long before medical assistance arrived. The Japanese lady recovered but it could have been a lot worse, nobody thanked us and the next day the Japanese lady was back in the sauna.

All this probably has the potential to put you off travelling independently and to choose the relative safety of group travel. This is not the intention of the book but exactly the opposite. Do not let the scaremongers get to you and ruin your travel plans. If you take care and put all this advice into practice you can minimise your chances of encountering problems. No matter what age you are, the unlikely chances of being attacked or robbed are the same. You are older, wiser, more experienced and naturally more cautious.

Even if you are part of a group it will not stop you becoming a target, just make sure you are not an obvious one. All these recommended safety tips will become second nature to you very quickly and some seem so obvious that I am sure you implement them already.

Angkor Wat is where the strangler fig trees are maybe holding up the buildings. If the trees are cut down the stones will probably fall. When the trees die or are blown down in a storm then the building may collapse. Nobody really knows what to do about them. They are a menace but for the time being make for a great photo opportunity.

15 Preparation - Get Yourself Fit

"The journey of a thousand miles begins with a single step."
Lao Tzu 6th century B.C.

Travel is often going to take you into challenging environments where you will need to be nimble on your feet, well co-ordinated and balanced. If you are less fit than you should be you will be more likely to fall and sustain some sort of injury. You need to make some time available to get fit and your efforts will be rewarded, particularly if you are off on an active trip rather than just sight seeing.

Travelling often involves a lot of sitting around on various forms of transport so wherever possible get off and do some walking. On overland journeys set off before the truck leaves and see how far you can get. Setting off walking on your own until the truck catches up can create some unique experiences.

You do not need to be super fit but you will enjoy yourself more if you are reasonably fit. Remember that if you are back packing then you have to physically carry everything yourself. If you are overweight then you have to carry that much more. There is so much information on health and diet around at the moment that it can be confusing as to what is the best approach. Try not to console yourself by agreeing with others that being overweight is now the new normal. Basically if you smoke, then stop, get more exercise and reassess your diet. These are the three important steps to take and all of them should be a constant part of your life.

Taking those three suggestions in order, if you still smoke then you are a fool. Probably most of us who are now over sixty smoked at some stage when we were teenagers but the sensible ones gave up. I gave up on the day my first child was born and still consider it to be one of the best things I have ever done. Some old school friends have already died from smoking related diseases and others are beginning to look old and haggard before their time. Experts agree that smoking accelerates aging, so that on average, smokers look 1.4 years older than non-smokers. The skin wrinkles more because smoking hampers the blood supply that keeps skin tissue looking supple and healthy. Successive governments have not really tried hard enough to help people give up, but it still comes down to an individual's right to choose. It was not so long ago that cinemas allowed smoking and if you were a non smoker you got pushed to some remote corner of the auditorium only to have to breathe in the fumes from everyone else. I stopped going to pubs because the smell was so awful. In restaurants smoke from diners that had finished their meals wafted around whilst others were still eating. Smokers themselves smelt awful and continue to do so. There was an incident reported in the press many years ago that took place in an indoor public place where a couple could been seen having sex. Nobody took much notice or seemed unduly bothered, however, when they rolled over and lit a cigarette then there was a whole chorus of complaints. The thing is I really do not mind what people do, it is almost impossible to offend me, but if they do something that is going to have a detrimental effect upon my health then I am going to get annoyed. Many years ago I met the entertainer, Roy Castle, he was a lovely man but he spent his career working in smoky jazz clubs playing the trumpet. He died before his time from cancer caused by passive smoking, although he himself, did not smoke. There is now a lung cancer foundation in his name. I know some of the smokers out there will be thinking that they will not be affected and their dad or uncle smoked all his life and lived to ninety six and you may be one of those lucky ones. I should not go on about this too much but what exactly would stop smokers smoking? Being diagnosed with lung cancer would not stop everyone because then they can think,

'Well if I am going to die anyway then I might as well die happy.'

Supposing the government health warning on the side of the packets could be replaced with something like,

'Cigarettes will almost certainly kill you and if you continue to smoke twenty a day you will probably die in your sixties'.

Would that stop them? Probably not, but if a brand of cigarettes were made even more carcinogenic so that they really did kill smokers more quickly I wonder what the uptake would be? We have an ever expanding elderly population which is set to be a huge drain on resources, pensions and hospitals. Perhaps it would ease this problem if people died younger. Of course I am not really suggesting this as an option, it is not that simplistic, this is a serious issue and one that has improved enormously for the non smoker, who can now eat his meal in a pleasant smoke free environment. You will feel the benefits from giving up almost immediately and your life span will lengthen. A fifty year study revealed that smokers die on average ten years earlier. These figures are from the web:

- men who quit at 30 died at the same age as non smokers
- men who quit at 40 died 1 year earlier than non smokers

- men who quit at 50 died 4 years earlier than non smokers
- men who quit at 60 died 7 years earlier than non smokers.

So there you have it. If you are 60 and stop smoking now you will live for an extra three years. I tried a simple on line questionnaire which gave me a life expectancy of 88 years, however, if I had been a smoker that dropped to 83. Quite apart from all these benefits you'll save lots of money which can be spent on even more travelling.

Exercise

Next you need to get some exercise. If you suddenly start carrying a heavy rucksack or walking up steep hills when you are not used to it, then you could end up suffering from back ache, knee problems or just getting out of breath. Nothing could be worse than having to cut your travelling short and to come home to tell the grandchildren that you couldn't hack it. If you are not fully fit then you will miss out on so many of the good things that travelling can bring. You will not be able to get to those exciting, remote places that can only be reached on foot. As we get older all those niggling injuries from the past come back to haunt us. All mine I can trace back to an incident on the rugby field but the way to combat this is to do plenty of the right sort of exercise.

The gym is probably the best place to start and if you are not already a gym bunny then this is going to be a challenge in itself. It is hard enough for regular gym goers having to return to the gym after 3 months holiday or even after the weekend, so imagine what it is like for the unfit 'fatty'. I have been going to the same gym for over twelve years and I love it. During that time I have watched many people come and go. Very generally speaking almost everyone who attends this gym regularly seems to be fit enough already. Every year there is a recruitment drive, mainly in the form of local mail shots. For the following few weeks dozens of new faces appear full of good intentions, but very few of them actually become regular clients. Some attend for a few weeks, for others it is days and for one or two they do not even last a single session! The manager told me of one person who joined and only attended once in the entire year yet he renewed his membership. Maybe his wife thought he was at the gym when he was elsewhere? People join for all sorts of reasons, but popular ones are, to fulfil a New Year's resolution, retirement, to lose weight or simply because they are feeling guilty. What they do not realise is that it can be sheer hard work particularly if they are overweight. (Incidentally how many obese people do you know who have survived into old age?) At first you have to take it really easy and build up very gradually and expect your muscles to ache the following day. Get to know the other members so it can become a social thing as well. You need to be well motivated and determined, the very qualities that are needed for many aspects of travelling. It is not a competitive sport, the only challenge is against yourself. There will be fit young men in the weights corner who will just pump iron all the time. You need to avoid this and never, ever try to lift too much. If you are using weights then lift a weight that you find is quite easy, then repeat the lift until you find it becoming more difficult, then stop. If you are over sixty you only want a general sort of fitness and to keep up your strength levels. Try to use all of the equipment incorporating aerobic exercise as well as weights of some sort. Do not overdo things especially at first. Aim to get slightly out of breath and to feel that your muscles have all had a little bit of work to do. Getting back into shape again is going to take anything up to a year but the benefits will start to show up fairly quickly. Once you have got yourself fit then it is just a case of keeping up that level of fitness and maintaining your body shape. Try to go to the gym at least three times a week at the minimum. The big gyms will have something for everyone, lots of exercise classes to choose from such as zumba, yoga, circuit training and there will be special classes for the over fifties.

 If you do not like gyms then there are plenty of other forms of exercise and walking has long been considered one of the best. If you are lucky enough to live near the country side then get out there. A good way is to get a family member to drop you off somewhere near a country footpath, then you can wander around freely wherever your fancy takes you, occasionally exercising your 'right to roam'. When you have finished just use your cell phone and issue directions for the pick up. You need a friendly wife or husband, or at least a friend for this. Failing that, you are over sixty, you may already have a bus pass and could get the bus home for nothing. However, bus pass eligibility has changed at the time of writing and anyone born after 5/4/50 will need to calculate when they are entitled to one. As previously mentioned the added bonus here, is, if you use the car to get absolutely everywhere then travelling by bus will be a novelty and quite exciting, particularly on the top deck at the front. Though guess who will have already snaffled those seats; some more annoying pensioners. Walking over rough ground in the countryside is ideal if you are training for a trek and much better than the gym which cannot replicate the unique movements, twists and turns caused by uneven or muddy ground. Neither can you wear your walking boots to the gym. Another useful type of walking route is a circular one. There are plenty of local books around to give you ideas, some of which incorporate a pub, but better still get an ordinance survey map out and work out your own route. It is so nice being out and about in the countryside that I am always amazed as to how few people actually take advantage of it. You can be out there absolutely on your own with nature for hours.

Buy a bicycle and use it to cycle to your gym. All those sort of trips that are not really far enough to take the car but quite a distance to walk, can be done with a bicycle. Post your letters, go shopping, nip round to friends, accompany the grand children on their bikes or just have a nosey around the neighbourhood. We all had a bicycle when we were children and those skills will still be there. The amazing thing is that bicycles have changed beyond belief. One of my earlier bikes was made of steel, painted black with a green pin stripe and had a Sturney Archer three speed gear on the cross bar. I could hardly lift it up and cycling was much harder work. On today's modern bikes it is positively a joy, it is effortless, great fun and you get to see so much more than you would in a car. Parking is never a problem, but theft could be, so make sure you always lock it up securely with a chain around the frame. I bought mine on ebay and I love it. It is a hybrid Saracen with 21 gears. My wife also bought a Viking Glendale with 21 gears so we can go out on little trips together. They are nothing special but adequate for most things and as hybrid bicycles they can be ridden anywhere. You can of course go for a flat out racing bicycle or a dedicated mountain bicycle. Whatever you choose it is another way to get fitter for your travels, and that could even be a cycling holiday. It does not have to be too strenuous. Cycling alongside canals and rivers in England and Europe is always going to be on the flat and it is a wonderful way to get closer to nature and explore less accessible places. There are plenty of cycling holidays to choose from and if you are tempted then research the following links:

www.bike-express.co.uk
flexitreks.com

There are dozens of other ways to improve your fitness level. Swimming is an ideal sort of all round exercise which everyone should do. This requires a bit more effort, actually getting there, then having to change and finally getting wet. It is just as valid a form of exercise as a workout in the gym and exercises muscles all over your body. Plenty of the large gyms have swimming pools in them so there will be no excuses.

Try to make your day as active as possible. Both housework and gardening can involve a lot of exercise, but sitting in front of the computer or watching TV will not, unless you start getting involved in isometric exercise. Briefly these are static exercises such as pushing against an immovable object like a wall or pushing your hands together as you sit at your desk. Here are some additional ideas to getting fitter:

- There has to be a moment when you decide to turn it all around.
- Do not take it so seriously that you feel obliged to buy all the latest gear.
- Exercise just needs to be good fun, take it too seriously and it will become a chore.
- Join a gym that is near where you live, so you will be more likely to go.
- Join up for a month initially just to make sure.
- Try to fit it neatly into your daily routine.
- Be realistic about what you hope to achieve.
- Always walk up stairs in shops rather than taking the lift. Your body will need more oxygen making the heart and lungs work harder.
- Park your car as far away from the supermarket entrance as you can and enjoy the walk, every little helps. Even carrying the shopping is extra exercise.
- At first aim to do 3 hours moderate exercise a week and try to build up your strength.
- Within each hour at the gym try to get out of breath for 20 minutes.
- House work such as vacuuming uses all the large muscle groups of the legs, shoulders and arms.
- Switch on some music and dance around the house, although this may best be done on your own in private!
- Take the bicycle out for some aerobic exercise. 20 minutes cycling will burn 200 calories.

Diet

Finally diet has been the continuing problem for so many people in recent years. My own mother was constantly on one sort of a diet or another although we all liked her just the way she was. In the Renaissance it appeared that fatter women were considered to be more beautiful and desirable. Most ordinary people did not have enough food to be able to become fat. Artists portrayed women in the ideal shape of the time, with a fuller figure. It is only in the last hundred years or so that we have all been conditioned into regarding very slim women as the ideal. Women, particularly younger women have a lot of pressure put upon them regarding their appearance, some are overweight but there are just as many overweight men. It has become a problem for many developed countries. If your priority is to lose weight then it might be as simple as eating less and with any luck getting fitter will be a welcome side effect. Forget about most dieting fads because quite often they will work for a while only for the weight to pile back on again. I am not going to go on too much here about what should be painfully obvious. If you just ate whatever you wanted to, as long as you did so in moderation it would be a good start. I read somewhere once that it is 'surprising how little food the body actually needs', and it is a maxim that as a family we try to adhere to. Too many people will keep on eating even though their body has had enough, food is just too nice and enjoyable. We eat for pleasure and eat far more than we need to, almost everybody does. Try to continually reassess your diet and to tweak it regularly for the better. Salt and sugar should have been cut out long ago. Fry ups and takeaways should only be rare events or occasional treats. Make sure to cultivate a healthy respect for fruit and vegetables. I used to start the day with a fresh orange juice (okay it does contain sugar) and a small breakfast, often just one slice of toast, but this changed after we had been on a cruise. The food onboard was just fantastic and sometimes I ate more for breakfast than I would normally eat in a whole day! Then the same for lunch and again for dinner, plus there were afternoon cakes and late night snacks. As soon as I got home I got on the scales expecting the worst, but to my surprise I had lost weight. All I could put it down to was eating a bigger breakfast. What does seem clear is that skipping breakfast will not help you lose weight, but eating a larger breakfast just might help. You probably know all this already but I didn't. So many life style articles encourage you to eat a healthy breakfast to kick start your day. It gets the body's metabolism working early enabling it to better digest its entire food intake for the day and it also discourages taking snacks before eating again at lunch time.

If you are overweight, or dare I say it, obese, then you do not need this book to tell you that you really should lose weight. Essentially you will be carrying around with you much more than other people and it is going to be harder work just walking. Add a rucksack and walk up a hill then you may not make it. You are going to miss out on many of the nice things that life has to offer.

Obesity is generally measured through body mass index (BMI). This is a simple formula where weight in kilograms is divided by height in metres squared. If the resulting figure is 25 to 30 you are overweight and 30+ is obese. A male weighing 85kg and six foot in height (1.8288m squared = 3.3445) comes out as 25.11, or slightly overweight, and this is nothing much to worry about. Having said all that if you take the sizes of many of England's top rugby players, particularly in the scrum, it is not uncommon to find 6 foot players of up to and over 20 stone. A quick survey of the current England squad gave many players a BMI of 33 and one player 40. Yet these guys are super fit. A lot does depend upon body frame, but it would be wise not to use this as an excuse.

Every year I always sit down and write out my New Year's resolutions and I periodically review them throughout the year. One resolution I made every single year and always failed miserably with, was to drink more water. It is recommended that you drink between 6 and 8 glasses a day or three litres. I never did although I knew that I should. Then one year I made a special effort and forced myself to drink water regularly throughout the day even if I was not thirsty. The water was kept in the fridge, sometimes with a few slices of squeezed lemon. What happened is that after a while the body begins to expect and need this water. This should be part of any fitness regime, certainly at the gym you will need your water bottle with you. You always need to keep your body hydrated. When travelling abroad in temperatures of 30 degrees centigrade or more, we sometimes long to be at home just so we could switch on the tap and drink a glass of lovely cold water. At such times water is the most wonderful drink in the world that you can possibly imagine. Lovely ice cool refreshing water, nothing else will do. When you are at home the challenge is going to be choosing water over a glass of fresh orange or a cold beer.

The cruise that I have mentioned was a significant turning point in the way we cooked and ate. We attended a series of seminars on health and nutrition which although we did not totally agree with all the recommendations it did get us seriously thinking. Back on dry land I started reading up on various health and nutrition advice and below is a summary of my findings:

Your daily intake of food needs to be balanced
Protein 40% Carbohydrate 40% Fat 20%
We eat too much and for pleasure rather than for sustenance.
Caffeine, refined carbohydrates, additives (e.g. MSG, Aspartame) and preservatives are all bad for the body.

You need to eat the correct food in the right combinations
Healthy foods are any meats that walk around on 2 legs, e.g. chicken. Fish is also healthy, particularly oily fish and anything that is grown naturally such as fruit and vegetables. These foods are broken down in the gut by alkaline.

Unhealthy foods are red meats and anything that is processed or unnatural containing additives. These are broken down by acids in the gut.

Problems can occur when the 2 groups are combined. The body has to produce both acid and alkaline at the same time. The food is not processed properly and left stuck in the large colon. Thus it is supposedly better to eat a steak sandwich rather than one with chicken and lettuce. However, the two different food groups can be eaten for the same meal as long as a minimum of five minutes is left as a gap between them.

Breakfast is the most important meal of the day and should be the biggest so that the body can digest food throughout the day and has more energy. Breakfast will provide the fuel that your body needs for much of the day. It also gives us essential vitamins and minerals. People who skip breakfast often struggle to make up these missed nutrients later in the day. Kick-start your digestive system with a lemon water, a glass of fresh orange or at least water soon after getting up to replenish your body fluids, and then eat. Fruit, cereal and porridge are ideal and help keep your bowels in good working order and boost your vitamin and mineral intake.

You need to eat regularly throughout the day. Do not leave more than five hours (other research says three) between meals. This will prevent hunger pangs between meals and over indulging at main meal times. Spreading your food over five or six meals gives an even source of energy and is reckoned to be better than 3 main meals. All this is a lot easier to do when you are retired and free from the shackles of work.

Drink lots of water. Water is really important and you need to drink 2 to 3 litres per day, which will help to detoxify your body. Toxins are bad for you and enter the body mainly through food. We also absorb toxins throughout the day through tap water, the air, the skin, and they are breathed in through polluted air or even air conditioning. More toxins are absorbed through various products such as deodorants (particularly ones that contain Aluminium Chlorohydrate, which are particularly bad), hairsprays and air sprays, most sprays are toxic. A BCA test, Body Composition Analysis Test, will measure your water retention and hydration levels, which in turn will tell you how toxic you are.

The liver deals with all the toxins in the body. Sometimes it cannot cope with the number of toxins coming in and they are deposited elsewhere in and around the lymph nodes where they are then surrounded by fat to protect them. In men the lymph nodes are mainly around the stomach creating a 'pot belly' and in women they are mainly around the waist, creating a 'pear shape'. It is important that you detoxify your body as part of your fitness plan. To detoxify the liver fully it will take up to six months and then it is recommended to detoxify again properly, every five to eight years.

Tap water contains toxins, traces of chlorine and fluoride. To purify water boil it and then refrigerate and perhaps squeeze in a little lemon according to taste. If you drink a lot of tea, coffee or juice then still aim to drink one & a half litres of water on top of that.

Hydration is important, drinking it is the key element to good health. I know I am banging on about it a bit but I am convinced:

- Around 70% of our body is made up of water and it is vital for every chemical reaction in the body.
- We need around 2-3 litres a day to transport nutrients, help with cellular enzyme activity and digestion of food, to carry out waste and toxins and also to support brain function for mood, energy and concentration.

- We lose water and also body salts through urine but also when it evaporates as sweat when exercising. A resulting loss of only 1-2% of body weight can impair performance by around 10-20%.

Simply by drinking more water you can get slimmer, look younger, exercise better and avoid headaches among other benefits.

- You will lose weight because drinking water is believed to be an extremely effective appetite suppressant as it is filling. By drinking more, you're less likely to feel hungry and will eat less. Plenty of water makes it easier for your body to break down fat cells.
- Research has shown that drinking half a litre of water within 30-40 minutes can increase how fast your body burns calories by up to 30%.
- Water helps fuel your muscles, so drinking before or during exercise will boost energy, as well as reduce the likelihood of cramps and sprains.
- Recent research suggests that drinking water combats dry skin, flushing out toxins and bacteria. Dehydration is one of the most common causes of headaches. Maintaining a regular water intake should combat most headaches even those brought about by fatigue.
- A regular supply of water to your body helps your brain work at a better pace and helps you concentrate.
- Drinking water improves immunity and helps to fight against colds and flu. It prevents salts accumulating in the kidneys which form kidney stones. It maintains the thickness of blood plasma avoiding cardiovascular complications and also helps preserve the correct shape of bones preventing arthritis.
- Water assists in the removal of toxins and waste from your body encouraging regular bowel movements and is crucial for a healthy gut. Drinking enough water means less likelihood of constipation.
- Water increases your body's power to work to its full capacity helping you to avoid feeling tired.

- Water encourages the flow of nutrients and hormones around your body releasing endorphins which make you feel happier.

Detoxify your body

The body is naturally 7.356 on the PH scale, where acid is 0 % alkali 14, and this is where you need to keep it, slightly alkaline. PH is the measure of the potential hydrogen, the amount of hydroxyl ions that are alkaline forming as opposed to the hydrogen ions that are positive and acid forming. An unhealthy diet will create too much acid, which is toxic. This is relevant because cancer will be more likely to proliferate in acidic conditions and less likely to survive in an alkaline environment. The body can be kept at 7.356 by eating a healthy balance of the right food and you can change your body's PH balance by eating such foods. Algae and seaweed are 13 (97%) on the alkaline scale and are excellent in the detoxification process, but too much alkaline intake can in some cases also be bad for you. At the opposite end of the scale battery acid is 0% and the nearest drink to it on the PH scale is Coca Cola - never drink it.

There are four ways to detoxify, through perspiration, urination, respiration and excretion (PURE). Prepare to Detoxify your body by eliminating, or at least cutting down drastically upon the following:

- alcohol
- dairy products
- fried foods
- coffee
- eggs
- sugar & artificial sweeteners
- red meat
- processed foods
- hydrogenated oils (most vegetable oils)
- refined carbohydrates (white breads, pasta, white rice and pastries)

Increase consumption of the following:

- fresh fruits - All fruit is alkaline except banana which is slightly acidic. Pineapple is particularly good, healthy and high on the scale. It also lubricates the inside of your system

keeping everything flowing through smoothly.
- fresh vegetables
- whole grains (oats, whole wheat, rye, barley)
- olive oil
- legumes (lentils & beans)
- nuts & seeds
- green tea & oolong tea
- water

Other research suggests that fasting is of benefit even if only for one day a week or month. This could be water only or with some fruit in the morning. It is also suggested that one day fasting alternating with a day where you can eat what you wish is of benefit. One day fasting a month seems like a good idea as a starting point and beginning on a Monday, after the excesses of the weekend would be a sensible idea. You can build up from there to a more intensive regime. The 5-2 method is another excellent way of incorporating fasting into your life style, eat normally for 5 days and have a calorie restricted intake of about 500 calories for women and 600 for men for the next 2 days. That one day could be from 2pm to 2 pm. This way you do not go without food for a whole day and you are asleep for a big portion of that time. Equally fasting days can be whenever you want, consecutive or non consecutive. In theory you can eat what you like on feed days but apply commonsense with that one. Yet another variation is feasting & fasting on alternate days, but the message is the same. Research shows that we live much longer with a calorie restricted diet. In the great depression during the 1930's, one of the odd statistics was that people lived longer. Fasting in mice shows that new brain cells are generated and this also applies to humans. If the body is hungry the brain thinks you are too stupid to find food it will generate more brain cells to help you search. Research also shows that fasting slows down the aging process.

At the end of a fasting day, when you have used up all the glucose in your blood, the body resorts to energy stored in your liver. That's your main source of energy when you haven't eaten. After that the body switches to burning fat for energy.

Other research into the health benefits of fasting includes cutting down the risk of having a stroke, heart disease, type 2 diabetes and breast cancer, improving asthma symptoms and lowering the risk of Alzheimer's and other degenerative brain diseases. It is believed that both exercise and fasting can suppress the process that leads to these diseases. Fasting stimulates the production of antioxidants and proteins that protect cells from stress and disease. The internet provided the following further information and seems such a sensible approach:

- Research has shown that the weight loss and anti-aging health benefits that come from the fasting diet are related more to the changes that take place in the body as a result of fasting, rather than to the reduction in calories on the fast days.
- Short fasts give the digestive system and related organs some time to rest, especially the pancreas. This is the gland that produces insulin in response to carbohydrates and sugar. The body is helped to become more sensitive to insulin, which is one of the most important aspects of weight loss, because insulin regulates how the body uses and stores glucose and fat.
- Through regular, short term fasts, individuals report that on their 'non-fast days' they have a better sense of control over what they eat. They rarely eat out of boredom, and have a tendency to choose healthier foods.
- Often, rapid weight loss can be problematic, as people find they regain weight as soon as they return to 'normal' eating patterns. The 5-2 fast diet is a little different, as the calorie restriction only happens for two days a week. On the other five days, there is no dieting and no calorie counting, just normal eating, including a few treats, which is encouraged.
- The programme isn't presented as a short-term solution, but rather as a long-term way of eating, although once at your desired weight, you can choose to switch to a maintenance fast programme, which requires only one fast day per week.
- There appear to be many positive side effects and very few negative ones. The first couple of fast days can be a challenge, but once used to the way it feels to be hungry, many individuals say that the fast days become not only bearable, but enjoyable. Reports include feeling lighter, more alert, energetic and awake.
- Any food on the fast days should contain a reasonable amount of protein, as this helps to give the stomach a sense of fullness.

- Any diet that states that you can eat whatever you like on the other five days sounds too good to be true. Everyone should follow a balanced diet at all times, with plenty of vegetables, good quality protein, nuts, seeds, wholegrain, beans, legumes and fruit. By all means, enjoy the occasional treat, but don't make them an everyday occurrence.

In order for the body to successfully utilise the energy available within the food and use it properly, humans must take in the required amount of nutrients and minerals that our body requires and this can be done by having a balanced diet. A good diet will contain a balance of the following compounds:

Vitamins - Vitamins are required for various chemical reactions in the body. They can be found mostly in dairy products, fruits and vegetables.

Proteins - Proteins are also vitally important as part of a balanced diet. They have many functions, for example globular proteins in the body make enzymes, hormones and antibodies, all of which are essential to human existence. Proteins are the building blocks that grow and repair your body. They are needed not only for muscle but also for hair, skin and internal organs. Protein is found widely in meats with lean meat offering the best form of protein. Along with meat, nuts will provide a certain amount of protein.

Carbohydrates - Carbohydrates are compounds that consist of carbon, hydrogen and oxygen atoms. They are all about energy and are found in foods like fruits, vegetables, breads, pasta, and dairy products. Your body uses these foods to make glucose, which is it's main energy source. Glucose is a type of sugar that is broken down in the first step of respiration and can be used right away for energy or stored away to be used later.

Fats - Also known as lipids, fats produce twice the amount of energy that carbohydrates are capable of producing, due to the more complex nature of their structure. There are five different types of lipid, triglycerides, phospholipids, glycolipids, steroids and waxes. Once all fats were considered bad but things have changed.

Unsaturated fats are good and mostly found in cold water fish, nuts, oils, seeds, dark leafy greens and other vegetables. Pick your cooking oil carefully, either canola oil, sunflower or olive oil are best.

Not all fats were created equal, saturated fats are bad for you and are found in meat and dairy products, but they are still an important source of vitamins and minerals.

Minerals - These inorganic substances are required for a variety of reasons in the body. One such example is the requirement of iron, which is present in haemoglobin, in its role of absorbing oxygen from the lungs into the bloodstream. They are found naturally in the ground and soil. Therefore, primary food sources that contain the highest amount of minerals are foods that come from the ground, fruits, vegetables and grains. These food sources extract minerals from the soil as they grow. Secondary food sources for minerals are found in products from animals that eat plants, including meat and dairy products.

The following information is based upon an article in the Times, 'Eat Like an Olympian' that appeared after the Olympics Games and outlines some further ideas for you to consider:

- Exercise before breakfast to help your body become more efficient at burning fat. Ideally have dinner at 6pm and do some more light exercise an hour later.
- Eat more vegetables and less fruit. 9 portions a day comprising of 6 vegetable & 3 fruit.
- The latest research recommends eating butter instead of margarine. Margarine has been promoted as lowering cholesterol and blood pressure, as increasing weight loss and improving overall health. Now current thinking says it is one of the most chemically altered foods in our diets and cannot be promoted as healthy.
- Eat 4 meals a day rather than 3, such as an omelette for breakfast, a salad for lunch, soup in the afternoon, then meat and 2 vegetables, with no carbohydrate, for dinner.
- When cooking use virgin olive oil for salad dressings, but coconut oil, which has immune boosting effects, for frying.
- Avoid carbohydrates and fat in combination, such as in pizza.
- Have cottage cheese as an evening snack if hungry, it contains tryptophan which also helps you sleep.

- For weight loss, replace carbohydrates, such as rice, with vegetables, such as broccoli.
- A glass of red wine a day is good for you and you probably will not take too much convincing. Most research says that it is and it reduces the risk of coronary disease, however, too much and it is more likely to have a detrimental effect. Women are allowed one 5 ounce glass and men two glasses.

  Here are some additional suggestions for you to mull over and perhaps test out:

- Chewing your food 40 times is a simple way to lose weight. In an experiment those that chewed 40 times ate 12% less than those who chewed only 15 times. It is thought chewing for longer prevents overeating by giving the brain time to receive signals from the stomach that it is full.
- Walk an hour a day. Japanese scientists tracked 30,000 women over 12 years and those who walked for an hour a day and then went running, swimming or to the gym for a further hour once a week were less likely to get cancer. Fat tissue in the overweight produces more hormones than in slimmer people. Higher levels of these hormones including oestrogen and insulin can increase the risk of cancers.
- Breathing deeply can help to lower blood pressure. People who practice transcendental meditation have lower blood pressure than those who do not, as it keeps blood vessels open and lowers pressure on blood vessel walls.
- Smiling - the broader your smile the longer you live. Broad grins and wrinkles around the eyes reflect a positive outlook on life. That translates into better long term health. Research in the USA studied pictures of baseball players published in 1952 and ranked them according to whether they had no smile, a partial smile or a big grin. They then compared the photos to their life spans. Unsmiling 72.9 years, partial 75 and grin 79.9.
- As already stated always start your day with a solid healthy breakfast. Ideally fruit and fibre, perhaps cereal with a banana. Mix a variety of cereals with chopped up dry fruit, ground nuts, milk and low fat, low sugar pro-biotic yoghurt.
- Learn how to achieve balance in your diet. Alternate between fish and meat and eat salad with both.

- Eat in moderation. When eating out try either skipping the starters or afters.
- Eat fish at least twice a week, including salmon, sardines, mackerel or fresh tuna to get those essential omega 3 fatty acids. Oily fish are particularly beneficial.
- Vary your diet and remember your body does not need as much as you think it does. Eat fruit instead of biscuits and drink water instead of fizzy drinks.
- Have at least 5 portions of fruit and vegetables a day. A fruit juice at breakfast time counts as one. A salad at lunch and a piece of fruit as a snack all count. Aim to increase the number of portions to 9.
- Eat and drink most things in moderation. If you believe all the research you read then almost everything can be proved to be bad for you, for example, coffee. Perhaps the advantages may just about outweigh the disadvantages just use your commonsense.
- On special occasions or when out with friends do not be too hard on yourself. Life is here for you to enjoy and eating all the wrong things once in a while will not do too much harm. Do not deny yourself and try not to feel guilty.
- When you cut out sugar and salt you will miss them both at first. Coffee or tea without sugar will be unpleasant, chips without salt will not be so tasty, but if you persevere after a while everything will start to taste awful with sugar or salt as your body begins to adjust.
- On all days try to walk at least 10,000 steps. Buy a pedometer or fit band and wear it every day to give you an incentive.
- Walk or use a bicycle rather than the car for all your short journeys.
- Underpinning all these recommendations for diet is getting enough exercise. Go to the gym regularly and do enough work to get out of breath for at least 20 minutes. This needs to be a combination of aerobic and strengthening work.
- When over 40 you can get a free NHS health check.

Returning to exercise again you need to consider what and when to eat before and after exercise. Now that you are retired the ideal situation is to get up early and eat a light snack of mainly fruit, then go to the gym for your workout and return to a proper breakfast.

Various newspaper articles over many years have been unsupportive of almost all diets because even when combined with exercise they do not generally seem to work. Almost any change in life style works for the first 3-6 months then the weight comes rolling back. It is the type of food that we eat that is important. Successful diets do exist and have two things in common, they are low in sugar and high in fibre.

It could be a sad fact that some of today's children, our grandchildren, in the developed world could be the first to die younger than their parents because of their diet. This is partly our fault when a generation ago some off us were complicit in persisting with a diet containing too much sugar and dietary fat. Much has changed but even the pure 'Not from Concentrate' juices still contain too much sugar. It is far better to eat real fruit. The current diet of many children could result later on in diabetes, cancer, heart disease and possible dementia. The Mediterranean diet has always been championed as the ideal one. This includes olive oil, legumes (beans, lentils and peas), fruits, vegetables, salad (lettuce and tomatoes), unrefined grains, dairy products and eggs, fish and wine in moderation.

We release more insulin than we did thirty years ago caused by diets high in refined sugars. This in turn affects signals from the brain that tells us when to stop eating. In effect the brain sends out a signal to store more fat thereby allowing less stored fat to be burned. We all need to be eating more real food and cooking it from scratch just as our parents did after the Second World War. Cook your meals from fresh ingredients, meat and vegetables and cut down on all salt and sugar.

Sugar has recently been identified as the real evil baddie in our diets. In March 2014 the World Health Organisation advised adults to drastically reduce their intake from 22 teaspoons daily to just 6. As long ago as 1972 Professor John Yudkin raised concerns in his book 'Pure, White and Deadly'. He thought it was sugar and not fats that was causing the rising levels of heart disease because it had only relatively recently been introduced into our diets. Unfortunately the stakes were too high within the food industry, they claimed not believe him and sought to discredit his research. If you start reading more about it, one way or another it appears that sugar is going to help kill you.

Recent research suggests life expectancy is increasing so fast that half the babies born in 2007 will live to be at least 103, while half the

Japanese babies born in the same year will reach the age of 107. Other research claims that 85,000 people who are 65 today will go on to live to 100 and for women this represents one in seven. These are extraordinary statistics and life expectancy is apparently increasing by 5 hours per day in the UK. How living to 103 squares with the current obesity problem is beyond me. Figures from the NHS show that one in 10 children is obese when they start primary school and a third are obese by the time they leave. If you believe all the research 50% of 7 year olds are not doing enough exercise, particularly girls.

Essentially we, at our age, need to be thinking about the future and how we can maintain our independence. The aging process is more malleable (Check Newcastle 85+ study) than it was previously thought. It is important that you keep your body in good condition. It is vitally important to maintain the muscle that you have got and activity is the key factor. You need to use your muscles to keep you fit and healthy, it is a simple case of use it or lose it. If you can remain active in both mind and body you stay healthy in both mind and body. Strength training produces a growth hormone that is also an anti-aging hormone. You need to concentrate on keeping your muscles in good shape. It is well known that as you age you lose muscle, we all do. If you want to lead an active independent life then you have to keep it going and this requires some effort on your part.

Elderly people do have a reduced lung, heart and kidney function which can make us more vulnerable to travel-related illness. This vulnerability is all related to your level of fitness and where in the world you happen to be going. The fitter you are then the less likely you are to have any problems. Older travellers should get some sort of personal health risk assessment, particularly if you intend travelling to high risk areas, extreme climates, high altitude, tropical countries or even on long haul flights.

There is a lot of research going on at the moment and things are not as simple as they might seem but you will not go too far wrong if you just eat less and exercise more. Get yourself in good condition and you will find that a lot of much younger people that you meet on your travels, will be a lot less fit than you are. On several recent treks we have been by far the oldest in the group, but had to wait for younger members in the group to catch up. Incidents like that can give you a real boost.

Remember these 3 key facts:

- continue to exercise throughout your life
- always aim to eat a healthy diet
- steer well clear of tobacco

You have to be fit enough to carry your own rucksack

Exercise and diet go hand in hand and underpin each other, while smoking will hinder your progress in both.
As a summary take notice of the following maxims:

- drink more water, aim for at least 2 litres per day
- eat less - it is surprising how little food the human body really needs
- if you ate everything, but in moderation it would be a good start
- do more exercise
- eat more fruit - begin the day with some fruit as part of your breakfast
- if you feel hungry between meals eat fruit and feel free to eat fruit at any time
- eat more vegetables
- breakfast should be the biggest meal of the day
- eat regularly, say every 3 hours, rather than 5
- restrict your intake of refined sugar.
- eliminate salt from your diet as much as possible
- eat the correct combinations of food
- do not eat sweets, biscuits and cakes or anything with refined sugar, except on special occasions
- eat slowly and chew food properly
- drink less alcohol, ideally only one glass of wine per day - try to limit yourself to 2-3 units for women and 3-4 units for men - a pint of beer is almost 3 units and a glass of wine is 2.
- do not take in more calories than you actually need

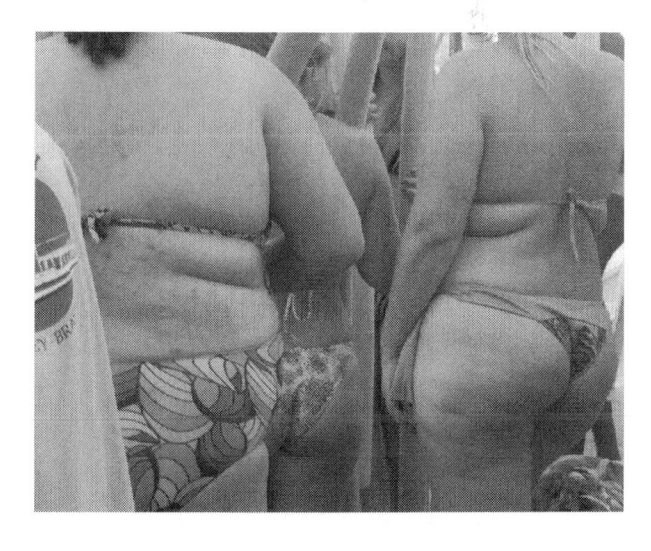

16 Communication

"Those who know nothing of foreign languages know nothing of their own."
Johann Wolfgang von Goethe 1749-1832

We were in one of the three museums in Annapadhura, the ancient capital of Sri Lanka. We love museums and can spent hours looking at ancient artefacts. One particular stone statue of a full size naked woman caught our attention mainly because her breasts had been broken off. This led to a discussion between us as to how this had happened. It was unlikely that it was accidental and was probably a deliberate act of vandalism. Against her better judgement my wife decided to ask the woman at the desk. She selected her words carefully pointing to the statue,

'Was it deliberately broken?'

'Do you speak English?' was the slow reply.

My wife then repeated her question and included some gestures, two slashing movements across her chest.

'You want the toilet?'

At this point she thanked the woman kindly and gave up. The lesson here is do not expect too much, Even if this woman had understood, it is unlikely she would have known such specific details.

If you are from an English speaking nation then you are at a massive advantage. English has become the world's main language. It may yet end up as a battle between English and Cantonese, but for the moment many people throughout the world are learning English and they want to practise it with someone like you.

After years of travelling you can become a bit sceptical when someone approaches and says, 'Hello'. The bottom line is that often they want something from you, probably money. If you are white, then automatically, they think you are rich and you might as well have 'ATM' stamped on your forehead. They may offer their services as a guide, ask you for a donation to some fictitious charity, sponsor the local football team or follow you saying that they just wish to practice their English, but in the end it is always about money. I must also say here that if you genuinely want a guide then some of these touts can be extremely good. It is not always like this, in Ho Chi Minh City we wandered into the park which was crowded with local university students. It was clear that they just wanted to talk and I was soon surrounded by twenty or so girls whilst all the boys clustered around my wife. Getting close to the locals in such a way can give you a deep insight into the country and the way people live. These students were learning English but realised the limitations of their professors. One of the questions that they asked was how many countries had I visited. I thought it to be over 40 and they were astounded. This got me thinking and I now keep this information as a list. (See chapter 26)

Almost anywhere in Asia away from tourist hotspots, people will want to talk to you. In India most people are naturally a little shy and always very polite. Lots of Indians will be on vacation themselves, exploring their own country. On the beach in Kerala we could see groups of students looking at us and giggling. An encouraging smile soon started a conversation and resulted in a lot of fun. They were all desperate to have a photograph of themselves with us, Europeans, white people. As it turned out they were all engineering students on a group vacation and never came into much contact with any foreigners. This happens throughout the world, when you get away from the main tourist areas, you become the centre of attraction. In rural Russia it was the Indian lady in a sari that became the big attraction.

Wherever you go it is best to learn a few simple words of the local language, it is always well appreciated and people will be more receptive to you. It may also be essential if say you happen to get lost, need the toilet or want a beer. In China we had a wonderful encounter using just sign language. People were hanging out of windows watching. What we have learnt is that everywhere almost everyone wants to talk, they just need you to create the opportunity. Just remember not to blow your nose as this is considered disgusting in public.

Learn some of the fundamental words and simple phrases, most of the major guide books will have a language section in the back giving you all the basic stuff:

- hello
- how much is it?
- I don't like it
- what is your name?
- please/thank you
- where is?
- goodbye

Even if you learnt just these few simple words it would be a good beginning. Phrase books may be old fashioned now but they still do the job and some might even linger on your bookshelf.

There is a big problem with accents. Even at home, in England regional accents can be hard to understand. Sometimes when watching a play on television set in Scotland we have to put the subtitles on, so what hope have foreigners got? Even if you speak good French, in rural France the locals will speak in their own patois, which is difficult to decipher, but go to Paris and there will be no problem at all. I have also found through experience, that women tend to listen more carefully and understand better than men. My wife understands French better than me, but I speak better French than her, so together we work well as a team.

There is an interesting app, 'iTranslate' that can be downloaded onto your iPad. Once set up if you speak into it, your sentence will be translated to a written and spoken form into any of about 25 different languages. It works well when translating English and is fun to use, particularly if you try speaking a foreign language in to it. You can then verify what exactly it was that you have said in French. I am sure your French accent will be better than mine but if you do not pronounce words correctly the results can leave your French friends somewhat perplexed. I tried asking the following in French,

'Ou puis-je trouver un hotel pas cher?' (Where can I find a cheap hotel?)

The first time it came back as,

'The simple when the club is partial author.'

Second attempt,

'Because when you go me cheap author.'

Third attempt,

'That when you'll maybe not expensive.'

At this point I thought that I was improving so tried once more,

'1009% than when I do my partial author.'

Well I blame the system, my French accent cannot be that bad. There is also an iPhone application with features that ensure the user pronounces words correctly. Google can also be used to translate, just copy and paste the text into the convenient online format of the Google Translate web service or free app. Unless you are a linguist or have a thorough command of a language then the problem is that every local person you meet abroad will know many more words than you do. You may be able to construct a simple sentence and be understood but will you understand the response? Because we are

English, one of the most widely spoken languages, many of us have become lazy with foreign languages. Wherever you travel in the world the locals will probably speak better English than you can speak their language. According to a recent survey two out of three British people admit that they cannot speak a single word of a foreign language. Another study put this figure at 22%, neither are probably correct but the inference is clear. One fifth did not even know what 'bonjour' meant. For many of us the incentive to learn is low, but this is the wrong attitude, you have to try a little and it will be appreciated.

It is amazing how some people just have a facility for language, the Dutch seem to be fluent in several and most Europeans will speak English with a clear well pronounced accent. We are lucky to have English as our mother tongue and could always get a job anywhere in the world teaching English as a foreign language. When speaking to foreigners or students visiting England try make every effort to speak slowly and clearly. I have seen English tourists abroad getting really frustrated because they cannot make themselves understood. The person I have in mind merely shouted louder and louder but needless to say it did not work. A poll of 2,000 adults conducted by travel website Hotels.com found that the over-55s were the age group most likely to have a go at speaking the local language. Younger people aged 16-24 were found to be some of the worst at phrase-making in an unfamiliar language, despite a foreign language being compulsory in schools up to the age of 14.

Merely pointing and gesturing can get you around most of the world successfully. Point to a beer and put up one finger, point to a lump of cheese and make a stroke down with your hand followed by one across and hopefully you will get half of it. For three slices of meat try three small swishes of the hand; if you are desperate enough you will find a way. In Russia a man asked us if we had an Elastoplast. He used his hands as if he was wrapping something around his finger and then held out two fingers crossed over, brilliant, we understood.

Some languages though, can be so difficult that our feeble attempts are hardly worth it. In Beijing as previously mentioned we took a taxi to the old town, which is the best place to go in the evening. It was easy, the concierge outside the hotel signalled for a taxi, gave the driver instructions, opened the door for us and off we went. The return journey was more difficult even though we had a map, knew where our hotel was and had the hotel's card. Nobody spoke English, they did not know where the hotel was and could not understand the map. It took seven taxis before we made ourselves understood and even then we got dropped off at the wrong place.

Blagging is a great skill to get you into places that are private, off limits or simply cost money. You can get in to lots of places just by talking a lot of persuasive nonsense, showing plenty of interest or using guile. It is a way of obtaining something by your powers of persuasion. It all sounds a bit devious and underhand but I am not talking about theft or deception, just talking people into doing things for you because you are such a nice person. The word arose in the late 19th century from the French 'blaguer' meaning to 'tell lies', although this is not going to be your intention either.

Apart from the Sir Donald Bradman museum we have blagged our way into lots of interesting places both public and private. A good strategy is just to walk in somewhere as if you own the place. Look confident and purposeful as you stride into your chosen destination and you might just surprise yourself.

In Bissau the capital of Guinea-Bissau there is not a great deal to see but there is an old Portuguese fort that is now occupied by the military. Looking through the gate the inside appeared to contain a few interesting buildings of some architectural merit. I strode in but never even got to the gate before an armed guard stopped me and sent me back. A few minutes later I approached from the other side. This time the guard was not sure what was going on and allowed me up to the entrance gate. The next guard let me through, and I was in, but not for long. One of the senior officers spotted me and I was taken to the check point. I did give a really good spiel, but the game was up and I was unceremoniously ejected, however, I did have a quick look around. Someone further down the chain of command was getting a little bit of a reprimand in the form of shouting, hopefully not due to me. The following day violence erupted inside the fort and four people were shot.

What cannot be said in words can always be done with photographs. Locals everywhere will be genuinely interested in you, your homeland and family. Keep some pictures of your children, grandchildren, house, garden and anything else of interest on your camera, phone or computer. This is an easy way to communicate, get to meet more local people and give them an insight into your culture. Here are some points about communication to consider further:

- Carry a pen and notepaper with you, so that you can write down figures and draw little pictures to explain things beyond your language skills. This can be more effective than speaking and avoids problems with accents. Then pass your pen and paper to the other person. There is a picture dictionary, 'Point it' that you could buy. This is a traveller's language kit consisting of a book of photographs of everything you could ever want. There is also, 'The Wordless Travel Book' and both are available on amazon.co.uk

- Never assume that someone will be able to speak English. Why should they? Apparently 82% of the world's population don't.
- Use body language, pointing, gesturing, miming, sounds, anything to get your message across.
- Never embarrass anyone by speaking slowly in a mocking tone just because you are getting impatient.
- Jokes are notoriously difficult to understand and explain in a foreign language. Be wary of offending people and their customs. 'Dublin' means something entirely different in Russian.
- Learn how to say 'do you speak English?' in the local language.
- You are the foreigner so do not get upset if the waiter brings the wrong dish, things get lost in translation, it is all part of the cultural experience and will make a great story on your return home.
- If you have an important question, like where do I get my bus that happens to be leaving in 5 minutes, remain calm.
- Even if you speak English slower and louder with a local accent, it is still English and you will not be understood. It is insulting and they are not deaf. This will of course not apply to readers of this book who will know better.
- Always be patient, when speaking in a foreign language, it will take longer to make yourself understood.
- If you cannot make yourself understood waving your arms around will not help, it is more likely to frighten locals away.
- Do not pretend you have understood something, simply nodding in agreement is pointless.
- There is no getting away from the fact that it is really the responsibility of the traveller to learn the local language of the country they visit.
- Faced with a communication breakdown always try to

remain humble with an open mind. You are the outsider, perhaps even a tourist!
- Remember that a smile never needs a translation.

Communication can be easy

17 Solo travelling

"I travel not to go anywhere, but to go. I travel for travel's sake. The great affair is to move." Robert Louis Stevenson 1850-1894

A national newspaper headline in 2011 said that almost half of the over-60s lived by themselves. On closer reading this was only 43% within a telephone survey of 3,000 adults. Another survey in 2009 concluded that age increased the likelihood of someone living alone, with 20% of 60-79 year-olds living alone compared to 34% of those 80 years and over. Most newly retired people are living with someone but there are a significant number of us coping on our own who still want to travel. Quite apart from all that happily married couples may want to go their separate ways when it comes to certain holidays. My wife is more than happy to let me do some serious trekking on my own as she would hate it. Quite often the majority of people on overland and trekking holidays are single travellers many of whom have a partner at home. Not everyone wants to suffer the hardships that such trips might entail. When my daughter went off travelling alone with very little money she cut a lonely figure as she tramped away with her huge rucksack on her back. We were proud of the way she managed to find jobs on route to fund it all, and after 3 years the inevitable happened, she met someone and never came back. As previously stated she had the confidence of youth on her side, but there is no reason why you cannot do something similar. You have greater experience and, hopefully, more money. Everything that has already been covered in this book still applies to solo travellers, but they do have some distinct advantages and problems.

For:
- One of the main advantages to travelling alone is the independence that it brings. You can fully indulge yourself and do exactly what you want, when you want, without having to think about the needs of others. Your time and budget are your own, there is no need to co-ordinate schedules with anyone else and you can just please yourself without consideration to others. If you want to get up late there will be no one waiting for you and complaining. Travelling alone allows you to be totally selfish and satisfy your every desire.

- All of the above means that you can be truly flexible. There will be no need to discuss any itinerary changes before implementing them, you only have your own opinion to consider. Deciding where to go and planning is all a lot easier if there you are on your own. Whatever your specific needs and wants are, they can be met more easily. If you want to travel, with only vague plans made beforehand, travelling alone will be perfect as you can decide exactly where and how you want to travel and adjust your trip accordingly.

- When travelling solo you will often get much more out of your holiday. You do not have to wait whilst your companion, or companions, bathe, get up, get ready, read the paper and indulge in their own whims. How you spend your day is your decision. No need to be trailing around the shops when you really want to be hiking in the hills. Travelling alone gives you total control and choice, and both of these enable you to use your time effectively. You will not have to go to places that you do not really want to visit. Free from the distractions of daily life, you will notice new things and can focus your full attention on absorbing what is really happening around you.

- One of the other great advantages to travelling alone is that there will be no one to argue or quarrel with. Arguments often happen when you travel and they can spoil the experience. Try six weeks with a friend in a small tent overlanding, that will test out the strength of your relationship. If you change your mind nobody will argue or question your decision. If there are two of you then one always has to consider the needs of the other. More than two then things get even trickier and a leader may have to emerge.

- You are dependent upon yourself and nobody can blame you if things do not work out as expected. You can be far more flexible with nobody to blame but yourself for mistakes. You become more curious and active in a different environment. Any unique discoveries you make will add to your individual experiences and they will be yours alone.

- You can keep going until you are tired and rest for as long as you need to. It is not necessary to travel at the pace of the slowest and if you want to search out an art gallery, botanical gardens or remote waterfall then it is your decision alone. Solo travel can be a great opportunity for reflection when you are moving at your own pace.

- Being on your own will lead to more communication with other people, such as the locals and other travellers. You are bound to meet interesting people and they will tell you about the best sights that are off the beaten track and away from the tourist traps. You will be more likely to meet and make new friends and this is one of the joys of travelling alone, maybe you will team up with them for a short time. As a solo traveller more backpackers or other independent travellers will be inclined to strike up conversations with you, and maybe invite you along on their adventures. On your own the initiative will also be with you to strike up new conversations and friendships; if you are in a group you will be far less approachable. It is only possible to build up a certain amount of trust with your new found friends, it may be alright to have dinner with them but keep your money and valuables close to you.

- Travelling solo on your trip can give you the best of both worlds, the option to meet new people and socialize whenever you want and the freedom to decide when you want some time alone.

- Travelling alone will give you the unique opportunity to discover yourself. It all sounds a bit fanciful, but it could be a life changing experience, as you set off on your journey of self-discovery. Your stress levels will drop as you have more time and solitude for reflection. How will you react in certain situations and face up to the challenges and problems that will inevitably occur? From this you should gain a deeper understanding of yourself and what really matters to you. Maybe you will end up more self-assured, calmer and confident. It is truly satisfying to know that you have done something quite challenging all on your own. No one has been there to help or back you up, it was all down to you.

The important thing is that you know your own limits, discover your own personality and keep an open mind. You will grow in confidence as you create your own adventures.

- With only yourself you will begin to enjoy your own company, start to understand yourself in a new way that was not possible before you stepped out of your comfort zone. You will have more time to observe people in your surroundings whereas in a group communication is invariably inwards.

- There will be no need to compromise on the price level of the facilities you use or the places you visit. If you want to go to an expensive restaurant one night and eat in the street the next you will not be upsetting anyone one a different travel budget to yours.

- There is a growing trend for women to be travelling on their own. This can only be a good sign, that world is a safer place to travel around, as long as the right precautions are taken. Older women on their own tend to avoid unwanted male attention and people in general can be more helpful.

- Although we are retired sometimes it seems that the one thing we still do not have is time. Solo travelling will create time for reflection and for testing yourself out in new situations.
  http://solotravelerblog.com
  www.solosholidays.co.uk
  www.justyou.co.uk

Against:
- Travelling alone is not for the fainthearted. Everything will be your responsibility and there is no safety blanket of a companion. If you lose your money or your passport, there will be no friend to help. If you become sick you will still have to try and get through each day on your own. You alone will have to sort out such problems.

Wander around interesting places on your own

- Having had all those wonderful experiences there will be nobody to share them with. Nobody to talk over the day with at the restaurant or in the hotel, nobody to share the expenses or take photos of you.

- Renting a car will always be expensive. Even when getting a taxi there will be nobody to split the fare with.

- Travelling alone may not be the first choice for the less confident traveller. You need to be self assured about meeting and speaking to new people and involving yourself in new situations. If this is not you, you might be better off in a group, it all comes down to your individual character.

- One big disadvantage is the single supplement charged by most companies. Some companies do not charge extra but normally you will have to pay an additional amount to cover a company's extra costs, even if it is for the privacy of your own tent. At worst you could end up paying double. A single room in a hotel is always more than half the cost of a double. If you are happy to stay in a hostel you will pay for a bed rather than a room. If you intend travelling with a company

then check out companies that offer to match you up with another solo traveller. A quick internet search will throw up some ideas.
www.gadventures.com
www.intrepidtravel.com

- There will be times when you feel lonely. It will not always be comfortable dining alone in a crowded restaurant. Loneliness is inevitable but can be turned to your advantage if you allocate this time for meditation.

- There are some activities that are difficult do alone, such as isolated hikes but in a densely populated area like a major city, then it may well be an advantage being able to do as you please.

- There will be nobody to push you out of your comfort zone or perhaps be the voice of reason.

- Perhaps the biggest problem is the question of safety. There is always greater safety in numbers. However, there is also greater danger to a group of unprepared travellers rather than a single prepared one. Try to stay in public areas and be wary about who you tell where you are staying.

- It is safer if you choose who to befriend rather than someone else choosing you. There will be nobody to watch your back or your luggage when you nip in to the toilet, and you are more vulnerable to theft, scams and criminals. Keep to open and public places particularly at night.

- You are an easier target particularly if you are a female alone. You have to carry all your own gear, but always be wary of anyone who approaches you offering to help. Lying a little can be a good tactic, such as, 'I am waiting for a friend.'

- You need to act confidently even if you aren't and if you are unsure about something then don't do it. Try to make sure that you already know where you are going and plan all your journeys ahead. Leave a detailed itinerary with someone at home and contact them regularly.

- Avoid looking like a tourist and try to blend in with the locals.

If you decide to go it alone the world is yours. You do not have to think of anyone except yourself. Go to the places that you have always dreamed about. There can be no excuses. You will often return home from travel with a transformed view of the world and as a slightly changed and enriched person.

Not everyone may want to go to Highgate cemetery with you. To go to the most interesting section you must book in advance. It has some of the finest funerary architecture in the world and is the final resting place of Karl Marx.

18 Insurance

"See the world. It's more fantastic than any dream made or paid for in factories. Ask for no guarantees, ask for no security."
Ray Bradbury 1920-2012

Everybody needs to have travel insurance. Normally it is more economical to buy it for the whole year and it will cover all your trips abroad. If you are only going for a weekend to Paris then you might just consider your European Health Insurance Card (It used to be known as E111) to be enough. It probably will be, but you are still taking a small risk. If you 'Google' it, plenty of unofficial sites will charge you £20 for obtaining it for you. The quickest and easiest way to obtain an EHIC is online where it will cost you nothing at:

www.dh.gov.uk/travellers
www.nhs.uk/ehic

The EHIC really is not a substitute for travel insurance. It may not cover all your health costs should you fall ill, it does not cover repatriation costs and only entitles you to reduced cost, or sometimes free, healthcare in state-run hospitals in any EEC country. It entitles you to the same treatment as a local. This is extremely useful in emergencies, and means if it's free for them, it's free for you. Keep it on you at all times when you're away to ensure you're covered.

Do not even think of going on a long trip abroad without adequate cover. You never know what could happen, it is not just for medical cover but cancellations, loss of luggage, theft and all sorts of other things that probably will not happen, but just might. Insurance is not for things that you plan for, it is for all the other things, delayed flights, other reckless idiots unwittingly involving you in an accident, things that you do not plan for. It is often long term travellers and budget travellers who feel they are invincible, which is of course so far from the truth. Loss of your personal belongings is often the main reason most people buy travel insurance, but is arguably the least important; your things can be replaced, but your health often cannot.

It may be unpleasant but try to imagine you have become seriously ill, or had a car accident whilst travelling, would you be covered for treatment in the country you are in? Would you have the support of an emergency assistance team to make sure you get the best treatment? Good travel insurance should provide you with this peace of mind. Perhaps a close family member becomes ill or a catastrophe wipes out your destination, there are all sorts of things that could just happen. How much would a specially chartered medical flight, with medical assistance on board cost? It is no longer, 'hope I die before I get old', but more like, 'I wanna live forever'.

The following are examples of what you may be charged for minor medical care on a cruise ship:

- An abscess that had to be lanced, £250 and it only took 2 minutes.
- An elderly gentleman fell injuring his arm. He went to get it checked but nothing was broken. An injection and some painkillers cost him £500.
- A woman came out with a rash following an allergic reaction. She had some blood tests and steroid injection plus another injection the following day. Total cost £2000.

Pick your insurance company with care and make sure it covers your needs. Do not automatically accept the insurance offered to you by your travel company as you will probably be paying well over the odds, up to three times as much. You may be able to get a year's cover for the same cost. Some cheap airline and holiday websites may automatically add expensive travel cover when you book. Make sure you double-check the full cost, and remove any unwanted policies before paying, probably by un-ticking some boxes online.

Look at several companies and make a comparison. It is worthwhile spending a little more to ensure that all your requirements are fulfilled and it is tailored to suit your needs. 'Staysure' are a leading company that market themselves as over 50's insurance specialists and suit my own current personal requirements. Fortunately we have only ever had need to make two claims on the policy, once for the camera that was stolen in Ecuador when the company paid up without a quibble and secondly when my wife's rucksack was stolen, and they did not pay up. This was because the bag was left unattended by her. It was in a pile in the reception of a hotel along with other members of our group with lots of other bags. She was just unlucky, but we should not have left it out of our sight. A good insurance policy is going to give you that essential peace of mind when you are out there on the road where hundreds of different things just could happen to you. It is better to be safe than sorry. Most companies will offer single trip insurance, longer stay insurance plus annual multi-trip insurance. You can generally opt for some sort of basic cover or comprehensive for all your holiday needs. Some companies offer over 65's policies and special insurance for those with medical conditions. All companies put their premiums up as you become older, normally in 5 year stages starting at age 66. We are seen as a higher risk and more likely to suffer health problems no matter how fit we happen to be. It feels like discrimination, but the insurance industry only works on averages. You will get charged extra for medical conditions but will not get a discount for being fit and healthy. As you do get older be aware that policies may only be for a single trip, typically when you are over 80. Maybe you will have settled down by then, but if not you can still get cover, even up to age 100. Staysure advertise that they cover 220 pre-existing medical conditions as standard up to the age of 85, and most other companies offer similar conditions. All of them will be listed in the policy, from athletes' foot to umbilical hernia. You do need to consider your pre-existing medical conditions and you must declare them to the insurance company if you want cover. For example taking statins for high cholesterol may mean that you are more likely to have a heart problem, a stroke say, therefore you may have to pay a higher premium, high blood pressure though is one of the 'free' conditions. You can opt to not declare pre-existing conditions on the basis that you will not have cover for any problems arising from them. There is usually an easy medical screening process on line or over the phone for health issues such as high blood pressure, diabetes, heart conditions and arthritis. For travel outside of Europe premiums may double and cost even more to cover North America or the Caribbean.

A quick internet search for holiday insurance will throw up thousands of companies all clamouring for your business. The market has improved in recent years with more insurers looking for a slice of the baby boomer market. The problem is going to be finding the right company to suit your needs. Once you have investigated a few sites telephone for a quote. You will have to endure the tedium of dozens of questions but keep your requirements the same so that you can compare like for like. It is a competitive business and some companies will match or undercut other quotes just to get your business. Once they have you signed up you will be more likely to renew with them.

I met, Tony, a fit 78 year old, travelling semi-independently in Russia. He was a Barclays premium customer and a fee of £17 a quarter entitled him to world wide travel until he was 80. He was trying to fit in as much as possible during the next 2 years as he thought holiday insurance would become too difficult to obtain, and too expensive when he turned 80. This was a great deal that has now been withdrawn. If you find a good deal then grab it.

If you want to go on a really long trip, of say 3 months, and are aged over 65 then things become more difficult. Insurance companies will only cover shorter trips.

www.staysure.co.uk will cover over 65's for trips up to 35 days on an annual multi-trip policy and up to 9 months on a single trip long stay policy.

www.theaa.com/insurance/travel gives members a 10% discount but limit trips to 45 days. They will cover long stay single trips up to 185 days.

www.freedominsure.co.uk normally cover trips for 31 days but will consider longer single trips on an individual basis.

This is probably sufficient for most trips but not a lot of use if you plan to roam the world during the British winter. If you can, then do your longer more difficult trips before you hit 66, until this point you can often get up to a 100 day upgrade for a small extra premium.

When you turn 75 it will become even more difficult to find a company that will offer multi-trip policies, you may have to insure all your holidays separately. As you age it will become more and more expensive and is something we all have to face up to. Insurance costs could become a major part of the holiday cost. However, do not put off your travelling; the sooner you get started the better.

Check out these companies regularly as conditions change from time to time but were correct at the time of writing:

www.avantitravelinsurance.co.uk offer over 65's an annual multi-trip policy covering a trip of up to 60 days and a single trip of up to 365 days.

www.world-first.co.uk/home/travel-insurance/seniors.aspx has two levels of cover for their annual multi-trip policy, 31 days and 62 with an upper age limit of 75 years. This will allow any number of trips. A single trip is covered for up to 186 days with an age limit of 99 years.

www.ageuk.org.uk/products/insurance/travel-insurance offer cover for 31 days which can be extended up to 45 for an extra premium and up to 140 for a single trip. There is no upper age limit and costs depend upon medical conditions.

www.freespirittravelinsurance.com will cover anyone up to any age with pre-existing medical conditions but only up to 45 days or 94 on a single trip policy.

www.flexicover.co.uk have annual multi-trip that covers up to 35 days but can be extended to 50 and a single trip can be up to 100 days.

www.saga.co.uk offer up to 45 days cover for a trip within a maximum 120 travel days for the year. A single trip policy covers up to 90 days. There is no upper age limit but pre-existing medical conditions will determine the cost.

www.onestop4.co.uk/travel seems to offer just about everything if you have a pre-existing medical problem.

Make some comparisons before you decide who to go with:

www.money.co.uk/travel-insurance Make a comparison of all that is on offer. A worthwhile discount is offered by booking online.

www.moneysavingexpert.com/insurance/cheap-travel-insurance has a link to over 65's, 70's.80's and 85's insurance that is really worth exploring.

www.moneysupermarket.com/travel-insurance also make comparisons.

Whatever insurance you go for you need to make sure that the cover is adequate and thoroughly covers your needs. To begin with make certain that the medical expenses limit is high enough. Staysure offer a basic cover of £5,000,000 and a comprehensive of £10,000,000. Do not go for a cheap policy. Make sure the policy covers any extra charges, such as a hospital stay or emergency repatriation. Are you covered for being flown home, natural disasters or visiting certain countries? Never assume anything, read the small print in your policy and phone the company directly if necessary. For visiting any obscure and rarely visited countries ask your company directly. Losses incurred through terrorist activity could need clarifying. I asked my company about cover if I was taken hostage and held for ransom.

'No Sir, that is not the sort of thing we cover.' was the polite reply.

Do not try to economise, older people should pay the extra premium for additional insurance protection.

Most people now have lots of electronic gadgets that they travel with, phones, tablets, cameras and music players amongst others. Companies tend to only offer a low basic cover for such items with optional upgrades. Check with your basic home insurance to see if you already have cover.

Your company should issue you with a simple insurance certificate with all the essential information on it including all the twenty-four hour emergency telephone numbers. One simple reference number should be enough in an emergency.

Other basic things to check are:

- What is the amount of cover for cancellations, curtailment and trip interruption if you miss pre-paid organised excursions, transport connections or hotel bookings?
- What is covered in case of a missed departure? Is this going to be covered by the airline?
- What happens if your travel company goes bankrupt and you are stuck in another country?
- What is their policy cover for your personal luggage and valuables? Just in case of loss you should retain all receipts. Find out what the excess is on this and other possessions if you should make a claim.
- How much basic cover is provided for lost, damaged or stolen possessions like jewellery, baggage, documents, etc?
- Best not to lose any money or your passport but if you do you will need a police report. Most companies will have a relatively low limit on this.
- It is a good idea to use your credit card to pay for holidays you book directly yourself in the UK. If it is for an amount over £100 then you will be protected by the Consumer Credit Act.
- What happens if your travel provider goes bust before you leave?
- What is the maximum amount of legal expenses per person or per policy if there is a travel dispute?

- What cover is there for emergencies, civil unrest in the country visited, terrorism or anything similar that causes you to return home early? I phoned my company up and asked if I was covered for hi-jacking, and I was.
- Remember you will not be covered if you venture into any country not recommended by the Foreign and Commonwealth Office.
- What happens if you injure someone else?
- If you are going to North America then extra cover will be required to cover costly medical bills.
- There will be a number of general exclusions in your policy that you should be aware of, many of which will be down to your behaviour. These include, needless exposure to danger, claims arising from illegal activities, drugs, alcohol abuse and fighting. All fairly obvious and not applicable to sensible mature people like us. There are some grey areas involving taking due care, at some stage you may well have a swift pint but supposing you have your bag snatched whilst being somewhat pie-eyed?
- If you insure just before you leave for your holiday but after having booked you will have no cover for a cancellation. Take out your policy when a holiday is booked.
- What exactly is not covered by your policy? If you are the adventurous type, and I hope that you are, then you probably need to have a personal chat with your insurance provider. Are you covered for bungee-jumping, trekking, jet skiing, quad biking, scuba diving, horse riding and walking? The list could go on and on. Extreme activities such as hang gliding will not be covered or will at least incur an extra premium. My policy has three long lists of activities for which I have varying amounts of cover. It is quite revealing to see what is not covered and makes for interesting reading, so I have listed them in full. You may well already have unwittingly participated in several activities that you never realised you had no cover for. Trekking for example maybe one of the common activities we are all involved in but is only covered up to 2,000 metres altitude.

What sort of personal accident coverage is covered? My policy lists cover as £20,000 regardless if it is the loss of one eye, permanent total disablement or death for the following sports and activities on a non-competitive and non professional basis:

athletics	rambling
badminton	rollerblading
banana boating	rounders
baseball	running
basketball	safari
bmx cycling	scuba diving (up to 30 metres)
bowls	skate boarding
cricket	snorkelling
cross country running	squash
curling	surfing
cycling	swimming
fell running/walking	tennis
glacier walking	trekking (under 2,000 metres)
golf	triathlon
heptathlon	volleyball
hiking (Under 2,000 metres altitude)	walking
	water polo
jogging	wind surfing
netball	yachting (crewing-inside
orienteering	territorial waters)
ringos	

The following sports and activities are also covered but no cover is applied in respect of personal injury or personal liability claims. This means there is cover for medical treatment but not for permanent disablement to the insured and others:

archery	gaelic football
boxing training	go karting (recreational)
camel/elephant riding	horse riding (not polo, jumping or hunting)
canoeing/kayaking (inland/coastal)	
	jet skiing
field hockey	marathon running
fishing (fresh water and deep sea)	mountain biking
	parascending (over water)
flying as a passenger (private/small aircraft)	roller hockey/street hockey
	wake boarding
football	water skiing

white/black water rafting (grade 1-4)

zorbing/hydrozorbing

For this next group of activities no cover was offered for any claims arising from participation:

abseiling
American football
animal conservation/game reserve work
bungee jumping
boxing
canoeing/kayaking (white water)
canyoning
caving/cave diving
clay pigeon shooting
cross channel swimming
dry skiing
fencing
flying as a pilot
gliding
gymnastics
handball
hang gliding
high diving
horse jumping
horse racing
hot air ballooning
hunting/shooting
hunting-on-horseback
hurling
kite surfing/land boarding/buggying
lacrosse
team sports played in competitive contests
war games (non armed forces)
water skiing
weight-lifting

martial arts
microlighting
motorcycling
motor racing (all types)
mountaineering
mountain boarding
paintballing
parachuting
paragliding/parapenting
parasailing
parascending (over land)
point-to-point
polo
potholing
professional sports
quad biking
rock climbing
rock scrambling
rowing (inland and coastal)
rugby
sailboarding/sandboarding
sand yachting
scuba diving (unqualified)
scuba diving (over 30 metres qualified)
shark feeding/cage diving
sky diving
steeple chasing

white/black water rafting (grade 5-6)
wrestling
yachting

I am not even sure what some of these activities are, but as it is, I have regularly participated in fifteen of these uncovered activities and probably some more which are not even listed. How many have you engaged in?

If you have to make a claim then do it as soon as you possibly can. If possible get a police report and make sure that you have all the correct documentation. It is very useful if you have retained receipts for everything that you have bought over the years, but somewhat impractical. Even a photograph of you wearing the clothes you have had stolen is better than nothing. If you are really organised and obsessive, photograph all your gear just in case. Insurance companies are in business to make money and will find a loophole to avoid paying out if they can. If you left your bag unattended at the station then it is not worth the effort of filling in the forms. Most companies will expect you to take 'reasonable care' of your possessions, they may not pay out if you leave your iPad overnight in your car. If you lose your luggage then save any tags, boarding passes or any other related paper work.

You must make sure you get to the airport in time. Allow for any possible delays. You will not be covered if the alarm did not go off and you did not get out of bed in time. If you check in early you will not be the passenger that gets 'bumped', with the pressure to fill planes to capacity it is not uncommon for seats to be double-booked. If you are 'bumped' you will probably end up on a later flight and will be entitled to compensation. This will be determined by the length of your flight and when you eventually arrive.

If your flight is delayed your holiday insurance should cover you for any money spent on hotels and food. The airline also has responsibilities to you and can be pursued for a claim. They should make sure you have a ticket for a free meal and if the delay is a lengthy one, overnight accommodation. Consider the following case:

December 5th 2010- Our overnight flight from London Heathrow to Nairobi was cancelled at the last minute. 'Cancelled' was the official announcement. Disgruntled passengers were milling around asking questions and were told that there was a technical fault. The airline staff were talking amongst themselves and one of them mentioned to another passenger that the plane was now going to the USA. Effectively it appeared that we had all been 'bumped'. We were told nothing more, given meal vouchers and put up overnight in a hotel. In the morning a cancellation letter was put under the door and we were to take off 24 hours later than scheduled. All passengers were offered an amount of air miles according to the class of seat booked. Adult economy passengers were entitled to 12,500 miles.

December 6th 2010- Our plane was over full, some passengers could not get on and were offered alternative options of travel to Nairobi. Both the check in desk and the flight help desk told us that it wasn't the first time that this had happened. It looked like two under full flights had been lumped together.

February 17th 2011- On our return home a letter was sent to the airline outlining our complaints. It was a longish letter but the main thrust of it was,

'EC Regulation No 261/2004; Article 14.2 says that, passengers whose flights of 3500 or more kilometres are delayed for more than 4 hours are entitled to meals, calls and a €600 cash compensation - provided they fly out of or to a EU destination'.

March 11th 2011- The airline replied apologising for their unintentional delay. Basically they said that there was a 'technical problem that could affect the safety of the aircraft, therefore, we had no choice but to delay your flight to maintain your safety and our unblemished safety record'. In line with EU regulations they did not pay compensation for situations beyond their control including:

- weather conditions
- air traffic decision
- unforeseen flight safety shortcomings
- industrial dispute
- political instability
- security risks

They did express sorrow and regret and as such would credit us with a further 4,246 air miles, which we made sure not to accept.

March 2011 - The Air Transport Users Council was contacted by email who said that 'cancellation cases should be taken on an individual case to case basis'.

March 18th 2011 - The airline was contacted by email in which we questioned their explanations. 'You state that our plane delay was due to flight safety short comings but I do not believe that this is correct. We were not told whether the problem was completely out of the ordinary and something that you could have taken steps to avoid or whether you made adequate arrangements for a substitute plane to be available'. This confusion about what exactly was wrong with the plane was a key point.

Also while at the hotel several other passengers, who were with us at the airport, including one who was a friend of one of the crew, told us that there was in fact a technical problem but NOT with our plane. We were told that the plane going to America with a full passenger list had the technical problems and that our plane which was less than half full was switched to the American schedule. When we had checked in the next day we had asked the check in person if this was correct and he confirmed that it was indeed the case and that he was very sorry but assured us that we would 'definitely get some compensation from the airline as they always look after their customers'. We restarted our legitimate claim for compensation.

March 29th 2011 - The airline responded expressing regret, 'A non-routine defect developed that could not be rectified.' They went on further to say, 'I realise that you heard conversations that suggested otherwise, however, since the defect was one that affected the safety of our aircraft, we remain unable to comply with your request for compensation under EU 261/2004.'

April 5th 2011 - The CAA replied requesting copies of all correspondence relating to the claim and a reply time of about 4 months.

May 5th 2011 - The airline sent a letter of regret that they were 'unable to resolve this matter to your full satisfaction'.

November 17th 2011 - The Consumer Affairs Officer from the Civil Aviation Authority replied to us after discussing the case with the airline. Briefly the airline had changed their tack and were now saying that the flight had been delayed and not cancelled. 'Unfortunately EC Regulation 261/2004 does not make provision for compensation for flight delays'. However, in a recent, similar test case of November 2009, the European Court of Justice made a decision that 'passengers who are delayed suffer a similar damage to the damage suffered by passengers whose flights have been cancelled and therefore the compensation should be the same'. Some UK airlines asked for clarification upon this ruling and on August 10th 2010, the Administrative Court of the High Court of Justice granted permission for questions relating to the case to be referred to the ECJ. The Court placed a 'stay' on further proceedings giving airlines a legitimate, if not temporary excuse not to award compensation. Pending a definite ruling the CAA were unable to help. They suggested taking action in a County Court under Small Claims procedures.

December 2011 - The agents who booked the flight for us said that they would look into the matter for us, but not while anyone else was dealing with it.

October 23rd 2012 - A ruling by a Court of Justice European Union (CJEU) clarified that passengers on flights delayed for three or more hours should be entitled compensation, in the same way they can if their flight was cancelled. These rights apply to all flights from European Union airports.

November 22nd 2012 - The BBC Watchdog programme reported upon all the new changes brought in by the CJEU,

'Airlines carrying passengers within Europe or in to Europe are bound by these regulations that say they should compensate you if your flight is cancelled, overbooked or you are denied boarding. Following a court judgement last month you're now **also** entitled to a payout if your flight is held up for more than three hours. And, as that rule applies retrospectively, it affects delayed flights going back seven years. But some airlines don't always follow these rules, leaving passengers frustrated at best, and out of pocket at worst'.

January 5th 2013 - An email was sent to the airline 'Flight Consumer Rights' section restarting the complaint dated, February 17th 2011 which was previously on hold. The email re-outlined the case and further stated that, 'At the airport, our airline did not give us written details of our rights under the 'Denied Boarding Regulation', as I know they are obliged to do so'.

Now with the new ruling by the CJEU behind us we were in a stronger position.

'I have written to you on several occasions and people keep changing their minds about the reason for the delay and or cancellation. I was also told by you that all claims under the 216/2004 EU initiative were on hold and that nothing further could be done. I now understand that on 23 October 2012, the Court of Justice of the European Union re-opened this and passed a judgment which said consumers who arrived at their destination three or more hours late could claim compensation and that people can backdate any claim to February 2005'.

April 2013 - Further letter sent to the airline pointing out what the BBC Watchdog programme reported.

May 10th 2013 - It was reported that airlines were still avoiding paying compensation by exploiting a loophole. The wording that airlines are not responsible if the delay is caused by 'extraordinary circumstances' can be interpreted in various ways causing passengers to lose out on claims. 'Passengers who are delayed due to strikes and poor weather aren't entitled to compensation as it's widely accepted that those events are beyond the airlines control. However, airlines are also classing some mechanical faults found onboard the aircraft as 'extraordinary circumstances' to avoid payouts'.

June 1st 2013 - We received 2 cheques each for €600 as compensation. Enclosed with it was a note with just one sentence, 'Having reviewed your claim and in accordance with regulation EU261/2004 and in full acceptance of all your claims in this matter we enclose 2 cheques in the sum of £512.86 (equivalent to 600 Euros) payable to yourself and Mr Blewitt'.

The essential thing is to persevere, airlines will make it very difficult for passengers to claim, fobbing them off with offers of air miles, vouchers for free meals and filling their letters with legal jargon. When you make a claim it is unlikely that the airline company will roll over and compensate you adequately. You have to refuse their offers and it will take a lot of hard work and correspondence to persuade them otherwise. If you think that you have a valid claim then do not give up. Polite and well argued persistence will eventually work. Most people are going to give up fairly quickly and airlines rely upon this apathy. Remember that you now have up to six years to put in a claim.

www.moneysavingexpert.com/insurance/cheap-travel-insurance t for small claims advice.

www.bbc.co.uk/programmes/p00zkz1k/features/flight-compensation watchdog.

www.caa.co.uk The Civil Aviation Authority.

www.travelclaimsservices.com They may be able to help if you have a problem with your travel insurance company. TCS is an independent company that can operate either as an extension to an established claims handling operation, or as a full third party claims outsource facility.

Many years ago on a package holiday we arrived at our Spanish hotel to find it was fully booked. We spent several hours in the hotel lobby followed by even longer on the beach waiting until the travel company sorted out alternative arrangements, by which time it was late in the evening. That night was spent in a spare room further down the coast and the following morning we were flown out to a small villa in Majorca and had a wonderful time. On our return we put our complaints to the company even though we had really enjoyed what was in effect upgraded accommodation. The company initially offered us £50 off the next holiday, then 2 one-way tickets to Cairo. We declined both and decided to take the case to the Small Claims Court. At that time it cost £50 but is still a reasonably priced service. £25 -210 for the initial claim fee when done online, a £40 court allocation fee for claims over £1500 and a £25-325 hearing fee to be paid if and when your case gets to court. The travel company decided to settle out of court and gave all our money back to us - doubled!

Does your insurance cover you?

19 Looking after things back home

"We wish to learn all the curious, outlandish ways of all the different countries, so that we can "show off" and astonish people when we get home. We wish to excite the envy of our untraveled friends with our strange foreign fashions which we can't shake off."
Mark Twain 1835-1910

Leaving your house unoccupied for weeks or even months is worrying. What if someone breaks in? Who is going to look after all your house plants and garden? What about the cat or other pets? Do you disconnect the battery in the car? The mail? Bills to pay? Did you shut the front door properly? Alter the Central heating? What if?

If you are going away for any length of time your home insurance company will have some stipulations. We had to have a burglar alarm fitted and this has to be set. All the windows have to be locked and someone has to come and check inside the house regularly, ideally daily, and at the minimum weekly. This is to make sure there are no problems such as water leaks. The reasoning is that if there is a leak then the water can be turned off to prevent further damage. Insurance company policies will vary but ours states that we are only fully covered for the first 60 days of any holiday. The house would be still covered for say fire damage but not for damage caused by vandals breaking in and theft. What we did not realise for sometime was that these 60 days will recommence if someone stays at your house, even if it is just for one night. So offer a relative or friend a free weekend away.

You need to know exactly what your insurance company requires from you so that they cannot wriggle out of a claim. Going through all the questions on the phone for a house insurance quotation is absolutely necessary but mind numbingly tedious,

'Do you have window locks sir?'
'Yes.'
'They must be locked whenever you go away.'
'Supposing I go away for just the weekend?'
'Yes they must still be locked.'
'How about if the house is left empty for the day?'
'Yes sir they must be locked or any claim may be invalidated.'
'But my house is quite large and there are 46 separate locks.'

'If entry is gained through an insecure window you will not be covered.'

'Supposing I just pop round to a neighbours to borrow a cup of sugar?'

'Unfortunately sir that is the policy of the company.'

I did not pursue this particular application any further and I am sure that the words 'reasonable' or 'unreasonable' should have figured somewhere.

During a winter's absence the insurance company will require you to keep the house at a certain temperature to stop any possibility of pipes freezing up. Turn down the thermostats, time the central heating to come on for a short period first thing in the morning and in the evening, just to keep the system ticking over. That winter you will save a lot on your heating bills.

To begin with it helps if you get on very well with your neighbours. Most people will not mind at all doing some simple jobs, such as collecting your mail and keeping an eye open for anything strange; this can become a reciprocal arrangement for when they go on holiday. We let several neighbours know our travel arrangements and are lucky enough to have one wonderful neighbour who will collect all the post and check the inside of the house periodically. A relative nearby who is good at DIY is on call in case a fence blows down or there is some damage to the house. Another friend in the next street is more than happy to water all the plants because she wants us to do the same for her. So with a bit of social networking it is possible to get a lot of things covered. We send all our 'helpers' an email attachment giving all the vital details and how to contact us and each other.

I have close friends who at 60 retired to gated accommodation in an apartment within a country house. Despite my jibes about this being 'sheltered' accommodation at times I feel quite jealous of their situation. They have no garden to look after and no responsibility for house maintenance, apart from an annual fee. They have a perfect life style and can therefore, go away at the drop of a hat. All they need to do is lock up and enjoy their travels. It is a way of life that will suit many older people. They have large tended gardens surrounding their apartment, a gym, swimming pool and a golf driving range. They love it although it would not suit everyone. I like my garden and largish house but therein lies the problem. You are retired, but when you take that big trip, will everything back home look after itself?

We employ a woman, called Ramona, who sits and reads a book in the conservatory. She has been appointed 'head of security' and does a fantastic job. If any potential thief sneaked around the back of the house they would spot her immediately and make a run for it. Ramona works hard for little reward and the grandchildren are fascinated by her. She is of course a shop mannequin but has become part of the family.

A large garden can represent big problem particularly if you plan to go away in the summer. It is always better to take long trips over the winter when the garden is resting and there is less maintenance to do. During the winter most of the garden plants have died down and the house plants need the minimal of attention. From mid October right through to the beginning of March things will tick over nicely on their own. When you eventually get home everything can be tidied up and put right surprisingly quickly. However, some destinations are less practical to visit in the winter, for example, the Arctic, Russia or Alaska will be too cold and other destinations will be too wet or affected by hurricanes, typhoons or tornadoes. Always check the weather before you go, that holiday may be cheap because it is the monsoon season! If you have to go away in the summer months then sometimes you just have to resign yourself to the inevitable loss, but all plants are replaceable. A simple automatically timed watering system can help with a lot of problems. Potted plants can all be grouped together somewhere and put out of the sun.

You have to make a choice between travelling and pets. If you have a dog it would be inconsiderate and expensive to keep on leaving it in kennels. The same applies to most other pets, it is unfair on them.

We know other people who get someone to come and live in their house during their absence. You can get a stranger who does this professionally or a friend who just fancies a change. There are big advantages if you need someone to mollycoddle your prize Bonsai collection or feed the hamster.

www.trustedhousesitters.com
www.housesitters.co.uk

Here are some more ideas and key points:

- leave a front door key with a neighbour
- make sure you lock all the doors and windows when you leave the house

- get a neighbour to pick up the mail or free papers
- cancel the newspapers and other deliveries
- put some indoor side lights on timer switches to make it look like someone is home
- put a radio on a timer switch to imply someone is at home
- make sure all the room main lights are off
- join your neighbourhood watch and inform the organiser when you are on vacation
- 'pretend' to get a dog and put up a sign, 'Beware of the dog'
- do not leave anything valuable that is visible through the windows and doors of your home
- a permanent outdoor light operated by a light sensor switch or a security light activated by movement will act as a deterrent to potential thieves
- put up a dummy alarm box to deter the amateur thief
- don't post on social media sites informing everyone you're going away
- do not hide your front door key under a flower pot near the front door or mat
- do not cover up the car in the driveway, that would be a real give-away
- switch off the water
- if you have a safe use it
- set the answer phone
- turn off all stand-bys on appliances
- water all your plants as necessary
- unplug your computer
- cancel any TV package until you return, and this may need to be done one month in advance
- employ Ramona

With any luck you will not have any of the above problems. Your daughter will live just around the corner and look after everything for you. You may live in a flat, hate gardening, dislike dogs and a responsible adult lives with you who will be only too glad to see the back of you for a while.

20 Money

"When preparing to travel, lay out all your clothes and all your money. Then take half the clothes and twice the money."
Susan Heller, New York journalist

We were in Istanbul when a man came up to us asking if we wanted to change money. As it so happened we did and he was offering a good rate. This was prior to the introduction of the recent new notes and the exchange rate at the time was something like 1,000,000 TLR to the pound so the notes had a lot of noughts on them. We agreed to change some cash and he counted out the money. My wife took the money and checked it. Everything seemed OK so I took out the correct amount of sterling to exchange. At this point he took the money back to double check it, rolled it up, gave it back to us and held his hand out for our money. My wife said she would check the money again but he immediately took the money back again saying that he would check it for us. He showed us all the notes again, rolled them all up and handed them to us. It all looked perfectly alright but he did not want us to check the amount again. The trick was that he had two rolls of money, one in each hand which he could swap faster than the eye could see. We were suspicious because we could never make a final check on the money. Eventually he gave up and went off. You have to be very careful.

Normally you should be wary of changing money in the street but occasionally this is where you will get the best deal. In Buenos Aries at the airport the exchange rate was 4.96 Argentinean Pesos to the dollar. At the banks and hotels the rate was 5.5 but on every street corner there were money changers offering a rate of 7.30. Again it all seemed too good too be true, but it was true, change all your money in the streets of Florida and Lavalle and you will get an amazingly good deal. The Argentinean people are worried about the stability of their currency and are stocking up on dollars and this was a fantastic deal.

When you arrive in a new country usually the exchange rates offered at the airport are pretty low. Exchange just enough currency to get you to your hotel, for the first day or first leg of your journey. However, this is not always the case, in Senegal the rate at the airport was exactly the same as in the high street bureaus, at least for the euro but not the dollar. There is a set rate for the Euro and also a fluctuating rate for the pound. Other travellers have reported that Japanese airport banks have some of the best rates, the airport kiosks in Peru offered better rates than the money changers in Lima and the Hannah Bank exchange booth in Seoul Incheon Airport was the best place to change money. It definitely depends upon the country you visit and a little research is needed beforehand.

Sometimes when travelling overland you will be crossing borders and you may need to change money right away. In more remote areas there will be plenty of money changers offering all sorts of optimistic rates and you may be forced into negotiating a deal. In a lot of West African countries the exchange rate at the borders may be the best rate and it may be the only place you will find to actually change money at all. When moving swiftly from country to country the dilemma will be exactly how much currency to exchange.

Wherever possible get some of the local currency in the UK before you leave home. Follow the exchange rates and try to make the deal when the rate is most favourable. Put a currency exchange website into 'favourites' on your computer to monitor rates or download a free currency app to your smartphone. Rates and commissions do vary between individual banks and high street bureaus. Inevitably the best rates are going to be found online. The 'International Currency Exchange' offer much more competitive rates than the high street and the cash is delivered direct to your door by Royal Mail Special Delivery. To qualify for free delivery your order must be over £500. They have a price match guarantee and your delivery is fully insured to arrive at your door the next day. A survey by Which? magazine rated them ahead of 16 other currency providers. For most places in the world the US Dollar is the most universally accepted currency, followed by the Euro and Stirling. You could play safe and take some of all three. Wherever possible take new, clean, unmarked notes.

www.xe.com to check exchange rates.

www.iceplc.com for foreign currency online.

What do you take with you, cash, traveller's cheques or ATM cards? You almost always get the best rate of exchange if you have cash. For a long trip this may involve having anywhere between £1000 and £5000 strapped around your waist in a money belt. This is going to make you feel more vulnerable but you do need some cash. If you are considering taking a very large sum of money into or out of a country, check if there are any limits. Some countries do not allow their currency to be imported or exported so you must have sterling, dollars or euros to exchange when you get there. Take some emergency funds with you but try not to keep it all together in one place. Whenever possible split your money up between you and your travelling partner. Only carry enough on you for that day and leave the rest in the hotel safe. Failing that always use a money belt or a zipped inside pocket. We still see people with fat wallets stuffed into their back pockets. Just how naive can you get?

Traveller's cheques are not really worth considering. Not so long ago they were the preferred method of dealing with cash on your travels but not anymore. In some countries they are not welcome and are more trouble than they are worth. Throughout the world travellers have found it increasingly difficult to find banks which will change them mainly because ATMs are now almost everywhere. In their favour they avoid the necessity for you having to carry large amounts of cash. If you still want traveller's cheques then change them only as you need currency and countersign them only in front of the person who will cash them.

Everyone has to take at least one ATM card. Make sure your bank is big enough to have branches wherever in the world you travel to as using your own bank reduces charges. Try to reduce your transaction fees as much as possible. You will have to pay foreign transaction charges and take whatever exchange rate is on offer. Some banks in certain countries offer no ATM fees so check this out before you leave.

Notify your bank or credit card company before you leave and tell them all the countries that you intend to visit. It will not be very helpful if your card is cancelled through suspected fraudulent use. Some banks will freeze your account if they see activity from outside the usual region that it's used. Having to contact them from overseas won't be any fun. My own bank unaccountably limits me to 5 countries so if it is to be a major trip we have to put further countries on my wife's card. If you do have to make withdrawals then at least try and make fewer but bigger transactions. Fees are going to add up on a long journey.

Every time you use your card overseas, your local bank coverts the transaction into your local currency for billing purposes and they take a little off the top for doing so. Thus the official rate you see listed online is not what you get and you'll never be able to fully avoid losses on the exchange rate. Below are some suggestions relating to ATM cards and to reducing the amount you lose in conversion and on fees:

- Use a Credit Card for normal everyday purchases in shops and restaurants. Credit card companies get the best rates. Using a credit card will get you an exchange rate closest to the official rate.
- The majority of credit cards charge a 2.5% to 3% fee when you use them overseas for withdrawing cash. There are a few alternatives. To withdraw cash we use a zero rated credit card from Santander. They charge nothing at all but it is now only available to existing clients who already hold one. Somewhere along the line they realised that this offer was too good to be true. Take up any such offers as you spot them. Check out the Halifax clarity credit card that claims to have no foreign exchange fee anywhere in the world.
- Some travellers avoid using debit cards for purchases, because if someone does obtain all your details they could drain your bank account. Limit their use to official bank ATMs.
- Never access your accounts in public Wi-Fi areas such as cyber cafes.
- Use a credit card that offers cash back.
- Always have two bank or credit card accounts. It is good to have a backup in case one card is lost or stolen.
- Make sure your credit card is returned to you after each transaction and that it remains in your sight when making a purchase.
- In some places such as parts of Asia and South America transaction fees on credit card purchases can be up to 10%.
- With an ATM transaction you get to keep most of the money in your bank instead of having it at risk in your money belt. When you need it you will be able to get it in the local currency at the exact current exchange rate.
- Withdraw a lot if the exchange rate has moved in your favour. Fees are usually charged per transaction instead of a straight percentage. The big downside is the risk of getting mugged - your decision.
- For most travellers the ATM card is the main weapon of choice, but some kind of a mix of debit cards, credit cards, and a bit of cash is probably the best idea.

A pre-loaded travel card with multiple currencies is a good idea in principle and avoids the possibility of credit card fraud. They are also know as cash passports, travellers cash cards, currency cards and pre-paid travel cards, amongst other variations. Working like an ATM card drawing out local currency from ATMs within each country you travel, they are promoted as being safer and more convenient than carrying cash. They also provide better exchange rates than a credit or debit card when abroad. You load your travel money onto the card before you go. The exchange rates are locked in when you load or top up, you get the rate on the day you convert your cash, so you will always know your budget when travelling.

However, there are other charges that may more than wipe out any savings that are made. Some add on ATM fees and inactivity fees. Look out for application fees, top up fees, withdrawing cash over the counter, foreign exchange fees, currency transfer fees, shortfall fees and fees for cashing in your card when you no longer need it.

They are often issued by specialist money changing companies such as Travelex, ICE or FairFX and anyone with a UK bank account can apply for one. Simply apply online, choose the currency you want your card denominated in and load it up with funds from your current account. You can top up and check your balance online and by phone. Some cards allow multiple currencies on one card, though only the major world currencies.

ICE at the time of writing had the best deal with no fees attached to their US Dollar Travel Cashcard and Euro Travellers Cashcard. Their International Travellers Cashcard had a load and top up fee of 1.85%. They provide a back up card in case one is stolen and will transfer the balance from the lost one. As an extra with the dollar and euro cards there is a 1% cashback on all purchases. They will also buy back up to £300 of currency at the same rate upon your return to the UK.

www.moneysupermarket.com/credit-cards
www.moneysavingexpert.com
www.travelex.co
www.fairfx.com

How much money do you need is summed up in the opening quotation, probably more than you imagine. There is no straight answer, your flights will already be paid for and perhaps some accommodation. So it will depend on how many extra activities you want to do and how much you expect to spend on, hotels, food, drinks, laundry, souvenirs, taxis and restaurants. Take more than you need and you may also want to include some money for local tips. Good local guides and crew members can make your trip experience special, and tips, however modest, will be appreciated.

There is plenty of counterfeit money in circulation so check that your money is real. Take a good look at the money you receive. Compare a suspect note with a genuine note of the same denomination and series, paying attention to the quality of printing and paper characteristics. Look for differences, not similarities. The genuine portrait should appear lifelike and stand out distinctly from the background, whereas the counterfeit portrait is usually lifeless and flat. Details merge into the background which is often too dark or mottled.

Keep your money safe and do not flash large amounts around when paying a bill. Despite what has been said earlier, deal only with authorized agents when you exchange money, buy airline tickets or purchase souvenirs. Do not change money on the black market.

Finally you may need to change some foreign currency back again. During those final days on holiday it is always difficult to gauge how much money you will still need. As a general rule don't change money back at airports where the rates will generally be lowest. If you are going to return to the country or have euros or dollars then keep the money for next time. If you overestimated and have a large amount of obscure currency go to a bank or bureau in town before departing. They will require your passport and maybe your original exchange receipt. If possible try not to have any money left to exchange, or perhaps make a purchase in duty free and put the remainder into a charity box.

In some West African countries you will get a lot of cash for your dollars

21 Tipping, begging and taxis

"He who does not travel does not know the value of men."
Moorish proverb

There are increasingly fewer genuine experiences left in the world. So much has been spoilt by irresponsible tourists bringing gifts and money to hand out. Wherever tourists venture children are being brought up to see begging as a way of life. Whole communities are becoming reliant upon handouts and traditional ways of life are changing. The very things that brought tourists in the first place are reduced to a second hand performance just for an expected payment. The best advice is not to give anything to people with their hands out. Do not give anything despite how hard it may seem. You are encouraging begging and altering people's way of life to one of dependency. Give only to those who perform some sort of mutually agreed service for you. Well off western tourists who parade through poor communities doling out dollars are creating an expectation and ruining things for future travellers. It is particularly upsetting to see tourists throwing handfuls of sweets to children out of the window of their coach. It will not do their teeth any good, all the wrappers will be thrown on the ground and smaller children may well be harmed in the scramble.

In India we sat outside a restaurant and watched a woman begging. She had chosen a gutter by the road and had a sick looking baby along with a pet rabbit. Numerous people stopped to give money, sometimes quite a lot. White people in particularly knelt down to talk and look at the baby. She was doing very well with a steady stream of clients. At one time, a boy came along, who was obviously her son, to whom she gave some money, followed by a man who was probably her husband. After a brief discussion he was quickly shooed away, business was just too good to be interrupted. Of course there are many deserving cases but bear several things in mind. Things are not always as they seem. Many beggars in India are controlled by someone else. All the money is turned over to them in return for food and shelter. Other beggars have been deliberately mutilated by their family or others to provide a means of income.

When you meet beggars in the street never ever lose your temper despite how persistent and annoying they can be. Always keep calm, a firm 'no' or whatever language is appropriate is sometimes enough. Avoid eye contact and try to ignore them, however rude it may seem.

It can get really tedious as some keep tapping you on the arm or even pushing you to get your attention. In Ethiopia they have a habit of pinching you on the arm. You are seen as being rich and like a piggy bank, if they shake you enough, the money will drop out. All of us have had to work hard throughout our lives for our money, yet sometimes people that do not appear hard up at all expect a free handout. They touch their lips to indicate hunger and plead with their eyes even if they do not look at all undernourished. There is a look of disbelief or horror when we do not stop. You have to decide what to give and when to give, but you cannot give to everyone.

In Sri Lanka as we approached the temple several handicapped beggars saw us coming and arranged themselves to look as hard done by and deserving as possible. As foreign tourists we had to pay to get in, whereas all the locals got in free, which is quite acceptable. Once inside there were more sad looking deformed cases all wrapped up in bundles of rags. For each of the separate internal temples we were expected to make a cash offering. The temple was being painted and even the workmen downed their tools to ask for money. On our way out we had to run the same gauntlet of outstretched hands again. All this has the potential to detract from what should be a pleasant experience. Sometimes you have to make up your own mind as to what is an appropriate and deserving case.

If the situation merits it, tipping is a necessary part of travel but it should be deserved. Like many other travellers, particularly British, I am ill at ease with tipping, not because I am inherently mean but because I can never judge what is appropriate or whether it is even expected. How much do you leave? Too much and you are a sucker, too little is an insult and is worse than leaving nothing. Most of us never received any tips when we were working, it is mainly those working in service industries that expect tips, waiters, porters, taxi drivers and guides all expect something extra. The situation varies from country to country. Nobody tips in New Zealand, you do your job well, get paid, and that is the end of it. In such countries as Japan a tip could be regarded as an insult. On the other hand in America if you do not leave a tip in a restaurant then the waiter will be chasing you down the street directing some well chosen abuse at you.

Some research is essential for travellers to know exactly who deserves a tip and how much to give. Tipping must be done wisely and fairly so check out these 2 websites before you go for country-by-country tipping advice.

www.cntraveler.com/travel-tips/travel-etiquette/2008/12/Etiquette-101-Tipping-Guide
www.ccrainternational.com/tools/TippingGuidelines.htm

We chartered a boat in The Gambia to go and see the hippos. This was in Georgetown some 100 miles inland and only reached after a full day's dusty drive; the infrastructure has since been improved. It took a good hour or more to negotiate a price. The old man pretended not to be interested, after all his was the only boat available. He knew we wanted to go despite being the only tourists there. He did not even come with us, the boat was managed by two young lads. We saw the hippos and as soon as we turned around it became clear that the boys were being paid nothing and only did it for the tip. They were desperate, and had to be told quite clearly that they would be getting a tip but not until we had landed. They deserved the money as they had performed a service for us.

The ordinary tourists on their package holidays will book up a trip to see something like the local culture show. It could be a professional dance group or the local waiters dressed up. In this way local traditions are being preserved. Usually such performances are going to be quite good and some such as the 'fire dance' in Bali are outstanding. Tipping is at your discretion but generally not needed if you have already paid for a ticket. In more remote areas if you have been taken to see some sort of dance, performed by slightly embarrassed villagers dressed up especially for the occasion then you have no option but to offer some cash unless you have booked and paid for the trip already. It is increasingly unlikely that you will stumble upon a genuine village ceremony but impromptu performances can sometimes be the best ones. The absolute best will be events that are performed only for the sheer enjoyment of it where no tips are expected at all.

Some more points to consider:

- Never tip for anything that you did not ask for.
- At airports and hotels always keep a tight hold of your bags unless you are prepared to pay a porter to carry them. If they get snatched out of your grasp then make it clear that you are giving them nothing and give them nothing.
- Always have some loose change in your pocket so that you can tip the appropriate amount in cash.

If there is a service charge on the restaurant bill then there is absolutely no reason to tip at all. These guys have got your money already regardless of how the service was. In fact there is no incentive to provide any decent service. If you are really unhappy and a bit stroppy, then you could get them to take the charge off your bill. However, in some destinations such as Greece, Guatemala and Hong Kong maybe you should leave a tip in addition to a service charge, because the service charge may not necessarily go to the waiter:

- Generally waiters are poorly paid and tips are a universally accepted necessity.
- Use your own judgement. I was with a guide and driver for seventy days on an overland trip. They were both brilliant, went out of their way to help and got tipped well. They have satisfying and enjoyable jobs but not well paid. On another overland trip the guide was so bad that nobody tipped him. The porters who lugged all my gear to Everest Base Camp deserved every single rupee.
- Never ask an employee if they require a tip.

Tipping is a strange business. Why do we give people something extra just for doing their job? It is typically an American thing that has spread throughout the world. Restaurants are the places that most people feel compelled to give tips to the waiter for good service and it is justified because they are on low wages. We are in effect subsidising the restaurant that use this as an excuse to pay a minimum wage. In fast food restaurants nobody tips any of the workers who are also on a low wage but people feel a need to donate money in a posh restaurant. Sometimes it is maybe just to show off in front of guests but more likely to be because it is simply expected. In the worst cases the waiter will say,

'Shall I add the gratuity to your bill sir?'

On the other hand a waitress could be a single mum trying to make a living who relies upon tips just to make ends meet. Some tour guides in London offer free tours and only do it for the tips. Other tour guides will go out of their way to answer your questions and help. If you have a bad back a porter will take your cases right up into your hotel room. In such circumstances these guys all deserve their tips.

Years ago I remember the dustmen knocking on my parents' door for their Christmas bonus, this was accepted practice. The postman would have his Christmas bonus left in an envelope by the front door even though it was not the regular postman. These practices have long since disappeared.

Everywhere in the world western tourists are being pestered by 'guides'. They can be very persistent and try all sorts of approaches. In Morocco and other countries, a favourite tactic is to claim that they are studying English and just want to walk with you and to talk. It will sound very plausible, but they will almost certainly be guides and eventually demand some money. However, if you do want a guide many of these 'guides' can be excellent value and show you some parts of the city that ordinary travellers will struggle to find. It could be money well spent.

You have to make the decisions about tipping. Take no notice of what Americans might say, they are the people who caused all the problems associated with tipping and when it gets down to it, can be just plain stupid.

At some stage in most journeys you will have to get a taxi. The golden rule is to negotiate a price before you get in. Get the driver to agree the price and if necessary write it down. Enquire about prices before hand. Ask the locals what they would pay. Check it out on the internet before you leave home. Always have some sort of idea about the going rate before you start negotiations. If you are not happy with the price, move on to the next taxi in the rank or flag another one down. Do not give up and take note of the following story,

'We had disembarked from the cruise ship in Buenos Aries following a trip to Antarctica. The concierge on the ship could have booked us a transfer to the airport for $56. Locals had told us that the taxi fare should be $25 to $30, you just had to hail one for yourself in the street. Outside in the port it appeared to be mayhem as hundreds of bewildered passengers made their way out. There was a large sign for the crowds to follow, for taxis. The path then narrowed to a single file, at the end of which, was a big Russian looking chap. He had equally hard looking men frequently coming up to him kissing him on both cheeks. My guess was that the Russian mafia were in control of things. He offered us a taxi for $70. We ridiculed this price and told him we were going to find one for ourselves. He said that this was going to be difficult and asked us why we were prepared to take such a risk. The 'risk' was that we might be mugged or robbed. We were thinking well okay we would not get into a taxi with *him* but would be happy to do so with any of the other thousands of taxi drivers in Buenos Aries. We told him what we thought about his offer and he shrugged his shoulders as if to say, that if we wanted to put our lives and safety at risk so be it. We asked him who he worked for and he said that it was the Port Authority but after further questions he told us that it was his own company. We parted by saying words to the effect that he had a very good business fleecing rich tourists prepared to pay through the nose and he smiled knowingly. Other tourists were split in their decisions, most complained but feeling that they had no option got into a waiting taxi. A few like us complained bitterly and wandered off on their own. We walked a further 30 inches and were offered a ride for $65, which we declined, although the pressure was on. We did start wondering if it was worth it but decided to persevere. I wandered off down the road away from the chaos to check out the situation while my wife looked after the luggage. Meanwhile the Russian returned with an offer of $45 which she politely refused. Remember that this guy was not even a taxi driver, he was just finding a driver for you and skimming off the excess. It was my wife who walked across the road and found a driver dropping someone off and negotiated a ride for $30. He would have had to queue up for maybe an hour for another fare. All we did was walk across the road. The whole process took us about 10 minutes. We were happy that we got a fare price; it is never a good feeling knowing that you have been ripped off'.

On this same trip an American couple had paid $5 for the taxi from their hotel to the port but the return journey cost them $25. They said that they were not brave enough to walk to the nearest taxi stop. There will be other such cartels of pirates throughout the world so try not to give in.

A survey by skift.com and cheapflights gave the cost of a taxi from Narita airport to the centre of Tokyo as £191 which worked out as £4.70 per mile. Copenhagen was the most expensive at £34 or £6.82 per mile, London Heathrow came in at £60 and £3 per mile. The trip to the centre of Buenos Aries was only found to be £6 at a mere £0.31 per mile.

The main points with tipping taxis drivers are:

- Always negotiate a price beforehand and if necessary write it down, if you think you are being overcharged, no tip.
- If the driver makes you lift your own cases into the boot, no

tip.
- If it is a metered taxi and you think you are being driven around the houses, no tip.
- Make sure you have the correct money because the driver will definitely have no change.
- Why do you need to tip at all? In some parts of the world they are already overpriced. They get well paid to get you to your destination and you are unlikely to see them again.
- If you have a lot of luggage that the driver handles for you, he gives a running commentary on the local tourist attractions and generally goes out of his way to help then, yes give a tip.

On the other hand taxi drivers do have overhead costs. A lot of time can be wasted queuing up in a line of other taxis so that one is always waiting for you. They will pick you up at any time of the day or night, put up with drunken behaviour and get you to your destination safely.

In comparison to much of the world, we in western countries are rich, some of us more so than others. All western tourists are privileged, overfed and reasonably affluent. When visiting poor countries we should all be making some sort of a contribution but this needs to be done in a responsible way. Where practical this could be taking basic foods such as rice, flour and cooking oil to isolated communities. The Himba tribe in Namibia were desperate for water. The women had to walk miles overland just to get one bucket full of muddy water, which they then had to carry balanced on their heads back to the village, every single day. Any items of clothing are wanted in third world countries. Resist giving out pens to every child but take them to a local school along with other stationary and reading books. If you have any room left in your bags then fill it up with useful gifts.

Remember to check out:

www.stuffyourrucksack.com

In Cuba, as already mentioned they are far too proud to beg, but handing out toiletries and clothing such as bras and t-shirts to local women is appreciated. You will be a hero if you bring a football for the children. Check out what is needed at your destination before leaving and squeeze something in. Some more ideas include, toys, stationary, solar calculators, maths sets, basic literacy books, and alphabet flash cards.

Some items are useful as bargaining chips or 'sweeteners' to seal a deal. In Zimbabwe I swapped a pair of broken sandals for a $100,000,000,000,000 note. To me this was a perfect souvenir, a reminder of how hyperinflation can destroy an economy and it weighed next to nothing. Baseball caps, football shirts and T-shirts are always popular. At the end of your trip you can give everything away that you no longer have use for.

Money is altogether more difficult to donate. However, money is always what is really needed if you can verify that it will be well used. If necessary ask what the charity or school needs and go and buy it with them. Ideally they will have some sort of accounts book which lists donations. If you are still unsure you can always donate money before travelling, many travel companies have an associated charity.

The One Hundred Trillion Dollar note

Take appropriate gifts for children

22 Food

"If you reject the food, ignore the customs, fear the religion and avoid the people, you might better stay home."
James A. Michener 1907-1997

To begin with it is worth repeating warnings about water. If you catch travellers' diarrhoea whilst abroad, water is the most likely cause. In countries with poor sanitation don't drink tap water or even use it to brush your teeth. Never drink local water or eat anything that you suspect may have been washed in it. So beware of salads, uncooked fruit and vegetables, ice creams and ice cubes in drinks.
www.nathnac.org/ds/map

- Always carry a bottle of water around with you. Use your own bottle and fill it up from a reliable source at the beginning of the day to avoid buying more bottles and creating more waste. Always use tap water if it is reliable. If not treat it ideally by boiling for 10 minutes, or use sterilising tablets.
- Avoid any food that has been left standing for a long time in warm climates or outside exposed to flies. Buffets should be refrigerated and covered up.
- Ensure all food is cooked through and piping hot. Any raw or undercooked seafood, fish or meat could be unsafe.
- All milk and dairy products should have been pasteurised.
- Salads are the prime example that might carry a water-borne disease.
- Food from street traders should have been recently prepared and served on clean, hot plates.
- Be wary about any ingredients that you suspect may not have been cooked, if in any doubt, avoid it.
- Stick to the golden rule,

'Cook it, peel it, boil it or forget it!'

One of the nice things about travelling is being able to sample all the local food. Trying all those new and exciting tastes and flavours is enjoyable but always carries a small risk. However, with the above warnings in mind that is going to minimal. Always try the local specialities as it is part of the travelling experience. Through trying new foods you can learn more about the local culture and broaden your view of the world. With that in mind it may be wise to avoid restaurants catering for tourists, with western menus and 'fish and chips'. We spent a week in Buenos Aries and went to the same restaurant five nights running, to eat steak. They were the five best steaks I have ever had anywhere in the world. This restaurant was packed out with locals every night which is probably going to be the best recommendation. No longer do you have to plan and cook meals at home but someone else is going to do it all for you. It can often be the highlight of the day, relaxing over a long meal, in some idyllic spot, somewhere in the world.

- Wherever there are tourists there will be plenty of food outlets and you need to search out the best.
- In popular destinations restaurants can get away with serving up mediocre food at inflated prices or maybe the increased competition has forced up standards and lowered prices.
- Have a look through the windows and see what customers are eating and if they are enjoying themselves. Better still ask anyone who comes out what their meal was like.
- Check out the local restaurants beforehand on the web, with a smartphone app or in the guidebook.
- If the restaurant is busy assume that this is generally a good sign, especially if there are plenty of locals eating.
- The best restaurant is rarely the most expensive one. If the same meal is more expensive than elsewhere, what extra are you getting for your money? Ambient atmosphere, riverside view or some entertainment perhaps?
- If the restaurant is dirty on the outside then the kitchens may also be.
- Seafood dishes are notorious for causing intestinal problems, as fish accumulate contaminants from a wide variety of sources. Shellfish filter sea water and can accumulate all sorts of nasty bacteria. If you must eat them make sure they have been boiled really well for 10 minutes.
- Follow the recommendations of your local hotelier, fellow travellers and locals for the best places to eat.
- www.eatwith.com - to dine out in a local's home

- Take every opportunity to try new food as long as it passes your hygiene tests, it is better to be safe than sorry.

In many parts of the world, such as Asia, food in restaurants is so cheap that travellers hardly have to worry about their budgets. This in turn creates a feel good factor that contributes to the continent's popularity. In Europe and other westernised countries things are going to be somewhat pricier but you do not have to eat in an expensive restaurant every night. Sometimes there are inexpensive places where you can eat as much as you like for a set price and fill up for the day, for example the self service delis in New York provide good value. Some people like fast food as provided by such companies as McDonald's. Here food is cheap enough although I would never set foot inside one. This is not quite true as McDonalds is often the only place where there is a toilet, just walk in like you own the place and use the free facilities.

One of the joys of travelling is to eat out in the street, with the locals, sampling all those tempting dishes. In many places all over the world locals will be cooking up all sorts of delicious offerings, particularly in South East Asia and China. There is still the question of hygiene so take every precaution and always carry a small bottle of hand sanitizer to use before every meal. However, you may still end up with the vendor serving you a sausage with grubby hands on a plate that has been dunked in greyish water. In order to minimise the risk we often take our own plastic plates because street food is an experience not to be missed.

Even eating out every night can become tedious and sometimes we long for some home cooking. Also if you are on a budget then eating out everyday is going to be expensive. One big advantage of hostels is that there will be a kitchen where you can prepare your own food. If you are staying in a hostel for several days and cooking for yourself then all your purchases will go into a communal fridge. Take some sticky labels with you to identify your food and put it all together in a bag if possible. There will usually be some communal shelves where the food, spices or cooking oil is for anyone to use. At the end of your stay leave any unwanted food for other travellers.

For lunch prepare some sandwiches and snacks in the morning particularly if you will be on a bus or at some isolated spot. It is often more convenient than having to waste time in a restaurant.

Always try the local specialities however repulsive they may seem to you. At one time we had a 'maison rurale' in France, set up high on a hillside in the countryside. We grew various crops that were plagued by snails. Unable to bring myself to crush them underfoot I threw them down the hill where their fate was to be determined on the road. Later I discovered that my neighbour was down at the bottom of the hill trying to catch them. The French will have a go at eating anything. He put them all in a wire basket for 3 days to cleanse them and fried them up with garlic and butter. Apparently in England we have wonderful tasty snails, which could be a good business idea for someone, and gardeners would be delighted for you to take them away. To me snails are just bits of grizzle and God put them in the safety of a shell for a reason. Gizzards which form part of the digestive tracts in chickens, are also like grizzle and are another French delicacy.

Again in France, in a popular and noisy country restaurant I ordered some speciality cheese. This was a sheep's cheese, wrapped up in vine leaves and fermented until it had putrefied. As I unwrapped the bundle the whole restaurant went quiet. Maybe it was the all pervading rancid smell or more likely all the patrons wanted to see if I would actually eat it. The smell was not appealing, more like appalling, and the taste was extreme, the strongest cheese I had ever tasted by a country mile. The smell stayed with me for days, however many times I washed my hands the smell still lingered there.

We ordered a set menu in a French restaurant but were unsure what the starter was. It was savoury soft and 'strange'. Later we were told it was sheep's brains.

Like the French we should all be adventurous in what we choose to eat and take all the unique culinary opportunities as they come along. These are some of the strange foods from around the world that I have tasted:

Frogs legs in France taste a bit like chicken to begin with, after a while they don't.

In Australia the Aborigines eat ants, the big ones with green bodies. If you pick them up and lick the green sacks they taste strongly of lime. If you are gentle they can be released unharmed or eat them whole and get the full nutritious experience.

In Ecuador the speciality is guinea pig and out in the streets they are roasted on spits. It tastes a bit like duck but there is not much meat on them. All the head is eaten as well, but avoid looking it in the eye.

Driving through West African countries boys hold up what look like giant rats for sale. These are agouti, a rodent that is also found in

South and Central America. There are lots of recipes and it is a bit like rabbit. It is not a rat as it has no tail.

Durian is the world's smelliest fruit and one that tourists often come across. If you can overcome the psychological barrier of the rotting garbage smell it does taste sweet and fruity.

In various countries big fat larvae are an important source of protein. Seeing them all writhing around, I have never been able to bring myself to pop one in my mouth, but fried up they are tasty, if a little bit chewy, and the taste can hang around for a long time.

China is a wonderful place to try something really different. Go to a night food market and check out what is on offer. Silk worm larvae were a cheap and tasty snack and not too dissimilar to the locusts, all barbequed to perfection. Snake skin on skewers was very difficult to chew but snake meat itself was a lot more palatable. There are dozens of unusual things to try but my favourite was scorpion. They work out relatively expensive but tasted like the little bits of meat that get burnt to a crisp around the Sunday joint. There were several westerners around but very few tried anything. Have courage and do not miss out. All of this can be washed down with a bottle of wine containing a dog's penis floating in it, yummy.

It was rumoured the French, yes again the French, used to place a dead donkey in a huge vat of fermenting wine to give it 'body'. I seem to remember a tale from years gone by, but I might have made it up.

We do not have to travel too far to find strange food and the French will throw their hands up in horror when faced with English cooking. In England, spotted dick, custard and Marmite are well known and loved but to foreigners a source of curiosity, disgust or excitement. Most of our weird food seems to originate in the north. The most famous Scottish dish is haggis. Made from sheep's stomach stuffed with heart, liver and lungs combined with oats, suet and herbs, it is widely available in English supermarkets. We bought one, and cut a few slices for dinner; it was quite nice, at first, a bit like a bland meat loaf without the meat. The remainder got put in the fridge, but by the next day it had grown back to the original size. And so it went on each day as if it was alive, until at the end of the week when we gave up and binned it.

Tripe is the stomach tissue of ruminant animals. Dressed tripe used to be a cheap and nutritious meal for the working classes and is still popular in many parts of the world today. Nowadays with increased affluence it is best used as pet food. Stew it, fry it and eat it if you have the 'stomach' for it. I attempted to eat it boiled with salt and vinegar. It was like eating rubber, but the salt and vinegar was nice. 'It melts in your mouth', the old folk used to say.

Black pudding or blood pudding is a type of sausage made by cooking blood with various ingredients until it is thick enough to congeal when cool. Inside are meat, suet, fat, bread, cornmeal and onions among other things. It is really tasty fried for breakfast even though it sounds awful. I have heard foreigners muttering darkly about 'vampires'.

Pig's trotters are boiled to soften them and tiny little bits of meat and skin are picked out between the bones. It seems to be more useful for passing time than gaining nourishment. However, they are good for making stock and have increased in popularity since the financial crisis.

Being adventurous with food is all part of the travelling experience and will form great memories. When you get home your friends will be impressed, your children horrified and you will avoid telling the grandchildren that you ate guinea pig. Try some of these other strange foods from around the world if you dare:

- In Cambodia fried tarantulas were eaten by starving Cambodians in the days of Pol Pot. Now they are fried whole with legs and fangs and considered a delicacy, crispy on the outside with a gooey centre.
- In The Philippines there is a really disgusting sounding treat for those with a strong stomach, balut. Fertilized chicken or duck eggs are boiled just before they hatch. Not really a chicken or an egg but they are supposed to be an aphrodisiac.
- In Sardinia casu marzu is a putrefied cheese infested with live, insect larvae. The cheese fly is encouraged to lay its eggs and the maggots release an enzyme during their digestion that causes the purification. Recent health problems have rendered it illegal so it needs to be sought out on the black market.
- Why bother to kill an octopus when you can eat it alive in Korea. The tentacles are cut off and put on the plate still squirming. They will wrap themselves around your tongue and fight for their lives whilst being eaten.
- In Japan, ikizukari is the preparation of sashimi made from a fish whist it is still alive. It is filleted without actually killing it

and served with the heart still beating. Sometimes it is put back in the aquarium to swim around in between courses.
- In Iceland the puffin forms part of the national diet and is harvested in a sustainable way. The heart is eaten raw whilst it is still warm as a traditional Icelandic delicacy. 'Wild thing you make my heart sing'.
- Dog meat is consumed all over the world but the Chinese had to take it off the menu during the 2008 Olympics.

The Chinese believe that everything has a life force and this gradually diminishes after harvesting. This applies to all living things both animals and vegetables, the rational being to eat everything as fresh as possible. There is so much strange food to try all over the world and the above are just a few extreme examples. Always exercise caution but always be adventurous.

Tasty snacks in China

23 Car Hire

"The real voyage of discovery consists not in seeking new landscapes, but in having new eyes."
Marcel Proust 1871-1922

Sometimes you just have to hire a car as the best and most convenient way to get around. You can organise your own self-guided tour travelling at your own pace. Maybe a little run-around for a few days or perhaps it will be a camper van for several weeks. Could just be a scooter or motorbike that will get you to all those difficult places. Any way all sorts of problems can occur unless you take some precautions.

Recognise that when driving abroad you are going to be at a greater risk, particularly if it is a left hand drive car. Road traffic accidents are one of the main causes of death and injuries for travellers abroad. It will depend what country you are in, but hired cars can be poorly serviced, roads may be badly maintained, congested, poorly signed, shared with lots of other hazards, particularly other drivers who maybe less skilled than you. Whilst riding a motor scooter in Goa we encountered, carts pulled by animals and people, sacred cows which have total right of way, lorries on the wrong side of the road that forced us off the road into the dirt, plus the occasional elephant. The biggest vehicle has the ultimate right of way and all this apart from the regular hoards of pedestrians, cyclists, motorcycles and other cars.

Always book up car hire in advance to get the cheapest prices, and compare rates on several different sites. Take notice of any excess fees that apply for accidents and theft. This could easily be up to £1000, but for an extra payment, can be reduced. You will have to buy collision waiver separately in America whereas it is often included in the cost in Europe. If you wish to do this then it is best done before leaving home as the company will want a lot more when you are standing in their office ready to go. The best idea is to arrange a short term excess cover from a third party provider such as the AA:

www.theaa.com/insurance
insurance4carhire.com

- Ask about any discounts that could be applied to lower your rate, perhaps frequent flier programs and certain credit cards. There just may be a negotiated rate, even for a senior citizen.
- Before you book online, do an internet search for coupon or promotion codes to put into the booking engine of your car rental company's site. Just type the name of the company followed by 'coupon code' and you may find special promotion offer. Many of the best rates do not show up on agents' computer screens without a little prompting from you. However, often these coupons have restricted applications, but you may be lucky.
- If you search online for 'flight and hotel and car' packages and bundled discounts it could save both time and money.
- Ask about available discounts before you book.

Research the company you choose because if it sounds too good to be true there could be a catch somewhere. The major factor that you should never forget is to book the car as early as possible as it enables you to get the car of your choice as well as at the most competitive price. Leave it too late and the price will keep on increasing as the rental date approaches. The major reputable car rental companies such as Hertz and Avis will assure quality service but there are thousands of internet car hire sites to wade through:

www.hertz.co.uk
www.avis.com
www.skyscanner.net/carhire
www.rentalcars.com
www.economycarrentals.co.uk
www.travelsupermarket.com/c/cheap-car-hire
www.travelocity.com/Car-Rental
www.kayak.com/cars

When booking up for your car hire there could be a problem concerning a maximum age restriction. Drivers over the age of 70 may be lumped in with those under the age of 25 and face extra charges or not be permitted to rent at all. It is generally not a problem in most places but can be with some rental companies in certain countries, so check ahead. Cyprus, Ireland and Malta impose arbitrary age limits. Typically you may find restrictions at 70, 75 or 80 but these can usually be overcome by shopping around, Avis has no age restrictions worldwide. Sometimes you may need a note from your doctor to prove you are in good health and fit to drive, along with one from your insurance company. It is all a bit worrying but with a growing 'grey' market, things could swing our way with companies such as National Car Rentals imposing no such limits anywhere in the world.

www.nationalcar.co.uk

Once you have booked up and have been shown to your car make absolutely sure that you check everything and that it is agreed with the rental company on their tick sheet:

- Always check the car bodywork for damage however small the scratches may be. Point them out to the hire company, ensure they circle them on their diagram, and if necessary take a photograph of dents and scratches. To be extra cautious photograph every inch of the car when you pick it up and on returning it. The company will have your credit card details and there have been dozens of cases where customers discover only when they get home that they have been wrongly charged.
- Check all the tyres are in good condition. If any are damaged or split get the company to change them. Ignore it, and again you could be deemed liable.
- Check the petrol gauge. Normally you have to return the car with the same amount of fuel in the tank. This is most convenient if the tank is full and it is then easy to return it full.
- Check the mileage odometer and write it down.
- Check the general condition of the car, the brakes, lights and indicators.
- Test out the air-conditioning. This is very important in hot climates.
- Start the car and listen for any strange noises. At least pretend you know what you are listening for.
- Position all the mirrors to suit your driving position.
- Tune in the radio when the car is stationary.
- Consider the adequacy of the insurance agreement.
- Automatic cars are less strenuous to drive but usually a little more expensive.
- If you are renting a motorcycle then you should wear a safety helmet. In some places such as Goa it is not compulsory except on main roads. Motor scooters can be really good fun

but notorious for accidents. In Goa I found it to be an essential convenience, you just need to persuade the wife.
- Does the car have seat belts?
- Make sure you have an unlimited mileage agreement. Check that there is no separate daily limit.
- Ask the company what extra charges there are which you are liable for.
- If your car is not there waiting for you then you will probably get a free upgrade. This is quite a common occurrence and generally a good thing unless you are on a budget and the next car is less economical.
- When you return the vehicle make sure you see someone and get them to sign some sort of written declaration. Avoid situations where you post the keys through a letter box. You are responsible for the vehicle until they have inspected it. Remember they have your credit card details.
- Return the car clean or you will be at risk of incurring valeting charges.
- Make sure you have left no small things in the car such as your sunglasses or phone.
- If you have paid a deposit wait while they credit it back to your account.

Other points to consider are:

- If you are picking up a car from the airport the rental agency is contractually required to pay a concession fee to the airport. If you do not need a car on arrival then pick up one downtown the following day. Take the shuttle bus into town.
- For only a few days rental, the major companies may offer the best deals and for longer terms, local firms.
- Take your own sat nav with you as it will save you a lot of money. All companies will have systems to hire.
- Try to make your car as inconspicuous as possible. Choose one that is common locally and has nothing to identify it as a rental car to thieves.
- Ask the agency about any potential safety issues.
- Before you purchase any extra insurance, check to see if your regular car insurance covers you in a rental car. Certain credit

cards also provide some cover if you pay for your rental with that card.
- There will be a charge if you intend to return the car to a different location. One way car rentals have higher base rates and drop off charges.
- Return your car at the agreed time. If you are late then the company could charge you for an extra day.
- If you return the car a day early you could face an early return fee, particularly if your shortened rental period means that you no longer qualify for a weekly rate.
- Car rental at 'peak' times could be more expensive.
- Adding more than one driver to your rental agreement often carries an extra charge, but some companies, like Avis and Budget, will allow the renter's spouse or domestic partner to drive the vehicle for no extra charge.
- If you regularly rent a car abroad consider joining a company's loyalty scheme.
- The advertised rate maybe an off season price for an unsuitable car size.

Acquire an International Driving Permit before you leave home. Currently these are £5.50 from the Post Office or the AA and are valid for one year. For most countries you do not need one but check if you do on the RAC site. An IDP is not a licence to drive a vehicle and is just a translation of your own licence. Regard it as an extra insurance policy that the police cannot argue with:
www.theaa.com
www.postoffice.co.uk
www.rac.co.uk/travel/driving-abroad/international-driving-permit/where-do-i-need-an-idp/

- Even if you are on a driving holiday do not spoil your trip by trying to do too much driving. One or two long drives a week interspaced with very short drive days is the way to go.
- Book hotels in advance if you feel safer, but it is better just to wing it and rock up hoping for the best. It will cheaper that way and it will give you greater flexibility.
- If you are renting for a long time it may be better to buy a car. Up north in Australia garages desperately need 4 wheel drive vehicles. Why not buy one in say, Melbourne, tour the

country and then sell it, maybe at a profit if you get really lucky.

Now that the children are long gone and there are just the two of you, you could hire a small camper van rather than a big expensive 'recreational vehicle'. They come with a double bed and some camping gear. You can travel around as the mood takes or do some planning. Stop where you want to or at national park camping sites. This is a particularly good option in the States and New Zealand. (Refer to chapter 12)

    lostcampersusa.com
    escapecampervans.com
    wickedcampers.ca

Out and about on the road there are more potential hazards to try and minimise:

- Familiarize yourself with the workings of the car before you set off. Check which side your petrol tank is on, and test out all the dashboard instruments. Memorize the make, model and colour of your car, write it down or take a photo. You will feel very silly if you have parked it and forgotten what it looks like.
- Lock the doors and keep the windows shut at all times to prevent bag and purse snatchers, particularly in busy towns. This assumes you will have air-conditioning in hot countries.
- Always wear seat belts.
- Avoid driving at night.
- Do not leave any valuables in the car. Make sure everything is hidden away out of sight.
- Park only in well lit and well travelled areas, particularly at night. Ideally your accommodation will have a private parking area.
- Do not pick up hitch hikers. I always feel a bit guilty about this as it was my main form of transport in the sixties.
- Be suspicious of anyone that approaches you offering to help. If there are groups of unpleasant looking individuals nearby then drive away and do not get out of the car.
- Be extra careful at petrol stations.
- Be aware of any 'staged' accidents designed to divert your attention or get you to stop.

- If you find yourself unsure about an area, back into your parking space to facilitate a quick get-away.
- Familiarize yourself with the local rules of the road before you leave home. Which side of the road to drive on, who has the right of way on a round-a-bout and whether you're permitted to turn right on a red light? Once in France I slept overnight in the car and continued my journey at first light. I drove for several miles until I found someone heading towards me on the wrong side of the road!
- If you have not got a GPS device buy a good road map.

As you are already an experienced driver you will already know all these bits of advice, but it never hurts to refresh your memory. Mistakes are easily made and can be costly. If you take care and are sensible you are unlikely to have any problems at all. Having a car to get about with can add so much more to your travelling experience.

On Lake Ganvie children learn to paddle at a very young age

24 Places to get to soon

"Only it seems to me that once in your life before you die you ought to see a country where they don't talk in English and don't even want to."
Thornton Wilder 1897-1975

I have been to some of the places described below and others I have not yet got around to. They are or were, all high up on my never ending destinations list, but one only has a certain amount of time and money. There are always new articles in travel magazines and the travel sections of newspapers, revealing destinations that the traveller must get to before everyone else discovers them or before things change. These are just a few suggestions amongst many and I am reluctant to be sharing some of these ideas at all in case you get there before I do. Once the tourist masses arrive then like all travel experiences they will be continually devalued.

Gabon
Thirteen new national parks have opened up here safeguarding much of the wildlife. The Loango National Park is one of the highlights. Described as 'Africa's last Eden' almost 85% is covered by rainforest. Where else can you see hippos and elephants on the beach?

Cuba
At the moment Cuba and Havana in particular, have immense charm. Maybe it is because it has been isolated by America for so long and their citizens are not permitted to visit, that it has avoided the horrors American influence can bring, such as McDonalds. Americans still go there but have to arrive via another country. If caught they face big fines or up to 10 years in jail. The real attraction in Havana is the faded grandeur of the crumbling colonial buildings and the amazing American classic cars from the 1940's and 1950's. The American trade embargo with Cuba in 1960 had the effect of instantly halting car spare parts along with most other trade and imports. All these cars are still on the road patched up with Russian spares and Chinese tractor parts. At the moment the whole place is a wonderful living museum, but things are changing and this process will accelerate when Castro dies.

In Havana, there is very little hassle, lots of people are offering cigars, rooms and restaurants but they do not persist. The food outside of international hotels is dismal, shops are poorly stocked and art galleries and museums have little in them. Take a walk around all the back streets of Havana, it is safe enough and a magical experience.

The old American classic cars are a big attraction in Havana

Falkland Islands

If you like hiking, wild life and photography or are interested in past wars and conflicts, then this is the place for you. At present it is a unique group of islands that are very British with Union Jacks everywhere, but this could all change if Argentina get their hands on it. The weather is going to be the big problem for any visitor unless you like rain.

Madagascar

Possibly already too late to beat the crowds but there is no place on earth like it. After being isolated for 80 million years in the Indian Ocean it has developed a unique array of flora and fauna. It is the fourth largest island in the world and home to innumerable unique species including the wonderful lemurs. It is the second most biologically diverse country in the world after Brazil. Get there soon before they cut all the trees down or cane toads alter the ecological balance.

Antarctica

With the regulations for ships entering these waters continually changing fewer will be allowed to set sail, so prices will inevitably go up. Get a real sense of old fashioned adventure exploring the last great wilderness on earth.

Mozambique

This is now a peaceful country with plenty to do and see. You could be of the few people to get to the Quirimbas Islands before things change. The hidden gems of the country are in the north with lots of nice beaches and some game parks. They are even changing the official language from Portuguese to English. Make sure you go in the dry season between the end of July and October.

Ethiopia

Some of sub-Saharan Africa's greatest historical sites are here. Plenty of tourists make the trip but there is still lots of room left for you. Travelling around is quite easy and the people are friendly.

Mountain Gorillas

You can go Gorilla tracking in several African countries. This remarkable primate shares nearly 98% of its genetic make-up with us. The remaining population of mountain gorillas is about 750. Numbers are slowly rising although they are still on the critically endangered list and they can be seen in 3 countries.

In Rwanda the dreadful war in 1994 between the Tutsis and Hutus that left one million dead is long over. The north of the country is home to about 280 mountain gorillas in 'the land of a thousand hills'. Right up on the border with Uganda and Congo is a ring of volcanoes where the mountain gorillas live. Unfortunately they occupy a fertile and densely populated area shared with man, although the locals are now more aware of the associated problems. Guides take small groups of tourists up into the hills to spend one hour with the gorillas and permits are $750.

In Uganda gorilla tracking is the top attraction. They are found in the Bwindi Impenetrable National Park. The permit alone costs $500 a day and that may look cheap in years to come. Some friends sent me a video clip of their experience. They were very close to the animals when one turned and came towards them. The commentary was, 'Oh shit' and the scene suddenly looked like a clip from the Blair Witch Project. Uganda has two dry seasons, December to February and June to September; in the wet seasons roads may become impassable. If a gorilla does happen to charge at you, then a handy tip is to stay absolutely still, the last thing you should do is run away.

The Congo gorilla permits for the Virunga National Park are $400 but there are occasional special offers. Travelling in the Congo is a bit more limited but you can stay in Uganda or Rwanda and then go to the Congo for your trek.

Failing all the above go to Bristol Zoo where the new gorilla enclosure allows brilliant close up viewing.

Ssese Islands, Uganda

Once you have ticked off the Gorillas on your hit list then try and get to these islands in the middle of Lake Victoria. These tropical Islands in the middle of Africa just south of the Equator were almost inaccessible for many years and only visited by the most intrepid of backpackers. Now you can get a ferry from Entebbe.

Papua New Guinea

The best reason to go is because there are so few tourists. Most visitors go for the Goroka show every September where over 100 tribes meet up for three days of dancing, music and activities. There is also the Mount Hagen show in August bringing together sing song groups from all over the country in traditional costume. Get tickets well in advance. Most organised trips are very expensive so if you are on a budget go independently. Fly from Australia to Port Moresby and get a visa on arrival or in advance from the London embassy.

Guinea Bissau

What is delightful is that there are no tourists or tourist attractions. This is the appeal, nothing has been tainted by Western influence. It is a genuine experience where the people do not even understand the concept of tourism. The Chinese are trying to get a toe hold in there and once roads are built it will inevitably start to change.

Dominica

It has been saved from the mass tourism that has spoilt other Caribbean Islands because it has no really white sandy beaches. It is full of green mountains, waterfalls, hot springs and a boiling lake. It is not a destination for sun-lounging but more for taking advantage of the stunning scenery. It is great for hiking, walking and wild life. Go in May or June when it is slightly out of season or when everyone else is there from January to April, but take an umbrella.

Bahia

This Brazilian state has 625 miles of rugged coastline and unspoilt beaches. Another former Portuguese colony like Goa but it is being developed more sensibly. It is not just about the beach, there is also wonderful old colonial architecture. There is still time to get there but perhaps you are 10 years too late.

Kovalam

On the coast in Kerala, India it has a wonderful beach and places nearby to walk to and visit. There are plenty of tourists here but it is not too overcrowded. Just turn up on your own as it is extremely easy to find accommodation. One of the best experiences here is to be sitting in a restaurant with a cold beer overlooking the beach while your fish is being barbequed. Some of the best seafood meals we have had anywhere in the world were there. Kovalam was discovered by people of our age or so over 40 years ago, the hippies. Now it has been developed to provide a sanitised Indian experience. It is still perfect, so try to fit it into your Indian itinerary.

Varkala

Again on the coast in Kerala and slightly north of Kovalam it is another place discovered by the hippies. You might have been one of them. It is still a fabulous bohemian place strung out along the top of a cliff overlooking the beach and the Arabian Sea. It retains a lot of charm and locals still pull in the fishing nets along the beach. Relax and get an ayervedic massage, you may never want to leave. While you are swimming eagles pluck fish from the water all around you. It is just another day in paradise for you and me. Beware when swimming as every twenty minutes or so a big wave arrives catching you unawares. When the wave hits it is just like being in a tumble drier and you have to wait until the ocean releases you. It might sound like fun but I was stupid enough to be wearing my sunglasses. Not only did I lose them but also my headband and even the bracelets on my wrist were ripped off. You have been warned.

Burma

Myanmar as it is now called has seen an incredible rise in tourist numbers since it has all opened up to the world again, however numbers are still relatively low compared to its neighbour, Thailand. You can now go with a clear conscience since the release of Aung San Suu Kyi from house arrest and the lifting of the recommended tourist boycott. Things are bound to change as the influence of Western culture starts creeping in and international companies establish outlets. There is a slow and ancient train that goes from Thazi, in the Mandalay region to Kalaw winding its way along the wooded mountainside. Described as a 'hidden gem' it leaves at 5.30am to serve the local population and arrives at 10.30am. Get to the station early to buy a ticket and take lots of US Dollars as ATMs are few and far between.

Albania

This country has not long emerged from the isolation of extreme Communism. It is hard to believe it is just up the road from Greece and that tourists have only just broken down the doors to Europe's final frontier. It has a lot going for it with Roman and Greek ruins, an unspoilt coastline and mountains inland. The backpackers have already paved the way for you.

Rodrigues

This is a tiny island 600 kilometres east of Mauritius in the Indian Ocean. It gained independence from the UK in 1968 and is like Mauritius used to be. It is so remote that hardly anyone has heard of it let alone been there. You can fly there from Mauritius and it takes only 90 minutes. It is not tropical like Mauritius but drier and rockier with no tourists. There are deserted beaches, coral reefs and great walks in the rugged interior. Next winter we fly to Reunion, Mauritius and Rodrigues. Trailfinders priced out all the flights and getting there will confer serious bragging rights. It is best to avoid the cyclone season from December to March.
www.tourism-rodrigues.mu

Sao Tome and Principe

I guess this is another place that you are going to need money, time and endurance to get to, but will be worth while. 200miles off the coast of West Africa it is somewhat isolated with very few tourists. The two tiny volcanic islands straddling the Equator are linked by a small plane. They are former slave centres and gained independence from Portugal in 1975, creating one of the world's smallest independent countries. The most straight forward flight goes from Portugal.

www.flytap.com

Kilimanjaro

I mention this because there is a magnificent glacier at the top that is rapidly melting. Between 1912 and 2007 it lost 85% of its volume. Another statistic states that it lost 26% of its volume between 2000 and 2009 alone. The ice reflects the heat of the sun back into the sky but as more rock is exposed more heat is absorbed by the bare rock speeding up the melting process. Global warming seems to be a likely cause, some experts disagree, but this is what I was told on my journey up. What does seem likely is that the glacier could be gone by 2030 so you have limited time left.

China

Things are changing fast as the Chinese people move from the country to the cities. Wages are increasing and the middle classes are expanding. More and more tourists are swarming over the main sites such as the unbelievable 'Emperors Army' at Xian. A lot of these people are going to be the Chinese themselves exploring their own country. The Great Wall is awesome but you must make a real effort to escape from the crowds. We went to the Mutianyu section where you take a cable car and then walk. It is steep in parts and assuming you are fit enough, for the best experience, set off on your own. I had two hours allocated to explore before my coach departed. Set your watch and get as far as you can in one hour before turning back. Some of the sections are very steep so most tourists get left behind quickly and you will soon be in splendid isolation. After 45 minutes I got to the end of the renovated section, there was only one person there, an optimistic souvenir seller. Signs say not to go any further but there was nobody around to stop me. I walked for a further 15 minutes along the still ruined section. Here the wall is crumbling away and you can see the dilapidated wall tracing its way up over the mountains. There is not really a path as such but it is easy enough to scramble along. Trees, shrubs and flowers are growing out of it and along with the isolation it is perhaps nicer than the renovated bit. Are you fit enough?

Another unrenovated section of the Great Wall of China to explore, if you have time to get up there you will be on your own

The Emperor's Army in Xian, has to be seen to be believed.

Cocos Islands

These 27 tiny islands lie off the west coast of Australia are reached by a three hour flight from Perth. This is Australia's remotest national park. Fly to West Island, one of the two inhabited ones, then go on to North Keeling Island. Come to think of it Christmas Island is in the same bit of ocean.

Isle of Wight

It is like going back to how England was in the fifties. The southern coast is getting eroded away by the sea and will disappear in 20,000 years. If you last went 20 years ago and stayed in a hotel by the sea on the south coast it has possibly been washed away by now. Check out the annual walking festival.

Colca Canyon, Peru

Though it's overshadowed by the more famous Machu Picchu, Colca Canyon is worth seeing on any trip to Peru. It is not exactly undiscovered and is Peru's third most visited tourist destination. Located about 100 miles outside of Arequipa, it's more than twice as deep as the Grand Canyon, although virtually nobody makes it to the really deep bit. Keep an eye out for the Andean condor, a native bird that makes its home in and around the canyon.

Tasmania

Everyone has heard of Tasmania but few people actually get there. This is the only island in the world where you'll find the famous Tasmanian devil in the wild. There is no need to go to the zoo in Tasmania, when the sun goes down marsupials are all over the place.

East Timor

Very few travellers make it here and you need to check the advice of the FCO first. It is not a holiday hotspot yet, but it will be. Intrepid back packers are opening it up with its pristine beaches, mountains, rock formations and sleepy fishing villages.

St Helena

This UK governed island located 1,200 miles from the nearest land is only accessible by a mail ship. This makes it a unique experience and one that may soon change as there is talk of building an airstrip. Catch the RMS St Helena from Cape Town to this unspoilt destination and regard it as just another cruise. Better still you can fly from RAF Brize Norton to Ascension Island and pick up the boat from there to St Helena.

http://rms-st-helena.com

Tristan da Cunha

While you are in the area you could pop down to see this archipelago of small islands in the South Atlantic Ocean. The only way is by mail ship, again from Cape Town. It takes 6 days at sea and the world's most isolated community will give you a grand welcome.

www.tristandc.com/shipping.php

The Antarctic is the last great wilderness

The faded grandeur of Havana

25 Traveller's Tales

"The world is a book and those who do not travel read only one page."
St. Augustine of Hippo 354 - 430ad

Part of the joy of travelling is being able to come home and tell your friends all about your trip. As you become more well travelled you will accumulate a lot a traveller's tales which will gradually be elaborated upon to impress everyone. Wherever we go there is always an unexpected encounter and here are just a few.

'Michael row the boat ashore'

Whilst visiting Egypt, somewhere close to Luxor, my wife and I spotted what appeared to be a small temple on the other side of the Nile. It looked mysterious and isolated in the middle of nothing but a sea of sand. Like all travellers we were hoping for adventure and to discover that place where no tourists had got to. Along with another man we hired a boat to take us across. It was a big old iron boat of some fifty foot with a lot of rust and we negotiated a very cheap price. It was in the heat of the day and on the other side there were no paths or shade but we were well enough equipped with our sunhats and flasks of water. In splendid isolation we fought our way across the dunes and to our little temple. It was nothing special but was ours to explore for that moment. Why was it there and what was the history behind it? All these questions remained unanswered. The real adventure began on the way back across the Nile when the boat engine failed. It had already got up a little speed and was drifting quite quickly to the opposite bank, directly towards a posh restaurant on stilts jutting out into the water. As we got closer the diners left their tables and came up to the windows and door pointing at us in amazement. Our 'captain' was beginning to worry and began furiously pulling on the starter cable to the outboard motor. As we drifted within twenty feet of the restaurant the diners look of astonishment turned to fear as they began running away from the window. A collision was almost certain and as the restaurant was on stilts it appeared doomed. By now the captain was in a state of sheer panic as he yanked the cable and we braced ourselves for the impending impact. At the very last minute the engine fired up and the captain jammed it into reverse. Disaster was narrowly averted, but by then we were so close that we were able to step off the boat and into the restaurant. All eyes were upon us as we strolled through like characters from an Indiana Jones movie. First there was a stunned silence followed by an outbreak of spontaneous applause. The captain had still wanted a tip but on this occasion we kept our hands in our pockets.

'In The jungle, the mighty jungle'

There is a group of small islands just off the coast of Kota Kinabalu in Sabah called the Tunku Abdul Rahman National Park. Easily reachable by small boat, they make an excellent days outing. We got off the ferry and took the hiking trail across the island, even though a guide is recommended. There is only one path through the thick jungle so it is difficult to go wrong and it takes about 2 hours to reach the other side. Eventually we emerged to find an idyllic beach, which we had all to ourselves. We stripped off and jumped in the sea with not another soul around. Wandering further round along the beach we could see the little jetty where the boat had dropped us off and it did not seem too far away. The island was crescent shaped and this looked like a good short cut back. We set off along the beach but it quickly petered out changing into a coastline of impenetrable mango swamp. However, just off the coast a wooden platform had been built on stilts sunken into the seabed. This seem to lead directly back to the ferry. We waded out holding our rucksacks high above our heads. By the time we got to the platform we were up to our necks in water and the platform was much higher than we had anticipated. I just about managed to get up on top, however, my wife struggled but made it with a lot of help and a grazed knee. So far so good and we followed the platform for 50 metres or so until there was a gap we had not spotted, where it was broken. Further on we could see many more gaps and we were forced to abandon our plan. Getting off a high platform is just as difficult as getting on, especially when we were trying to keep our gear dry. It was then that we thought about salt water crocodiles. Were there any here or not? Probably not but we were not sure, so into the sea again we waded back to the shore by which time we were running a little late in order to catch the last ferry. Thinking about the hiking trail and the layout of the island it was obvious that if we cut through the jungle we would have to eventually find the path. It was hard going hiking up a steep wooded slope from the beach, with no path to follow, and by then we had run out of water. It was hot and we were both tired and thirsty. I could move a lot quicker than my wife so between us we decided that she should stay and rest while I struck out on my own to find the trail. We kept in touch by shouting and whistling as I moved further away. Fortunately I hit the trail before we became out of contact and it looked like we might make it back in time after all. It was then that a tropical cyclone began along with high winds. Branches and debris were falling down all around us and this was the last place we wanted to be. We stepped up our pace, not stopping and pushing ourselves to the very limit. So quickly did we move that we arrived back with 20 minutes to spare. There was a little bar, but all we wanted was water. Never have we drunk so much water in one go, it was expensive but worth every ringgit.

N.B. There are crocodiles but they are increasingly rare.

'Back in the USSR'

The Hermitage in St Petersburg is open from 10.30am to 6pm and we were determined to get our moneys worth. At 5.45pm the guard ordered us out and I protested explaining that we had another 15 minutes. He pulled out his gun and we left right away.

'Don't touch me I'm a real live wire'

We were in the Amazon jungle at an animal rehabilitation centre and I was sitting on a bench just waiting to go. On the bench with me a large ant was running around providing an interesting distraction. What I did not realise until later was that this was a Conga Ant, also known as the Bullet Ant and Lesser Giant Hunter Ant, the most dangerous ant in the jungle. It is the largest ant in the world and can grow up to one inch. If it bites it will cause intense pain, swelling and require hospital treatment, and there it was running around on my bench. The locals call it the Bullet Ant as the pain is likened to being shot with a bullet. It would be excruciating pain and intense throbbing for 24 hours. Incredibly the Satere-Mawe people of Brazil deliberately sting themselves multiple times, repeatedly over months as part of their initiation rites to become warriors. Be careful where you step in the jungle.

'We've gotta get out of this place'

It had been a nice family holiday to Tunisia, but sadly it was over and we were at customs checking in our luggage. I lifted up the cases to put them through the security machine expecting to be waived through, however, the machine stopped leaving my case inside. The official was studying the contents of my case carefully and looked clearly concerned, as if he had just stumbled upon a terrorist network.

He said, 'Just a minute sir, would you mind waiting there for a minute?'

He made a phone call and spoke agitatedly for a few minutes. Guards quickly arrived and a senior customs official came to study the scanner screen. I was told to step aside and was beginning to wonder what it was inside my case that had aroused their attention. I had read about criminals and drug couriers sneaking illegal things into unsuspecting tourists cases. The cases had not been left alone, they were locked and I had packed them. I stole a look at the screen, and there it was, for everyone to see, the clear outline of a sub-machine gun.

The case was moved out of the scanner and to the counter and other travellers were diverted to a different queue.

'Unlock your case sir.'

It was more of an order than a polite request.

With the case unlocked the customs team moved gingerly forward and one of them opened the case slowly. I guess it could have been booby trapped so they were taking no chances. With the case successfully opened they used some specially adapted long handled tongs to lift up the first item of clothing dumping it on the counter. As each article was removed the officials crowded around to see the incriminating evidence. All sorts of thoughts were whizzing around in my head, arrest, a night in jail or worse. I would not have been able to explain it away.

The final article was lifted up, the officials all looked at each other and broke into laughter. We had taken a small cricket bat on holiday with us and a water heating machine, a white plastic affair with a coiled element sticking out at the bottom. When the two were lined up, yes, they looked exactly like a gun.

'She's got a ticket to ride'

After the long flight to India we were glad to finally be at Dabolim International airport and soon to have two great weeks in Goa. Entering through customs after under going the necessary formalities we were each given a ticket and passed through into a sort of no man's land, a smallish confined area where everyone could be vetted. You cannot go back and for security measures the only way out is to present your ticket to the official at the end of a short queue. My wife dropped her ticket, it floated down in the air, rotated a few times and with perfect precision wafted straight under the only door in the room. We tried to blag our way out but with no ticket there was no exit. It took a lot of explaining to customs officer what had happened but in the end he understood. However, the door was locked, nobody had a key or knew where the key was. We had to sit down, on the floor and were effectively trapped. It was a full hour before the key was found. The door was opened and the ticket found. Following that experience I am now in charge of tickets for everything at all times.

'Hey hey we're the monkeys'

We were staying in a small hut, in the middle of the Sabah rain forest. There were some walking trails in the area, nobody said you couldn't go off on your own but normally a guide led the way. We got up at first light and set off up the hill on our own and after about 45 minutes we spotted an orangutan high up in the trees. We knew that you were not supposed to look at them directly in the eyes in case it provoked a confrontation so we had to be cautious. Later back in the camp we told the park warden and until then we had not realised how fortunate we had been to actually see one in the wild.

He said, 'What did it look like?'

'Well, it was hairy and had long arms.......'

To us it was an orangutan and all we could do was narrow it down to a medium sized male. The rangers knew every animal by sight.

'The times they are a changin'

We were lucky enough to get to Libya before Colonel Gaddafi's downfall and all the ensuing troubles. Leptis Magna is an amazingly well preserved Roman city and a UNESCO World Heritage Centre with very few visitors. What a wonderful place Libya is, however, they are just not geared up for tourism. When checking out of our hotel we had to collect our passports. There was a short line of guests also waiting and looking somewhat impatient. The man on reception had a pile of passports and for each customer went through the entire pile looking at the photos until he matched it up and triumphantly handed it over. Next one please.

'If you gotta make a fool of somebody'

The Temple of Artemis is one of the seven wonders of the ancient world located near Ephesus in Turkey. We decided to search it out and took the local bus from Bodrum, an unpleasant journey in the heat of the summer. Ephesus itself was wonderful but where was the Temple of Artemis? After and hour or so wandering around and asking we found it, in the middle of a field surrounded by cows. It was just a pile of stones with a few broken columns, and this was one of the Seven Wonders of the World. Unloved and unnoticed maybe the importance of the sight has been realised by now.

'Where do you go to my lovely?'

Of the 'big five' the leopard is the most difficult to spot in the wild. In Tanzania I did sort of see one whilst on Safari. Our guide spotted a black leopard sitting in a tree.

'There it is' he said, pointing to something in the distance.

'Where?' we all replied as there was really nothing to look at.

'Over there in the cleft of that tree.'

'What tree?'

The tree was so far away that I needed binoculars to actually see it and even then where was the leopard? Gradually it became clear, the leopard was sitting in a cleft of the tree and its tail was hanging down like an umbrella handle silhouetted against the horizon. These guides have good eyesight.

'This is the dawning of the Age of Aquarius'

The Banya or Sauna is a long standing rich Russian tradition. In St. Petersburg there is one that is popular with the expats called Krugliye Bani and will provide an interesting experience. At the door men and women have to separate. Once inside I stripped off naked and entered the Swedish sauna. There, I was befriended by three young army recruits who had brought in some dried fish, which they shared with me, but a few minutes later they were all thrown out for eating. The Swedish Sauna was hot but nothing compared to the next room.

The Swedish sauna is for 'wussies', the Russian sauna is so hot that you could quite easily cook to death. The challenge was to stay in as long as possible just before you might pass out. Naked Russians were running in and out all the time.

They were running out to a plunge pool, jumping in, and getting out fairly quick. I jumped in bashing blocks of ice out of the way as I submerged. At these temperatures in 15 minutes you could be unconscious and in 45 minutes dead. I too got out PDQ.

There was another cabin up some wooden steps where naked men were disappearing into, so I followed. Opening the door I was confronted with dozens of naked men crowded together in the steam. They held bunches of green birch twigs which they were beating each other with or self flagellating. I picked up some twigs and started flailing away at my back. This is a classic banya practice that is supposedly good for the skin.

Finally men were disappearing through another door into the open air. I opened the door and there before me was a round open air heated pool full of naked women and men. It was a bit like a Roman orgy except nobody was having sex, and there was my wife who had been through a similar experience. We lay there in the water under the starlit sky wishing there were such facilities in England.

'Shakin' all over'

There are lots of hamams or Turkish baths in Istanbul. Years ago in a men's magazine there was an article, '50 things to do before you die'. On the list was, 'Have the Sultans massage at the Cagaloglu Hamami in Istanbul.' This was a long time ago and things have changed, the experience has been toned down now to accommodate the ordinary tourist. They still claim to be one of the 1,000 places to see before you die, anyway this is how it was.

This hamam was built in 1741 and is a beautiful structure, comprising of a huge round heated marble slab under a massive dome. I had paid an exorbitant amount for this massage and wrapped only in a towel lay on the marble slab waiting for my masseur. The fires burn directly under the slab and in the middle it was far too hot to lie on.

The masseur arrived, a huge overweight man clad only in a loin cloth. He picked me up by one arm, with one arm, and gently shook me. Then for the next thirty minutes he proceeded to wrestle with me in a similar fashion to the ridiculous professional contests on television, except I was not fighting back. At one time he had me upside down in midair, with me stretched over his back, my legs held by his legs and his arms under my arms with his hands clasped behind my head and then he stretched me further. His arms and legs were all over the place entwined with my body and he tweaked, pulled, bent and stretched every single part of me.

I was hauled to the side of the building where there are various bowls of hot, warm and cold water where for the next thirty minutes I was washed and scrubbed in every little nook and cranny of my body. He washed my hair, scrubbed every inch of my body, washed between my toes, inside and out of my ears and nose, he cleaned between my buttocks around the anus, between my legs, under my penis and foreskin. Every now and then he would fill buckets of hot water and hurl them at me. Some people may see this as some sort of invasion of privacy but that is how it was, sometimes you have to 'take a walk on the wild side'.

The masseur, he just did it for the tip, another example of a gratuity well deserved. It was a unique experience and one that cannot be found elsewhere in the world.

'Come on baby light my fire'

Many years ago in Bali we hired a taxi for the day. It cost very little and the driver took us to lots of interesting places. In the evening he agreed to take us to watch the men walk on fire. We were going to book up at our hotel anyway but he got us in for free and sat us right down at the front, on the floor, so close to the fire that the heat was only just bearable. We had the best position in the venue while the other guests from our hotel were sat way back in the seats and had paid more for this outing than we had paid for the whole day.

The fire walker came on, he appeared to be in some sort of a trance and his feet were bare. By now the flames had died down and the glowing embers were raked into a long trough dug out from the ground. At first he walked quickly through the hot embers as if testing them out, then he shuffled though more slowly. He was clearly spaced out, and warmed to his task by standing on the red hot fire, kicking up sparks and glowing bits of wood all around him, some of which landed near to us. This was no imitation show, we were in some danger just sitting there. How he was not burnt remains an ongoing mystery.

'I'm gonna stick like glue
stick, because I'm
stuck on you'

The Sinharaja Forest in Sri Lanka is quite isolated but as pristine rain forest well worth visiting. However, in the wet season the forest is swarming with ferocious leeches which will try to attach themselves to you at every opportunity. We began by covering our shoes and socks with salt, but you cannot escape them. They can sense body heat and movement from 10 feet away, so we did not stand still for very long. It takes a leech 15 minutes to get comfortable and sink its teeth into your skin, so every 15 minutes we stopped to flick them off. In reality most of us checked far more regularly than that. Unlucky hikers had them on their arms, necks and faces. Once the leeches start sucking out your blood you can feel very little. After two hours or so of feeding they may fall off and leave a small bloody hole which may continue bleeding. In Colonial times leeches were rated as the worst enemy.

'I got you babe'

On the Gambian border my wife and I were approached by a woman who tried to give us her 6 month year old baby. She said,

'Please take my baby home with you. He would have a better life. Please give him a chance. Please do this as a humanitarian act.'

She already had 5 other children and wanted a better life for it. She had no means of support and did not realise the complications involved.

'Too much, the Magic Bus'

The buses in rural Peru are infrequent, you miss the bus and there may not be another one until the next day or even the following week. Many locals in the high Andes rely on this service and missing the bus is not an option. The Peruvian peasants, particularly the Peruvian 'hat' women, have a bit of a reputation for not having too high a standard of hygiene. Nature calls, but once on the bus it is not going to make a 'comfort' stop just for you. Blokes can just dangle their willies out of the bus window but for women it is slightly more difficult, but still possible. The woman in front sort of lifted up her skirts and wedged her arse out of the window with a certain degree of agility, but this wasn't just a 'number one'. A 'number 2' out of a bus window which is hurtling around hairpin bends is not a pretty sight but full marks for ingenuity.

'Help, I need somebody'

We were staying on the Atlantic coast in The Gambia. Hardly

anyone ventures out of the resort but we decided to take the local buses to the capital, Banjul, on the basis of an overheard conversation. The journey consisted of 3 separate trips in dilapidated minibuses each of which cost about 2p but got us there surprisingly easily. We made our way to the local market but were stopped on the way by 2 huge black thugs, (Thugs come in all colours)

'Where are you going?'
'We just want to look around the market.'
'No you cannot go in there alone it is too dangerous.'
'We just want to walk alone.'
'No, you will be attacked and robbed.'
'We will take that chance.'
'No, you must come with us, we will show you.'

At this point we tried to walk on but they blocked our path and nothing we said would deter them. These guys were seriously big and nasty. We tried side-stepping them but they physically blocked our way. Luckily we were saved by the appearance of a policeman and the thugs just melted away. We were so relieved to see him and he said,

'No you cannot go in there alone, I will show you.'

Finally after shaking him off we got into the market and had a lot of fun bartering with the locals.

These are some of my traveller's tales and I would be interested in hearing some of yours. Please send any interesting experiences and encounters you have had to - **timothy.blewitt@sky.com**

The male frigate puffs out his chest to attract the females.

26 We want the world and we want it - Now!

"Make voyages. Attempt them. There's nothing else."
Tennessee Williams 1911-1983

Exactly how many countries are there in the world for us to go and visit? It may seem strange but nobody is absolutely sure. It depends upon who you ask and what is recognised as a country, so do not believe anything that is written down here. This is due to the continually changing political landscape and the precise definition of what a country is. The most widely-accepted definition is derived from the 1933 Montevideo Convention. By these guidelines, a state must have a government, be in a position to interact with other states diplomatically, have a defined territory and possess a permanent population. Since South Sudan became an independent state on 9 July 2011, there are supposed to be 195 independent sovereign states in the world, including Taiwan, but due to political reasons it fails to be recognised by the international community as independent. There are about a further 60 dependent areas and five disputed areas, such as Kosovo. Apparently there are only 191 countries that are not disputed. Within the United Nations there are 193 countries but this does not include independent countries such as Vatican City. The USA recognises 195 independent countries but not Taiwan, although it really is independent and was a member of the United Nations until 1971. China claims that Taiwan is simply a province of China. Taiwan along with Western Sahara, Northern Cyprus, Somaliland, South Ossetia, Transnistria and Nagorno-Karabakh are all involved in a struggle for independence from a larger state. Some countries are part of a larger country such as, England, Scotland, Wales and Northern Ireland. As you can see it is all a bit confusing but 196 is the most frequent answer. The list below contains 197 independent countries, so another one crept in somewhere. I have put a tick next to the countries I have visited:

Afghanistan
Albania
Algeria
Andorra ✓
Angola
Antigua and Barbuda

Argentina ✓
Armenia
Australia ✓
Austria ✓
Azerbaijan
The Bahamas
Bahrain

Bangladesh
Barbados ✓
Belarus
Belgium ✓
Belize
Benin ✓
Bhutan

Bolivia
Bosnia and Herzegovina
Botswana ✓
Brazil ✓
Brunei
Bulgaria ✓
Burkina Faso
Burundi
Cambodia ✓
Cameroon ✓
Canada ✓
Cape Verde ✓
Central African Republic
Chad
Chile ✓
China ✓
Colombia
Comoros
Congo Republic
Congo D. R.
Costa Rica
Cote d'Ivoire ✓
Croatia ✓
Cuba ✓
Cyprus ✓
Czech Republic
Denmark ✓
Djibouti
Dominica
Dominican Republic
East Timor
Ecuador ✓
Egypt ✓

El Salvador
Equatorial Guinea
Eritrea
Estonia
Ethiopia
Fiji
Finland
France ✓
Gabon
The Gambia ✓
Georgia
Germany ✓
Ghana ✓
Greece ✓
Grenada ✓
Guatemala
Guinea ✓
Guinea-Bissau ✓
Guyana Fr. ✓
Haiti
Honduras
Hungary ✓
Iceland ✓
India ✓
Indonesia ✓
Iran
Iraq
Ireland ✓
Israel
Italy ✓
Jamaica
Japan
Jordan
Kazakhstan
Kenya ✓
Kiribati

Korea North
Korea South
Kosovo
Kuwait
Kyrgyzstan
Laos
Latvia
Lebanon
Lesotho
Liberia
Libya ✓
Liechtenstein
Lithuania
Luxembourg ✓
Macedonia
Madagascar ✓
Malawi ✓
Malaysia
Maldives ✓
Mali
Malta ✓
Marshall Islands
Mauritania
Mauritius ✓
Mexico
Micronesia
Moldova
Monaco
Mongolia
Montenegro
Morocco ✓
Mozambique
Myanmar
Namibia ✓
Nauru
Nepal ✓
Netherlands ✓
New Zealand
Nicaragua

Niger
Nigeria ✓
Norway ✓
Oman
Pakistan
Palau
Panama ✓
Papua N Guinea
Paraguay
Peru ✓
Philippines
Poland ✓
Portugal ✓
Qatar
Romania
Russia ✓
Rwanda ✓
St Kitts & Nevis
Saint Lucia ✓
Saint Vincent & Grenadines ✓
Samoa
San Marino
Sao Tome and Principe
Saudi Arabia
Senegal ✓
Serbia
Seychelles ✓
Sierra Leone
Singapore ✓
Slovakia
Slovenia
Solomon Islands
Somalia
South Africa ✓
South Sudan
Spain ✓
Sri Lanka ✓
Sudan
Suriname
Swaziland
Sweden
Switzerland ✓
Syria
Taiwan
Tajikistan
Tanzania ✓
Thailand ✓
Togo ✓
Tonga
Trinidad and Tobago
Tunisia ✓
Turkey ✓
Turkmenistan
Tuvalu
Uganda ✓
Ukraine ✓
U A Emirates ✓
U.K. ✓
USA. ✓
Uruguay ✓
Uzbekistan
Vanuatu
Vatican City ✓
Venezuela
Vietnam ✓
Yemen
Zambia ✓
Zimbabwe ✓

While the listing above gives the independent countries of the world, it is important to remember that there are also more than sixty territories, colonies, and dependencies of independent countries. Below are some more countries of the world, islands and places that could be included in your own personal list of countries you have visited. There are probably several more that you could add:

Akrotiri
American Samoa
Anguilla
Antarctica ✓
Aruba ✓
Ashmore & Cartier Isles
Bassas da India
Bermuda ✓
Bouvet Island
British Indian Ocean Territory
British Virgin Islands
Cayman Islands

Christmas Island
Clipperton Island
Cocos Islands
Cook Islands
Coral Sea Islands
Dhekelia
Easter Island ✓
Europa Island
Falklands Islands ✓
Faroe Islands ✓
French Polynesia ✓
French & S Antarctic Lands
Gaza Strip
Gibraltar
Glorioso Islands
Greenland
Guadeloupe
Guam
Guernsey ✓
Heard Isle & McDonald.
Hong Kong ✓
Isle of Man
Jan Mayan
Jersey
Juan de Nova Island
Macau

Martinique
Mayotte
Montserrat
Navassa Island
Netherland Antilles
New Caledonia
Niue
Norfolk Island
Northern Mariana
Paracel Islands
Pitcairn Islands
Puerto Rico
Reunion ✓
Saint Helena
Saint Pierre & Miquelon
S Georgia & S Sandwich Isles.
Spratly Islands
Svalbard ✓
Timor Leste
Tokelau
Tromelin Island
Turks & Caicos Islands
Virgin Islands
Wake Island
Wallis and Futuna
West Bank
Western Sahara

Clearly I have a lot of places left to visit and I shall never visit them all, but there are reckoned to be 100 or so travellers have visited all the countries in the world. Back in 2009 an Indian businessman visited all 194 countries in the world. In 2012 Graham Hughes became the first person to visit all 201 countries in the world, without using a plane. His journey of 160,000 miles took just 1,426 days and will take some beating. There are two basic requirements, time and money plus an awful lot of research, motivation, determination, patience and sacrifice.

The Travellers' Century Club is an organisation for people who have visited 100 or more places on their list. Founded in 1954 they have identified 321 eligible countries and territories. It is a very comprehensive list of including some great destinations, if you can get to them. The club has no requirements as to how long the traveller must have stayed in a country to qualify, even a port-of-call or a plane fuel stop is enough.

http://travelerscenturyclub.org/countries-and-territories

However, this is not a competition, it is much better to travel slowly, at your own pace, enjoy each moment and go to the places that you really want to go to.

Where is the frog?

27 Memories

"Like all great travellers, I have seen more than I remember, and remember more than I have seen."
Benjamin Disraeli 1804-1881

When you return home the memories of your travels will be clear in your mind and this is the most important reason for the journey. You can regale your children and grand children with fascinating traveller's tales. In time memories will begin to fade and at our age that might be quite soon so it is wise to have a back up plan.

We keep a diary for all our major trips which gets filled in religiously every evening at some convenient point. Preferably during a pre-dinner aperitif but sometimes whilst awaiting dinner at some restaurant or maybe just before turning off the light, torch or candle. I dictate to my wife, mainly because she writes quickly and clearly, and because sometimes, I cannot even read my own writing. She reminds me of events that I have forgotten and modifies my content, so it is something of a joint effort. Ours is only a small pocket sized book, mainly because we travel light, but we get a lot into it. If you choose to do this your efforts will be rewarded later on when you have been to so many places that they are all beginning to get confused and start merging together. A quick read through and all your memories will come flooding back. We see lots of people writing diaries on our travels, some call them journals and are much more elaborate than ours. One thing I really wish I had done was to keep all the entrance tickets to museums, historical sites and parks. They tell a story on their own and are often nice little souvenirs with a picture and information on the front. They can then be pasted into your diary as an added memento. I do keep all the tickets from rock concerts and put them into the relevant CD covers, but have only just started with travel tickets. If you have a journal there will be more room to paste them in. There is a limit to what you might want to include but some of the best journals I have seen contain some wonderful drawings and cut out pictures, along with interesting written accounts. A journal could almost become a family heirloom and an important part of the travelling experience. Anything that is flat or can be flattened can be added, pressed flowers, minor value bank notes, articles cut from travel brochures, use your imagination.

Another idea might be to continue each diary into the next trip as it will generally end up with some empty pages at the back. I now do this and as life goes on I would on reflection have included all the other minor 'holidays' I have been on. We do this now but as it was we only wrote a diary for the major annual trips.

Choose your diary carefully, it almost certainly needs a hard cover for when it gets bashed around in your rucksack. If you discover one that you really like then buy a few of them particularly if you are going down the 'continuous' route. They look much nicer in a neat row on the book shelf and you will not be trawling round the shops before each new trip. I find that a lined one suits us but if every other page was plain it could accommodate cut out scraps and sketches.

I have a political world map which I have pasted to a pin board, framed and put up on my study wall. There is a black headed pin pressed in to every place visited. I love just standing there looking at it and one of the great pleasures in returning home is to add a few more pins. When my daughters saw it they immediately knew what they wanted for Christmas!

Alternatively you could purchase a scratch map. This is first and foremost a map of the world but a map with a difference. The surface is covered in a gold foil that can be scraped off to keep a record of your trips. It all seems a bit gimmicky but decide for yourself.

www.luckies.co.uk

The most important form of recording your unique travelling experiences will be photography. Digital cameras have made things so much easier than in the past. We can just snap away willy-nilly and delete the ones that don't come up to standard. There is a danger that too much time can be taken up with composing pictures and not enough actually looking at whatever it happens to be. But you are a traveller, you are on your own with plenty of time and you can do it all. I remember seeing groups of tourists, often Americans, who arrive, take their photos, and then it's a case of, 'Okay, we've done that lets go'. We have often been at some wonderful places on our own just absorbing the atmosphere, when suddenly a coach load of tourists arrive to disturb the peace. Not only do they have to rush around but they cannot get any sort of photo without crowds of other tourists in the background. We just sit back and wait until they have gone. I have only met one couple who did not take any photos at all, he was in remission from cancer and taking pictures seemed to them of little value any more. Much more important was to be living and absorbing everything around them.

It is wise to sort out your photos as soon as you can. Back them up by storing them in some way, of which there are now many. Bitter experience has shown that compact discs can get corrupted over time. Back your pictures up in at least two ways, we use an external hard drive and cloud storage. Apparently 38% of us only store our photos on the computer and they will all be lost when the hard drive eventually dies. I always carry a net book, and sometimes an iPad, with me and try to download them on a daily basis, creating folders and sub folders to store them. If you wait until you get home then you are never going to remember exactly where you took that picture. With digital photography, as it is, if you are anything like me, then after two months travelling you may have several thousand pictures and it will be a nightmare to sort them out. It is pleasant at the end of each day to have a slide show, either on the camera or computer, as a satisfying way to relive the day and at the same time you can delete all the shots that did not work out. After doing all this and verifying you have copies then don't forget to delete the images from the camera card. What I also do is create a 'developing' or a 'best of' folder so that when I do get home all I have to do is download them on to a flash drive and take them in for printing.

Printing the best photographs gives you a hard copy which makes it easier to bore or entrance your family and friends and to bring back those unique memories. All the others will get stored on your computer hard drive and backed up on an external hard drive, or wherever you choose, possibly never to be seen again. There are lots of storage ideas online and the electronic photo viewer is another great idea.

Remember that sometimes it is best to ask before taking photos of people. In popular tourist spots the locals get fed up with cameras being pointed at them. In Ganvie, a lake dwelling, in the Republic of Benin, the children have been taught to hide their faces and the women turn their heads away from the camera. In Ecuador it is even worse, if you sneak a photo and get caught the locals will shake their fists at you. They believe that for every photo a little bit of their soul is taken. On the other hand in less explored areas of the world many people love having their photos taken and are intrigued to see it for themselves. Usually children everywhere are happy to have their picture taken and a huge crowd will gather. In China it was us that were the centre of attention. I had a Chinese tourist with a video camera pointed in my face, walking backwards along with me, as if I were a celebrity. Nobody had bothered to ask me for permission and it did feel a bit intrusive. There is a similar situation in many countries where white tourists are less common. It is the locals who want a photo of you, and one of you with them.

I have travelled with people who have taken a photo of their shoes or a teddy bear in every place they have visited and with others who never take many photos at all.

Try to send emails regularly to friends and family to keep them up to date with your travels and possibly make them extremely jealous. What did we all do before the wonders of email? If you keep a regular written travel account on the iPad, netbook or the device of your choosing it can easily be transferred as an email. Always take a flash drive in case you have to go to an internet cafe. Emails can form the basis for the diary. My wife and I do not do blogs as such and refuse to become involved in social networking sites. It all seems a bit desperate and we have no desire to share the tiny details of our lives with the rest of the world. However, many people seem to want to and great if you have a big enough audience.

I do keep a website just for family members which has proved to be invaluable especially when we have forgotten what holiday we took several years ago. It was intended mainly just for holiday photographs along with a written account but now covers much more including the family history. It all started years ago when I read an article in a women's magazine entitled, 'Create your own website in 15 minutes'. Six weeks later I still had not figured how to do it, so I enrolled in an evening class at the local sixth form college. A further six weeks later and I could set up a basic website in 15 minutes or so but putting in the content does take a lot longer. I find it to be a great way of storing information in an easily accessible form, even if you do not publish it and just leave it as a document on the computer. The only drawback with publishing is that you have to pay a small annual fee to an ISP provider, but then anyone can access it anywhere in the world. There used to be more free website providers but they are notorious for disappearing quickly.

The only memories that can be bought are souvenirs and there is no accounting for taste. Plastic Eiffel towers, resin Buddhas, donkeys made from shells, stuffed leather camels, plastic cats that nod their heads and wave their arms are amongst the thousands of tourist tat that some mug will buy. Not people like us of course and all this stuff will turn up later at your local car boot sale.

Why not go the whole hog and write a book to record your memories. Whatever you decide to do the best memories are those inside your head. It is looking back on things with pride, satisfaction and knowing that you have faced up to the challenge. Maybe you were out of your comfort zone, but these are the longest lasting memories. Such memories cannot be bought, you have to make the effort to create them.

I have listed my top travel experiences. It is a very subjective list and governed to a large extent by my own personal interests, who I was with, the weather and all sorts of other influences. As I travel more widely I add in new encounters in the appropriate spot and it is already out of date. You must have been to some of them but your list will undoubtedly be a lot different. These are the top 100:

1. Everest Base Camp trek in the winter - Nepal.
2. The Devil's Pool in Zambia - sitting on the edge of Victoria Falls after swimming and scrambling across the top.
3. Angkor Wat and Beng Mealea - real Indiana Jones stuff.
4. The Victoria Falls on the Zambian side. The roar of the water and enjoying getting absolutely drenched from the spray.
5. Walking along the Great Wall of China until the end of the restored section and then further over the ruined parts.
6. Visiting the Himba Tribe women in Namibia.
7. The Terracotta army at Xian - how did they do it?
8. The Maui on Easter Island.
9. The Pyramids & the Sphinx - walking in a circle right around them.
10. Karnak Temple, Luxor, Egypt.
11. The crater on Easter Island - soon the sea will destroy it.
12. Swimming with a shark in the Galapagos Islands.
13. Antarctica - just being there.
14. Turtle Island, Borneo - watching them lay their eggs in the early hours of the morning.
15. Climbing Kilimanjaro - the Machame route to the highest point in Africa.
16. Seeing an orangutan in the wild, on our own, in Borneo.
17. 'The Sultans massage' in Istanbul.
18. Taking a microlight flight over The Victoria Falls.
19. Sigiriya, Sri Lanka - the eighth wonder of the ancient world.
20. Bathing in the hot volcanic waters of the Blue Lagoon in Iceland.
21. Seeing giant tortoises roaming in the wild up in the highlands

of Santa Cruz, Galapagos Islands.

22. Climbing Kinabalu, Borneo - from sea level to 14,000' in less than 24 hours, to watch the sunrise.
23. Bali - walking down through the paddy fields and seeing local women stripped to the waist washing clothes. (This was in 1986 so unlikely to be the same now)
24. Swimming with seahorses on the private beach of The Princess Hotel in Bermuda.
25. Abu Symbel in Northern Egypt - how did they move it?
26. Ephesus in Turkey - walk in the footsteps of Anthony & Cleopatra.
27. The Turkish baths in St. Petersburg - do what the locals do.
28. Quad biking in the sand dunes, Namibia - 'wall of death' stuff.
29. The Valley of the Kings, Egypt - arriving by donkey over the mountains.
30. Leptis Magna, Libya - the largest and most complete Roman city and the tourists have not yet arrived.
31. The Sagrada Familia in Barcelona - Gaudi's masterpiece.
32. Havana, Cuba - stay at the Ambus Mundus Hotel (where Hemmingway stayed) and explore the faded grandeur of the old town and the amazing old American cars. Remember to order a frozen Daiquiri.
33. Gliding over Sussex in a hot air balloon.
34. Taking a light aircraft flight over the Ocavango Delta.
35. Having tea at the Ritz in London.
36. Arriving at Anjuna market, Goa on a motor scooter.
37. Snorkeling in the Red Sea - more fish here than you can shake a stick at.
38. Crib Goch - the finest walk in Wales. Continue right around the Horseshoe for a great day out.
39. Tryfan in Wales - a great trek and jump from Adam to Eve at the top, if you dare.
40. Ayers Rock - walk round it, climb up it and watch the sun set on it.
41. Climbing up the Statue of Liberty - well worth the long queues.
42. High tea at The Galle Face Hotel, Colombo, Sri Lanka - not as formal as The Ritz but a more sumptuous banquet. One of the top 10 hotels in the world.

43. Climbing Dune 45 in Namibia.
44. The Recoletta in Buenos Aries - the amazing cemetery that has the memorial to Eva Peron.
45. Standing inside the Sahara dessert and feeling the hot wind.
46. Longyearbyen in Spitzbergen - the furthest north permanent settlement in the world.
47. Exploring the souk in Marrakesh & Djemaa El Fna Square.
48. Bangkok - the golden Buddha, emerald Buddha and other Buddhas
49. Walking the levadas in Madeira.
50. Crawling through the Vietcong tunnels in Vietnam.
51. Botswana - sleeping in a tent in the middle of nowhere surrounded by wild animals, including lions.
52. Scuba diving off the Great Barrier Reef.
53. Experiencing the fire dance in Bali.
54. Watching the Tango in Buenos Aries.
55. The golden onion domes of St. Basil's in Moscow.
56. Eating fish & dancing at Oistens, Barbados.
57. Taking a trip through the Kerala Backwaters.
58. Herculaneum, near Pompeii - smaller but better with fewer tourists.
59. Pompeii - the most famous Roman ruined city.
60. Driving The Great Ocean Road in Australia.
61. Walking the South Downs Way.
62. Crawling through the Cango Caves in South Africa.
63. Watching a herd of elephants crossing the river in the jungle in Borneo.
64. Having a Singapore sling in Raffles Hotel.
65. Standing on the spot where the Russian royal family were slaughtered in Yekaterinburg.
66. Taking a bus trip down the Amalfi Coast.
67. The Norwegian fjords whilst sitting in a Jacuzzi on top of a cruise ship.
68. St. Mary's gardens in the Scilly Isles - 'The Garden of Eden'.
69. The Kremlin armoury seemingly containing some of the 'secrets of the world'.
70. The Falkland Islands with all the recent history.
71. The Maldives - flying above the atolls in a sea plane.
72. Eating a steak in Buenos Aries - the best in the world.
73. Athens, the Parthenon - go on world heritage day & it's free.

74. The Prado in Madrid - looking at Hieronymus Bosch's masterpiece, 'The Garden of Earthly Delights'.
75. Cave No. 2. Royal Rock Temple, Dambulla, Sri Lanka.
76. Taking a boat trip down St. Katherine's Gorge in Australia.
77. Halicarnassus, the tomb of Mausolus - now a ruin but once one of the seven wonders of the ancient world.
78. The Sultans Palace, Bangkok.
79. Polonnaruwa - the ancient capital of Sri Lanka.
80. Walking the Samarian Gorge in Crete.
81. Climbing Sydney Harbour Bridge - spectacular views.
82. Oradour-sur-Glane, France - walk round in silence.
83. Going up the Eiffel Tower.
84. Yapahuwa, Sri Lanka - half the height of Sigiriya and far fewer tourists.
85. Staying in a nunnery near St. Peters in Rome along with the wonderful Sistine Chapel.
86. The baths at Banos in Ecuador.
87. The Camel Market in Sousse, Tunisia.
88. The Sinharaja Rainforest in Sri Lanka - trekking through the forest infested with ferocious leeches.
89. The Daintree rainforest in Australia.
90. Exploring the Amazon jungle in Ecuador.
91. The boat trip across the Tonle Sap Lake to Ho Chi Min City.
92. The fetish market in Togo - love it or hate it.
93. Highgate cemetery, London - Karl Marx and others are buried there.
94. Walking alone in the Guinea Highlands.
95. The Bambarakanda Falls - walk to the base of the highest falls in Sri Lanka at 240m.
96. Exploring Christiana in Copenhagen - do not take a photo in Pusher Street.
97. Listening to nightingales in a Sussex wood.
98. The Hermitage in St. Petersburg - you need at least a day.
99. Otavalo market in Ecuador - get up at 6am to see the animal market.
100. The walk to Little Adams Peak in Sri Lanka.

28 Who are the worst Tourists?

"Travelling is a brutality. It forces you to trust strangers and to lose sight of all that familiar comfort of home and friends."
Cesare Pavese 1908-1950

Who are the worst tourists to meet abroad? This is all a bit subjective but it always used to be the Germans. They are the nicest people you could possibly wish to meet in their own country but put them on a package holiday in Spain and then, yes, one member of their group will get up at the crack of dawn and lay a beach towel on every sun bed by the hotel pool. The Americans get everywhere and you tend to hear them before you see them. Loud and brash, they just do not care if you can hear every word of their private conversations. They appear unable to understand how their behaviour affects others and sometimes they only think of themselves. Once they have got the photo they have 'been there and done that'. The Japanese swarm around in groups together, briefly taking over every photo opportunity possible but they do not stay long before it is back in the coach and on to the next sight seeing opportunity. Then came the Russians, easily distinguished by their expensive but tasteless dress sense and loud aggressive behaviour. Isolated for so long and unable to travel they have yet to learn the basic rules. Tourists have posted on the internet, 'We went to Turkey and it was ruined by the Russian people who are simply rude to the staff, rude to other holidaymakers and have absolutely no concept of waiting for anything.' That mantle of inconsideration is now shifting to the Chinese. Flush with new money they have yet to learn that they are not the only tourists. They will actually push you out of the way, 'I have paid for this holiday so what right have you got to be here in my way?' Newly rich and rude younger Indians are also in the running, who think it is cool to use constant bad language and treat the service industry workers as servants to carry out their orders. This does not apply to their parents who have actually earned the money for their children to take these vacations. The worst tourists though, can at times be the British, not us personally of course, but the younger Brits who have enough money to go somewhere where the booze is cheap, get drunk, behave badly and get us all a bad name. They are an embarrassment to the likes of you and me.

Right at the other end of the scale are those tourists who are welcome everywhere. Those that are friendly, good company, able to blend in and not offend anyone. It is only my personal opinion of course but these would be Australians and Kiwis. There are a lot of sweeping statements here but this is my list of the top 6 worst tourists:

1. Russians.
2. Chinese.
3. Germans.
4. British.
5. Americans.
6. Indians.

Havana

29 A final word

"There are no foreign lands. It is the traveller only who is foreign."
Robert Louis Stevenson 1850-1894

The good news is that a 2013 study by the Centre for Economic Performance at the London School of Economics revealed that at the ages of both 23 and 69, people reach their peak years for satisfaction, before declining further after turning 75. This was based upon 23,161 German individuals aged between 17 and 85 but the same pattern has been observed in over 50 countries and within all socio-economic groups.

More good news, we are the baby boomers, the chosen ones. Some of us, like fine wine, get better with age, while others already seem to be a generation apart, content just to fade away. As a generation we kick started a revolution and for a short time took over the world. We invented teenagers and some of us are destined to spend our entire lives growing up; to remain in a permanent state of adolescence, a sort of 'Peter Pan syndrome'. The future is now, so take every experience you can get, and very few are more important than travelling. You may look in the mirror and gradually see your father or mother looking back at you so take the opportunities that they never had. I remember my father at 70 saying to me,

'But I feel so fit.'

My mother at 67 said,

'I still feel in my mind as if I am 25.'

Each generation has the same thoughts, but it takes a little bit of effort to get out there in the world and start travelling. 'Hope I die before I get old', still rings true when 'talkin' 'bout my generation'. If you think you are old then that is what you will be, travelling, meeting people and experiencing new countries and cultures, will help to keep you young. It will help to keep you alert, fit and alive. Being over 60, with the children now mercifully independent you can enjoy some adventurous travel and be spontaneous in your choices. Enjoy the world while you still can.

30 Directory

accommodation-budget
www.expedia.co.uk
www.travelsupermarket.com
www.booking.com
www.hotelshopuk.com
accommodation-community hospitality
airbnb.co.uk
www.couchsurfing.com
www.globalfreeloaders.com
www.wwoof.org
www.helpx.net
www.servasbritain.org
www.servas.org
accommodation-hostels
www.hostelworld.com
www.hostelbookers.com
www.booking.com
accommodation-youth hostels
www.yha.org.uk
www.hihostels.com
advice
www.silvertraveladvisor.com
tripadvisor.co.uk
www.fco.gov.uk/travel
campervans
www.cruiseamerica.com
www.cruisecanada.com
www.motorhomeroadtrip.com
www.unbeatablehire.com
www.wickedcampers.com
www.hippiecamper.com
www.juicyrentals.com
lostcampersusa.com
escapecampervans.com
wickedcampers.ca
campervan exchange
www.motorhomeholidayswap.com
car hire
www.hertz.co.uk
www.avis.com
www.skyscanner.net/carhire
www.rentalcars.com
www.economycarrentals.co.uk
www.travelsupermarket.com
www.travelocity.com/Car-Rental
www.kayak.com/cars
www.nationalcar.co.uk

car hire-insurance
www.theaa.com/insurance
insurance4carhire.com
car hire-international driving
www.theaa.com
www.postoffice.co.uk
www.rac.co.uk/travel
cargo ships
www.freightervoyages.eu
www.strandtravelltd.co.uk
clothing
www.travellinglight.co.uk
www.rohan.co.uk
cruises
www.iglucruise.com
www.cruisecritic.co.uk
www.fredolsencruises.com
www.cruiseandmaritime.com
www.princess.com
www.celebritycruises.com
cycling holidays
www.bike-express.co.uk
flexitreks.com
flights-air miles/alliances
www.staralliance.com
www.skyteam.com
www.oneworld.com
flights-budget
www.ryanair.com
www.easyjet.com
www.flybe.com
flights-charter
www.avro.co.uk
www.cheapflights.co.uk
flights-compensation
www.caa.co.uk
www.travelclaimsservices.com
flights-ideas
kayak.co.uk/explore
www.whichbudget.com
flight packages
www.ebookers.com
www.lastminute.com
www.moneysavingexpert.com
www.expedia.com
flights-round the world
www.trailfinders.com
www.staralliance.com

www.oneworld.com
flights-safety
www.airlineratings.com
flights-Sao Tome & Principe
www.flytap.com
flights-screenscrapers/comparisons
www.kayak.com
www.kelkoo.co.uk
www.skyscanner.com
flights-seats
www.seatguru.com
food
www.eatwith.com
gifts
stuffyourrucksack.com
health
www.fitfortravel.nhs.uk
www.nathnac.org/ds/map
homestay- Russia
www.hofa.ru   Home Exchange
www.homebase-hols.com
www.homelink.org.uk
www.lovehomeswap.com
house sitters
www.trustedhousesitters.com
www.housesitters.co.uk
mail boats
http://rms-st-helena.com
www.tristandc.com/shipping.php
maps
www.luckies.co.uk scraper maps
money-exchange rates
www.xe.com
money-cash cards
www.iceplc.com
www.moneysupermarket.com
www.moneysavingexpert.com
www.travelex.co
www.fairfx.com
organised adventure travel
www.gadventures
www.adventurecompany.co.uk
www.explore.co.uk
overlanding
www.dragoman.com
www.intrepidtravel.com
www.gadventures.co.uk
www.journeylatinamerica.com
www.africa-in-focus.com
property bonds
www.hpb.co.uk

www.sherpareport.com
Rodrigues
tourism-rodrigues.mu
solo travel
http://solotravelerblog.com
www.solosholidays.co.uk
www.justyou.co.uk
solo travel-matching partners
www.gadventures.com
www.intrepidtravel.com
special offers
dealchecker.co.uk
travelzoo.com
tipping guidelines
www.cntraveler.com
www.ccrainternational.com
trains-Australia
www.greatsouthernrail.com/au
www.freedomaustralia.co.uk
www.gsr.com.au   Ghan railway
trains-Burma
www.orient-express.com
trains-Canada
www.seat61,com/Canada.htm
www.canadaforvisitor.com
trains-Europe
www.danube-express.com
www.tcdd.gov.tr
www.orient-express.com
www.seat61.com
trains-India
www.seat61.com/India.htm
www.indianrail.gov.in
www.palaceonwheels-train.com
www.irctc.co.in
trains-Luxury Trans Siberia
www.goldeneagleluxurytrains.com
www.sundownersoverland.com
Trains-South Africa
www.rovos.com
www.bluetrain.co.za
Trains-trans Siberia with the locals
www.transsiberianexpress.net
www.justgorussia.com
www.trans-siberian.co.uk
www.intouristuk.com
trains-USA
www.amtrak.com
travel insurance
www.staysure.co.uk
www.theaa.com/insurance/travel

www.freedominsure.co.uk
www.avantitravelinsurance.co.uk
www.world-first.co.uk
www.ageuk.org.uk
www.freespirittravelinsurance.com
www.flexicover.co.uk
www.saga.co.uk
www.onestop4.co.uk/travel
travel insurance comparisons
www.moneysavingexpert.com
www.money.co.uk
www.moneysupermarket.com
travel insurance E111
www.dh.gov.uk/travellers
www.nhs.uk/ehic
traveller's club
http://travelerscenturyclub.org
trekking
www.adventurecompany.co.uk
www.explore.co.uk
visas
www.doyouneedvisa.com
www.worldtravelguide.net
weather-where you are travelling
weather2travel.com
worldweather.wmo.int
weather.com

31 Index

Aborigines 44, 80
accommodation 20, **176**
  airbnb 179
  camper vans 181, 291
  camping 183
  couch surfing 178
  helpx 180
  home exchange 181
  hostels 31, 177
  hotels 176
  property bonds 183
  servas 178
  time share 185
  youth hostels 177
Adelaide 44
adventure travel 13
Albania 298
albatross 130
Alice Springs 44
all inclusive 115
altitude sickness 49, 51, 53, **57**
Amsterdam 125
Angkor Wat 38
Antarctica 125, 131, 295
Antarctic Convergence 132
Australia 29, 31, 41
autism/Asperger 154
baby boomers 8, 329
back packing 15, 31, 32
backpackers 31
Bahia 297
Bali 311
Bangkok 36
Barramundi fish 43
Beagle Channel 129
beggars 40, 101, 270
Beijing 111
Beng Mealea 39
Benin 18
best experiences 322
big five 71, 309
Blue Mountains 46
BMI 215
bragging rights 12, 103, 298

breaking down 149
Broome 43
Buenos Aries 47, 136
Burma 298
bus passes 62
bush camping 147
bushmen 80
Cairns 41
Cambodia 27
camping 16, 65, 69
Cameroon 18
Canberra 46
Cango Caves 89
Caodaism 40
Cape Horn 129
Captain Cook 133
car hire **286**
  age problems 287
  booking 286
  check the car 288
  companies 287
  insurance 182
  international driving licence 27, 290
  security 291
  The Garden Route 89
cargo ship 143
century club 317
charities/money 30
Channel Islands 121
cheetah sanctuary 82
Chimborrozo 114
China 111, 283, 299
Choeung Ek 40
Chowpatty beach 36
climate 23
clothing 23, **25,** 53
  bikinis 22
  shoes 25
  sarongs 28
Cocos Islands 301
cod liver oil 8
Colca Canyon 301
comfort zone 12

communication **230**
  accents 232
  blagging 234
  foreign languages 233
  gestures 233
  pictures 234
  translation 232
compression bags 28
computers 17, 28
confidence 9, 23
Copenhagen 124
Cote d'Ivoire 18
countries 314
Crawford market 35
crocodiles 43, 81
cruises 15, **119**
  Celebrity 'Infinity' 128
  dangers 139
  Grand Princess 125
  Marco Polo 120
  medical costs 245
  Stornaway 120
  Tobermory 121
Cu Chi Tunnels 40
Cuba 29, 276, 293
cycling 212
Daintree 41
dangers 158
  bullet ants 306
  driving 286
  Islamic extremists 151
  muggings **194**
  pickpockets 69, 101, 199
  police 161
  roads 164
  taxis 145
  thugs 312
Darwin 42
dementia 28
Devil's Pool 77
diaries 19, 320
diet 8, **214**, 222, 225
  breakfast 214, **216**
  detoxify **218**
  fasting **220**
  nutrition 216
  sugar 226

  toxins 217
  water 215, **217**
discounts 34
Dominica 296
Drake Passage 130
drill monkey 162
Dr David Lipschitz 9
Dr Samuel Johnson 133, 134
Dubai 35
Dublin 121
Easter Island 34, **46**
East Timor 301
East Africa 68
  Botswana 80
  Cape Town 88
  Johannesburg 90
  Kande Beach 75
  Kenya 69
  Malawi 75,
  Nairobi 69
  Okavango Delta 80
  Sossusvlei 86
  South Africa 88
  Swakopmund 86
  Tanzania 70
  Trucks 69
  Victoria Falls 76
  Zambia 75
  Zanzibar 73
  Zimbabwe 77
Ecuador 114
Edith Falls 43
Egypt 304
Elephant Island 36
email 322
emergency contacts 29
Ethiopia 271, 295
exercise **210**
  fitness 213, 227
Fakirs 36
Falklands 133, 294
fetish market 154
FCO 34, 67, 201
fitness maxims 228
flights 15, 32, **171**
  air alliance 174
  baggage 171

334

charter flights 172
insurance 174
jet lag 192
long haul 172
parking 173
price predictor 173
round the world 32
safety 175
screenscrapers 172
seats 172
short haul 171
upgrades 174
when to book 171
food 104, **279**
black pudding 284
haggis 283
local specialities 281
pig's trotters 284
restaurants 280
strange food 282, 284
street food 186, 281
tripe 283
Freemantle 44
Gabon 293
Gamina Yama 102
G Adventures 111, 114
Galapagos Islands 112
gap year 8, 12, 13, 31
garden 261
gifts 29, 276
glucosamine 190
Goa 9, 15, 111
Goffman 10
grammar schools 8
Grampians 45
gratuities 123
Great Alpine Highway 45
Great Barrier Reef 41
Great Ocean Road 45
Greyhound bus 42
group dynamics 68, 73, 75, 76, 79, 105, 153, 169
guide books 16
guides 67, 115, 274
Guinness 121
gyms 210

health **186**
aeroplanes 192
dengue fever 189
dentistry 191
diarrhoea 186, 189
first aid kit 190
hepatitis 186
HIV/AIDS 186
malaria 187
meningitis 189
rabies 188
sunburn 191
tetanus 188
ticks 190
tuberculosis 189
typhoid 189
water 186, 279
yellow fever 189
Herero women 86
highest mountains 51
Himba tribe 83
Ho Chi Minh City 40
Honfleur 121
Humboldt current 113
icebergs 131, 132
iguanas 117
Iguazu Falls 136
insurance
car 182
claims **253,** 257
companies 245
comparisons 248
cover for activities 251
EHIC 244
home 259
travel 192, **244**
what is covered 249
Irkutsk 104
Islam 157
Isle of Wight 301
itinerary 17
journals 319
Kakadu 42
Katherine Gorge 43
Kilimanjaro 51, 299
Kindle 16
Kings Canyon 44

335

Khmer Rouge 40
Kiel canal 125
Kovalam 297
Kremlin 99
Kumba Icefall 56
lady boys 37
Lake Baikal 105
Libya 11, 308
leeches 312
life expectancy 226
lists 28
llamas 135
Lord Carnegie 12
Lukla 54, 57, 58
Madagascar 294
Mai Lai 40
Marrakech 115
Martial Glacier 129
'mate' 136
medication 29
Mekong Delta 40
Melbourne 45
Miss World 6
mobile phone 19, 26
money 12, **263**
   cash cards 267
   counterfeit 268
   credit cards 265
   exchange rates 263
   ICE 264
   traveller's cheques 265
Montevideo 135
Moscow 99
mountain gorillas 295
Mozambique 295
mugging 48
Mumbai 35
neighbours 260
netbook 19
Nigeria 18
norovirus 122, 139
Norwegian Fjords 124
oneworld 32
omega 3 8
organised trips 111
Oslo 124
Otavalo 115

overlanding 15, **63**
   Africa-in-Focus 64
   Dragoman 64, 67
   The kitty 68, 88
   Ngorongoro crater 71
   Serengeti 70
palm oil wine 11
package holidays 15, 111, 115
packing 22, 23, 24
   toiletries 26
Papua New Guinea 49, 296
party trucks 63, 82, 169, 170
parking at airports 20
Perth 44
Peru 301
Phnom Penh 39
photography 320
planning 15, 16
Pol Pot 39
Pompeii 115
Poms 45
post war Britain 7
poverty 36
Puerto Madryn 135
Pussy club 37
pygmy tribes 163
quad-biking 86
Quechan people 114
Queen Victoria 8
Quito 194
Ramadan 35
research 20
Roaring twenties 7
Rodrigues 298
round the world 15, 32, 34
Roy Castle 209
rucksacks 22, **24**
Russia 18
safaris 71
   Chobe National Park 80
   Etosha National Park 81
safety **194**
   precautions 196, 200, **201**
SAGA 10
Santiago 47
saunas 309
Sao Tome 298

scams 37, 70, 74, 136, 263
Scilly Isles 121
scooters 43, 111
Scotland 120
   midges 120
   Invergordon 120
seasickness 122, 139
secret seven 81
security at home 61
Shackleton 133
Siem Reap 38, 39
silver surfers 8
sixties 7,8, 31
slavery 156
smoking **208**
snorkelling 113
solo travel 11, **237**
   advantages 237
   disadvantages 240
South East Asia 31, 37
souvenirs 322
spike Milligan 8
Spitzbergen 125
Sri Lanka 271, 312
Ssese Islands 296
St. Helena 301
Surrey puma 71
swimming 212
swinging sixties 7
Sydney 46
table tennis 10
Tahiti 46
tango 48
Tasmania 301
taxis 20, 77, 274
time speeds up 7
tipping **271**
Titanic 128
Tonle Sap 39
Toul Sleng 39
tourists 38
Trailfinders 17, 32
trains 20, **94**
   America 108
   Australia 108
   Burma 108
   Canada 108

Europe 107
Ghan railway 44, 94
India 107
South Africa 107
Trans Siberian Railway 15, 94
trekking 49
   Alps 61
   Annapurna Sanctuary 61
   Crete 61
   Dolomites 61
   Everest Base Camp 54
   Kala Patthar 56
   Kilimanjaro 51
   Kinabalu 49
   Madeira/levadas 60
   Mallorca 61
   Naxos 61
   Tenerife/Mt. Teide 60
   United Kingdom 61
   Wales 61
trekking poles 50
tripadvisor 20
triposa 16
Tristan da Cunha 302
travelling 9,10
travel magazines 17
travel shows 21
tuk-tuk 38, 39
Uluru 44
Ushuaia 128
Valparaiso 47
Varkala 297
Vimanmek Mansion 37
visas 18, 145
Vladivostok 106
voodoo 155, 156
walking 211
weather 16
West Africa 18, **144**
   Benin 156
   Cameroon 162
   Cote d'Ivoire 151
   Dakar 144
   Gambia 146, 312
   Ganvie 157
   Ghana 152
   Guinea Bissau 147, 234, 296

Guinea Conakry 148
Nigeria 159
Senegal 146
Togo 154
when to travel 33

world maps 16, 320
worst tourists 327
Yekaterinburg 102
YHA 45

Tim Blewitt grew up in the Surrey countryside. He now lives in Goring-by-Sea, West Sussex and is married with two daughters. He taught art and ceramics for many years.

Made in the USA
Charleston, SC
09 June 2014